Language contact and bilingualism

Language contact and bilingualism

René Appel and Pieter Muysken

Institute for General Linguistics, University of Amsterdam

Edward Arnold
A division of Hodder & Stoughton
LONDON NEW YORK MELBOURNE AUCKLAND

© 1987 René Appel and Pieter Muysken

First published in Great Britain 1987
Reprinted 1988, 1989 (with corrections) 1990, 1992, 1993

Distributed in the USA by Routledge, Chapman and Hall, Inc.
29 West 35th Street, New York, NY 10001

British Library Cataloguing in Publication Data

Appel, René
  Language contact and bilingualism.
  1. Bilingualism
  I. Title   II. Muysken, Pieter
  404'.2   P115

ISBN 0-7131-6491-3

Typeset in 10/11pt Plantin Compugraphic
by Colset Private Ltd, Singapore
Printed and bound in Great Britain for Edward Arnold,
a division of Hodder and Stoughton Limited, Mill Road, Dunton Green,
Sevenoaks, Kent TN13 2YA by Athenaeum Press Ltd,
Newcastle upon Tyne.

Contents

1 **Introduction: bilingualism and language contact**   1

I **Social aspects of the bilingual community**   11

2 **Language and identity**   11
  2.1 Language and ethnicity   12
  2.2 Language attitudes   16
  Further reading   20

3 **The sociology of language choice**   22
  3.1 Deterministic perspectives   23
  3.2 Person-oriented approaches   27
  3.3 Functional specialization   29
  Further reading   31

4 **Language maintenance and shift**   32
  4.1 Factors influencing language maintenance   33
  4.2 The process of language shift   38
  4.3 Language loss   42
  Further reading   45

5 **Language planning**   46
  5.1 Types and theories of language planning   47
  5.2 Stages and activities in language planning   50
  5.3 Factors influencing language planning   56
  Further reading   58

6 **Bilingual education**   59
  6.1 Minority languages in the school   60
  6.2 Types of bilingual education   64
  6.3 Results of bilingual programmes   67
  Further reading   71

II The bilingual speaker   73

7 Psychological dimensions of bilingualism   73
7.1 The bilingual brain   73
7.2 The mental representation of two languages   75
7.3 The use of two languages   79
Further reading   81

8 Second-language acquisition   82
8.1 Features of interlanguage   83
8.2 Social-psychological factors and second-language acquisition   92
8.3 The problem of age and the simultaneous acquisition of two languages   94
Further reading   100

9 The effects of bilingualism   101
9.1 Linguistic and educational aspects   102
9.2 Cognitive effects   108
9.3 Effects on personality development   113
Further reading   115

III Language use in the bilingual community   117

10 Code switching and code mixing   117
10.1 Why do people switch between languages?   118
10.2 Where in the sentence is code mixing possible?   121
10.3 Further reading   128

11 Strategies of neutrality   129
11.1 Neutralization of linguistic identity   130
11.2 Neutralization of communicative mode in intergroup communication   133
11.3 An integrative perspective   135
Further reading   137

12 Strategies and problems in bilingual interaction   138
12.1 Adaptive strategies: foreigner talk   139
12.2 Problems and misunderstandings in native–non-native interaction   143
12.3 An integrative perspective   150
Further reading   151

IV Linguistic consequences   153

13 Language contact and language change   153
13.1 Five scenarios   154
13.2 Is there syntactic borrowing: The case of relative clauses   156
13.3 Grammatical borrowing and linguistic change   162
Further reading   163

14 Lexical borrowing   164
14.1 Typology   164
14.2 Social and cultural determinants   165
14.3 Grammatical constraints   170
14.4 Borrowing and integration: can we distinguish borrowing
    from code mixing?   172
14.5 Lexical borrowing and language death   173
Further reading   174

15 Pidgins and creoles   175
15.1 A survey of pidgin and creole languages   176
15.2 Creole studies   180
15.3 The social position of the creole languages   184
Further reading   186

References   187
Index to languages and countries   201
Subject index   206
Author index   210

Preface

For a number of years we have been doing research and teaching courses on different aspects of language contact. René Appel has worked on minority languages and particularly on the educational problems of children of migrant workers in the Netherlands. Pieter Muysken has focused on Quechua–Spanish language contact in the Andes, relating this to more general aspects of creolization and language mixture.

Particularly in planning our courses on language contact, however, we felt that the problems and concepts both of us had been dealing with were closely interrelated. It came to be a challenge to explore the relations between social, psychological and (socio) linguistic aspects of language contact more explicitly in this book. We are not certain that our exploration has been successful everywhere, given that so many disciplines with different research traditions are involved.

We would like to thank all the students and fellow researchers at the Institute of General Linguistics of the University of Amsterdam who have commented on earlier versions of material contained in this book. To conclude, we would like to acknowledge an indebtedness that will be obvious to all insiders: we have named our book with the title of Uriel Weinreich's pioneering work, *Languages in contact*, in mind. We are quite aware that it remains difficult to go beyond the depth of insight achieved in Weinreich's writings.

Amsterdam, September 1986

1 Introduction: Bilingualism and language contact

Imagine the history of mankind, not as a history of peoples or nations, but of the languages they speak. A history of 5000 languages, thrown together on this planet, constantly interacting. Imagine the treaty of Versailles not as an event of international diplomacy, but in terms of people putting on their best French to make themselves understood and achieve the greatest advantage. Think of Cortes' conquest of Mexico in 1532 not as an outrageous narrative of bravery, cruelty and betrayal, but in terms of the crucial role of his Indian mistress Malinche, interpreter between Aztec and Spanish. Think of the sugar plantations, where the uprooted slaves were thrown together, as meeting places for many African languages.

Imagining all this, two things come to mind: first, how closely the history of languages is tied up with and is a reflection of the history of peoples and nations. Second, how little we know of languages in contact. Far more is known about the economic consequences of Balkanization, the disintegration of the Austrian empire, than of what happened to all the languages of the *Kaiserliche und Königliche Reich* when it fell apart in 1918. This book tries to provide the concepts needed to understand what it means for two languages to come into contact. What happens in communities where several languages are spoken? How can speakers handle these languages simultaneously? When and why will the different languages actually be used? Which consequences does language contact have for the languages involved? These are the main issues we address here.

In this chapter we will give a bit of background to the discussion by sketching a few of the conceptual problems, listing some of the reasons why researchers have wanted to look at language contact (hoping that these may be valid for the reader as well), describing some of the major types of language contact in the world, giving a brief history of the field and presenting, finally, a sketch of the different contributing sub-disciplines and an outline of the book.

1.1 Bilingualism: concepts and definitions

Language contact inevitably leads to bilingualism. Generally, two types of bilingualism are distinguished: *societal* and *individual* bilingualism. Roughly speaking, societal bilingualism occurs when in a given society two or more languages are spoken. In this sense, nearly all societies are bilingual, but they can differ with regard

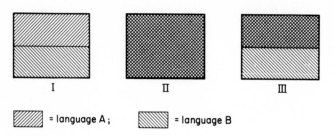

Figure 1.1 Schematically represented forms of societal bilingualism

to the degree or form of bilingualism. Theoretically, the following forms can be distinguished (see Figure 1.1).

In situation I the two languages are spoken by two different groups and each group is monolingual; a few bilingual individuals take care of the necessary intergroup communication. This form of societal bilingualism often occurred in former colonial countries, where the colonizer spoke English, for instance, and the native people a local language. In societies of type II all people are bilingual. Approximations to such a form of societal bilingualism can be found in African countries and in India. Often people have command of more than two languages.

In the third form of societal bilingualism one group is monolingual, and the other bilingual. In most cases this last group will form a minority, perhaps not in the numerical or statistical, but in the sociological sense: it is a non-dominant or oppressed group. Situations like III can be observed in Greenland, for example, where the people who speak Greenlandic Inuit must become bilingual, i.e. learn Danish, while the Danish-speaking group, which is sociologically dominant, can remain monolingual.

Of course, forms I, II and III are only theoretical types which do not exist in a pure form in the world we live in: different mixtures are much more common. The linguistic situation of most countries is far more complex, with more than two groups and more than two languages involved. It is useful, however, to keep the ideal typology in mind when we describe complex bilingual societies.

It is fairly clear what *individual* bilingualism is, but determining whether a given person is bilingual or not is far from simple. Many people in Britain have learned some French in school and practice it on their annual holiday, but are they bilingual in the same way as young Puerto Ricans in New York, who use both Spanish and English with equal ease? To what extent must a speaker have command over the two languages in order to be labelled a bilingual? Must he or she have fluent oral and writing skills in both languages? Must a true bilingual be proficient in productive (speaking, writing) as well as receptive tasks (listening, reading)? Which components of the language are the criteria: vocabulary, pronunciation, syntax, pragmatics?

In the history of the study of bilingualism various definitions have been proposed. We will give two extreme, but well-known variants. Bloomfield made the highest demands. According to him, a bilingual should possess 'native-like control of two or more languages' (1933: 56). At the other extreme, Macnamara (1969) proposed that somebody should be called bilingual if he has some second-language skills in one of the four modalities (speaking, listening, writing, reading), in addition to his first-language skills.

The problem of a *psychological* definition, in terms of proficiency, seems to be unsurmountable, not because of measurement problems (which are complex enough by themselves), but because it is impossible to find a general norm or standard for proficiency. Therefore we prefer a *sociological* definition, in line with Weinreich (1953: 5), who said that 'the practice of alternatively using two languages will be called here bilingualism, and the persons involved bilinguals'. Somebody who regularly uses two or more languages in alternation is a bilingual. Within this definition speakers may still differ widely in their actual linguistic skills, of course, but we should be careful not to impose standards for bilinguals that go much beyond those for monolinguals. The very fact that bilinguals use various languages in different circumstances suggests that it is their *overall* linguistic competence that should be compared to that of monolinguals. All too often imposing Bloomfield's criteria on bilinguals has led to their stigmatization as being somehow deficient in their language capacities.

With regard to the terminology used in this book, two more things:
(1) The terms *bi*lingual and *bi*lingualism also apply to situations where more than two languages are involved. Only in obviously appropriate cases will we sometimes use the terms multilingual and multilingualism. (2) In this book the terms bilingual/ism refer to conventionally recognized languages and *not* to dialects of languages (for instance, London Cockney and Received Pronunciation), although we are quite aware of the fact that many research findings and concepts in the study of bilingualism carry over to bidialectism.

Any definition of bilingualism has to come to grips with a central problem in the social sciences: that of scale and of aggregation. Are we talking about individuals, about families, neighbourhoods or whole societies? What can 'language contact' possibly mean, since 'language' is an abstraction? Speakers can be in contact, metaphorically speaking two grammars might be said to be in contact in the brain of an individual, but languages as whole entities? We do find bilingual societies where many individual speakers are not bilingual, particularly societies organized along caste lines, or with very strong social divisions. An example of the latter would be the province of Quebec before the Second World War, where an English-speaking urban bourgeoisie coexisted with a French-speaking farming community (cf. form I in Figure 1.1).

A second problem has to do with our definition of languages as well. Is it meaningful to speak of language contact given the fact that we do not know how to distinguish between languages and dialects? Hindi and Urdu are two, religiously differentiated, varieties of essentially the same language: Hindi is spoken by Hindus and Urdu by Moslems. Is there a possibility of language contact here, or just of dialect mixture? The same holds for Dutch and German along the eastern border of the Netherlands. Where does it become meaningful to speak of the two languages being in contact? How different do the two codes have to be?

A third set of problems has to do with the level of grammatical analysis that we deal with. If we accept the replacement of the central notion of 'language' by that of 'grammar', then we surely should speak of 'grammars in contact'. Then again, if we accept the notion common in generative grammar since the late 1970s that grammars consist of a number of independent components, (the phrase structure component, the transformational component, the lexicon, the phonological component), then the question is whether we should not be dealing with components of grammars in contact. This problem may seem very academic, but in chapters 10 and 13 we will argue that it is crucial for understanding what is going on.

1.2 Reasons for studying language contact

Turning now to reasons for studying language contact, we can discern strong impulses both from social concerns and from developments in language studies. Countries such as Belgium and Canada, both with language groups that are sometimes opposed to each other, have created centres for the study of bilingualism, stimulated research and produced outstanding scholars. It is hoped that a thorough and dispassionate analysis of bilingual language behaviour will help us to gain insight into the language problems of groups and individuals and thus support language planning and educational policies. This type of research has been recognized as crucial in countries such as India, which faces a combination of languages spoken of daunting complexity, and has become one of the world's centres for language-contact research. Sometimes it is called 'the laboratory of multilingualism'.

In addition to these countries, characterized by a long history of bilingualism, a large number of countries, particularly in the industrialized West, have become bilingual on a large scale in the last 20 years due to migration. The presence of groups of migrants has had a great impact on these societies: suddenly a number of myths about monolingual and monocultural national identity were shattered. The political emancipation and educational needs of the migrant groups have stimulated in turn a whole new series of language-contact studies, both in Europe and in the US and Canada.

It is not only minorities of migrants that have participated in these processes of political and cultural emancipation, however, but also a number of traditional minority groups. These groups have clamoured for political decentralization, recognition of their own language and culture and bilingual education. This, in turn, has led to a number of studies on language-contact issues.

On the level of ideology, these developments have not remained without repercussions. The process of decolonization has left the former colonial powers, one might say, with a lot to think about. A strong tradition of historical research has emerged that focuses on the conditions, processes and consequences of colonialism, both for the colonizing powers and for the Third World. This tradition has enriched our perception of colonization itself considerably, and allows us to look at the propagation and expansion of the European languages in a wider perspective. It also allows us to develop a vocabulary and conceptual model for talking about systems, including languages, influencing each other.

The cultural developments in the West of the 1960s led to a return to the study of the vernacular languages, away from purism, including the spoken languages of minority groups. An early manifestation of this was the emergence of Black and Amerindian studies in the US in the early 1970s, and certainly the study of language-contact phenomena has profited from this development. Here phenomena such as creole languages were involved that clearly did not fit into a purist conception.

When we turn to linguistics itself, the study of language contact has developed into a paradigm for sociolinguistics as a whole. Sociolinguistics as a discipline has stressed the diversity in language use. The study of diversity leads, of course, to a focus on the clearest example of diversity: multilingualism. All the major issues in the sociolinguistic study of the so-called monolingual speech communities reappear in enlarged form in the study of language contact: style shift, linguistic change, code selection and speech repertoire, attitudes, and perhaps variation. Both societal pressures, then, and trends internal to our cultural perceptions and internal to linguistics have fostered the study of language contact from a number of different perspectives. We will turn to these shortly.

1.3 Situations of language contact

In section 1.1 we presented a schematic typology of bilingualism. Here we will attempt to describe what the dominant language contact situations in recent history are. Such a survey can only be very provisional and tentative, particularly because space and time play tricks on us. What seems like a stable situation now may rapidly change in the future, or be the interim result of an extremely drastic change that escapes our view.

A first historical situation of language contact is the linguistic archipelago: many often unrelated languages, each with few speakers, spoken in the same ecosphere. Such situations are rare at this moment, but must have been frequent in the precolonial era. Examples now are the Amazon basin and the Australian desert, where many aboriginal peoples still live in tribal groups. Sociolinguistically these areas are characterized by extensive bilingualism, linguistically by widespread diffusion of words and elements of grammar from language to language.

A second setting for language contact involves more or less stable borders between language families. One such border runs between the Romance and Germanic languages through Switzerland (where French and Romansch are spoken in the South, and Swiss German in the North) and Belgium (where Dutch and German are spoken in the North and French in the South). Another example is the border between the Indo-European and Dravidian languages running through India. It is hard to generalize across these cases: for India extensive borrowing is reported, and this does not seem to exist in Switzerland, and only marginally in Belgium. These differences appear to be due to the very different power and status relationships obtaining between the languages involved. In this book we return to such differences repeatedly. If one thing can be learned from language-contact studies it is how important the overall social context is. Sociolinguistics is not like chemistry, and when you put two languages together the same thing does not always happen.

The third type of situation in which language contact occurs is the result of European colonial expansion. Colonialism has not only created a number of societies in which high-prestige European languages coexist with the native languages of the conquered peoples. New varieties of the colonial languages were created also, resembling the original in the case of English, French, Portuguese and Spanish in the New World and in Australia, but also in often unrecognizable form, as in the Creole languages of the Caribbean, West Africa and the Pacific. Very roughly, the spread of the colonial languages can be represented as shown in Map 1.1.

Map 1.1   Schematic representation of the European colonial expansion

A fourth situation reflects individual pockets of speakers of minority languages, cut off by the surrounding national languages. Examples include Welsh and Gaelic in Great Britain, Frisian in the Netherlands, Basque in France and Spain. Often these groups reflect traditional populations, already in existence when new peoples and languages swept in.

The final situation is in some sense the result of a reverse migratory movement: the influx of people from the post-colonial Third World societies into the industrial world. People from the Caribbean have migrated to North America and Europe, people from Central America predominantly to the US, and people from the Mediterranean predominantly to Western Europe. Again, Map 1.2 gives some idea of these movements.

The result of these migratory patterns has been mentioned already: newly and uneasily multicultural and multilingual societies, faced with hitherto unknown educational problems but also with cultural enrichment and new possibilities.

The history of peoples and languages is very rich. Of many developments and languages all traces have disappeared. These types of language-contact situation are certainly not the only ones. Imagine all the sociolinguistic upheavals caused by the conquests of the Romans or the Mongols. When we look at a region such as the Balkans, which now is relatively stable, we realize how many linguistic changes involving many different languages must have taken place there. Present stability is the result of movement in the past.

1.4 The history of the field

The roots of the linguistic study of language contact go back at least to the comparative and historical tradition of the nineteenth century. William Dwight

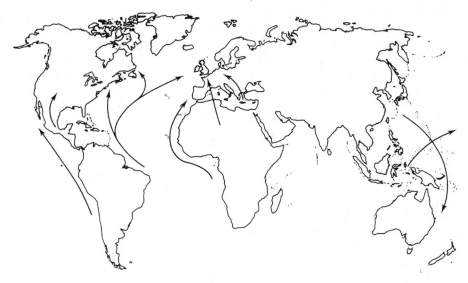

Map 1.2 Schematic representation of the post-colonial migration to Europe and North America

Whitney (1881) explicitly discusses the role of borrowing in language change, and we will return to his views on the matter in chapter 14. Hugo Schuchardt documented a number of complex situations of language contact in publications from 1880 onward, and was the founder of modern creole language studies. His most complex contribution to this field, part of *Kreolische Studien* IX (1890), has not been followed up. In the wake of Schuchardt's work a number of other creolists, including Hesseling (e.g. 1899, 1905) and Turner (1949) have continued to develop the linguistic study of language-contact phenomena. Their work will be discussed in chapter 15, on pidgins and creoles.

Finally, work that can be viewed as presenting the first truly comprehensive view of language contact dates from the early 1950s, including both Weinreich's seminal *Languages in Contact* (1953) and Haugen's detailed study, *The Norwegian Language in America* (1953). These contributions can be considered at the same time as laying the foundation for what later came to be called the discipline of sociolinguistics. Quite independent of these scholars, we should mention Marcel Cohen's work in France, who started out as an Arabist and whose work gradually came to include a strong concern for language-contact phenomena, as shown e.g. in his *Pour une sociologie du langage* (1956).

1.5 Contributing disciplines and structure of the book

Bilingualism or *language contact* in itself is not a scientific discipline. It is an issue, a subject or a field of study to which various disciplines can contribute. The disciplines can interact or, on the other hand, function independently, because of differing viewpoints, methodologies or terminologies.

When in a given society languages are in contact this may be of interest for socio-
logists or social anthropologists. Languages are social phenomena or social
institutions, and the division of a society into social groups is often reflected in
linguistic divisions. Linguistic behaviour and attitudes towards languages in a
bilingual society often give further insight into social norms and values. In most
cases, the sociological approach to bilingualism involves a language as a whole,
disregarding its different varieties, processes of internal change and structural
aspects. In the first part of this book we will deal with data, viewpoints and theories
from this 'sociology of bilingualism'.

More general topics such as the relation between language and (social) identity and
the functioning of two languages in a community will be discussed in addition to
more specific topics such as the position of minority languages in the school, the
effects of bilingual education, and the problem of language planning.

Earlier in this chapter we made a distinction between societal and individual
bilingualism. The bilingual individual can be profitably studied from the perspective
of psychology. The second part of this book, *The bilingual speaker*, discusses psychological aspects of bilingualism, such as the different ways in which the two languages
may be stored in the bilingual brain, the way in which a second language is acquired,
and the psychological consequences of being bilingual.

The third part of this book is called *Language use in the bilingual community*. Here
especially the contribution of sociolinguistics *per se*, i.e. the study of socially governed
linguistic behaviour, will be presented. The chapters in this part will contain
information on the languages people choose in interaction situations, or how they
avoid making a specific choice, on ways in which people with different language
backgrounds interact, and on the social consequences of specific interaction patterns.

The discipline of linguistics proper can contribute by discovering what happens to
the structure of languages when they are in contact. This linguistic perspective is
presented in the last part of this book. Do languages change when they are in contact
with other languages? Can they borrow rules of grammar, or just words? Can
languages mix, and how can new languages emerge out of language contact?

Distinguishing between sociological, psychological, sociolinguistic and linguistic
contributions to the study of bilingualism and language contact is in many ways
unsatisfactory and artificial, because they are so intricately interrelated. It is
impossible to study a psychological topic such as the cognitive consequences of
individual bilingualism without taking social factors into account such as the relative
status of the languages involved. In the same way it is impossible to study the
phenomenon of transfer in second-language acquisition without making a detailed
comparison of the two linguistic systems involved. Therefore we will often refer to
chapters in other parts of the book.

The subject matter of this book is a complex one, with societal, psychological and
(socio)linguistic aspects that can only be separated on an abstract analytical level.
This separation is reflected in the organization of this book because for us it was the
only way to present an overview of research results from different disciplines. We
hope it will not hinder the reader in developing a coherent view on the subject of
language contact. Whatever the reason that there are so many languages spoken in the
world (and people have been pondering this question since the Old Testament), the
fact is that there are; and another fact is that many people find themselves at the

frontier of two languages. What we try to show in this book is that there are many ways of coping with this situation. The structural characteristics of the languages involved impose an outer limit on the possible linguistic outcomes of language contact. Which strategy is chosen by any one speaker depends on many factors: the relation between the speaker and the languages, and the societal context in which the speaker finds himself. We continue to be amazed at the versatility and resourcefulness of speakers: multilingualism is not just a problem, it can be a triumph of the human spirit.

Further reading

People interested in modern studies of language contact should consult Mackey's *Bilinguisme et contact des langues* (1976), an encyclopaedic survey with much relevant material and Grosjean's *Life with Two Languages* (1982), a highly readable book with many accounts of personal bilingual experiences. Fasold's *The Sociolinguistics of Society* (1984) documents the relations between the study of language contact and sociolinguistics in general. Baetens Beardsmore's *Bilingualism; Basic Principles* (1982) stresses psycholinguistic aspects, and the title of Skutnabb-Kangas's *Bilingualism or not: The education of minorities* (1983) is self-explanatory. In addition there are a number of collections of articles, of which we mention Fishman (1978) and Mackey and Ornstein (1979), both focusing on sociological subjects: demography, language maintenance and language and education, and finally McCormack and Wurm (1979), which contains articles on a variety of subjects, including code switching and language planning.

I   Social aspects of the bilingual community

2   Language and identity

Sançak is an eight-year-old Turkish boy who has lived in the Netherlands for about five years. Approximately half of the children of the school he attends are of Turkish or Moroccan nationality. Their fathers had come to the Netherlands as migrant workers, and later on their families came over. The language of the classroom is Dutch, but the four Turkish children have one morning per week instruction in Turkish by a Turkish teacher (in a separate classroom). Sançak is a very sociable child, but most of the time he seeks the company of Mamouta, another Turkish boy. Although Mamouta generally prefers to speak Dutch, Sançak always speaks Turkish with him. Furthermore, he also counts in Turkish when he is doing arithmetic. In his view his family will 'soon' return to Turkey, Turkish is a more beautiful language than Dutch, and he longs to live in Turkey. He is delighted when a Dutch-speaking person asks something about Turkish or tries to learn a few Turkish words from him. Sançak is a lively, expressive child, but sometimes rather disobedient. When he goes against the rules of the classroom, and the teacher reprimands him, or when something is going on which he does not like at all, he can suddenly burst out in a stream of Turkish (though he always speaks Dutch with the Dutch teacher). When children are singing Dutch songs with the teacher Sançak may jump up from his chair and start singing (and dancing) a Turkish song.

Evidently, Turkish has a special meaning for Sançak. It is the language in which he is most fluent, and when he uses it with Mamouta, he can have Mamouta (who is his best friend) all to himself, because there are no other Turkish boys in the classroom. But perhaps more importantly, sometimes he does not use Turkish to convey a message but only to mark his own identity as a Turkish boy who does not agree with the course of events in the Dutch classroom. In singing a Turkish song Sançak demonstrates a part of Turkish culture, of which he seems to be rather proud.

Language is not only an instrument for the communication of messages. This becomes especially clear in multilingual communities where various groups have their own language: e.g. the Flemish in Belgium and the Gujeratis in India. With its language a group distinguishes itself. The cultural norms and values of a group are transmitted by its language. Group feelings are emphasized by using the group's own language, and members of the outgroup are excluded from its internal transactions (cf. Giles et al., 1977).

Therefore it is a common assumption in sociolinguistics – an assumption which is validated by many personal observations and research data – that languages carry social meanings or social connotations. In this chapter we will deal with this assumption from the perspective of the relation between language and identity in bilingual communities. In the sociological and sociolinguistic literature a group's identity is often called its *cultural* or *ethnic identity*, or its ethnicity. In section 2.1. we will discuss the concept of ethnicity and its potential links with language. The main question to be answered here is: is there always a categorical and necessary relation between language and ethnicity?

If a language has social meaning, people will evaluate it in relation to the social status of its users. Their language attitudes will be social attitudes. Section 2.2. reports on studies of language attitudes.

2.1 Language and ethnicity

Everything that differentiates a group from another group constitutes the group's identity. Although there are no fixed criteria, a group is considered to be an ethnic group with a specific ethnic identity when it is sufficiently distinct from other groups. For instance, sailors certainly constitute a group, but they would not qualify as an ethnic group. The group of Spanish-speaking people living in the USA and coming from Mexico (often called Chicanos) on the other hand, definitely constitute an ethnic group. They have their own native language, and such a group is therefore often called an 'ethnolinguistic group'. For quite some time it was assumed that the ethnic groups we find in our modern societies were dying out, because they were expected to integrate into mainstream society and give up their own life style, culture, language and identity. But the perspective on ethnic groups and ethnic identity has changed. Glazer and Moynihan (1975:4) argue that ethnic groups were formerly seen as relics from an earlier age, but that there is 'a growing sense that they may be *forms* of social life that are capable of renewing and transforming themselves'. Glazer and Moynihan also note that a new word reflects this new social reality: *ethnicity*.

Many scholars have tried to define the concept of ethnicity, i.e. they have tried to establish which features are characteristic of an ethnic group. We will not try to reproduce or summarize the often heated debate on the definition of ethnicity, but confine ourselves to the views of two scholars who are especially relevant here because they discuss ethnicity in relation to language.

According to Fishman (1977) we must take three dimensions into account when we think of ethnicity. The most important dimension is termed *paternity*: ethnicity is 'in part, but at its core, experienced as an inherited constellation acquired from one's parents as they acquired it from theirs, and so on back further and further, *ad infinitum*' (Fishman, 1977:17). In this way ethnicity is linked up with a feeling of continuity. The second dimension is that of *patrimony*, i.e. the legacy of collectivity – defining behaviours and views: pedagogic patterns, music, clothes, sexual behaviour, special occupations etc., which are somehow inherited from earlier generations. *Phenomenology* is the third dimension, and it refers to the meaning people attach to their paternity (their descent as members of a collectivity) and to their (ethnic) legacy. Phenomenology has to do with the subjective attitudes of people towards their membership of a potential ethnic group.

Another approach is represented by Ross (1979), who distinguishes two schools of thought with regard to the definition of ethnicity. The first one is *objectivist*, claiming that the ethnicity of a group is defined by its concrete cultural institutions and patterns: a distinctive language, distinctive folk tales, food, clothing, etc. In fact, this view restricts itself to Fishman's dimension of patrimony. The second school adheres to a *subjectivist approach*. Ethnicity is supposed to reflect a shared us-feeling, while the members of the group may differ considerably in clothing, religion or even language. In such a group, the subjective factor – the us-feeling or the us-against-them-feeling – overrides the importance of other objective factors not shared. LePage and Tabouret-Keller (1982) illustrate this point with the example of West Indians in Great Britain. Initially, West Indian immigrant groups were characterized by island labels and island identities but the attitudes of the majority of white Britons led to the development of a sense of a common enemy on which a new, general West Indian identity could be based. This subjective approach to the definition of identity cannot be seen in terms of Fishman's dimensions. Fishman stresses the origins of identity, even in his dimension of phenomenology which regards the meaning people attach to things they have inherited. The subjective view of ethnicity claims that it can develop as a reaction to actual circumstances. For Fishman (1977) language is the symbol *par excellence* of ethnicity: 'Language is the recorder of paternity, the expresser of patrimony and the carrier of phenomenology. Any vehicle carrying such a precious freight must come to be viewed as equally precious, as part of the freight, indeed as precious in and of itself' (Fishman, 1977:25). The importance of language is amplified by the fact that it is used to cope with other ethnic experiences. People talk about all kinds of cultural or ethnic activities and issues, and therefore language is connected with these. A kind of associative link is developed. Relevant cultural items – types of clothing, aspects of wedding rituals, etc. – find their expression in the language, and it is often thought that they cannot be expressed in another language.

In various studies the relation between language and ethnicity had been demonstrated. Mercer *et al.* (1979) studied a group of bilingual Gujerati and English-speaking students in Leicester. The students were either themselves immigrants or the first-generation offspring of immigrants from the Indian subcontinent or East Africa. With respect to identity, Mercer *et al.* could distinguish three groups: those who identified themselves as Indian, those who identified themselves as British, and those with a 'mixed' British–Indian identity, favouring a synthesis of British and Indian elements. Members of the Indian identity group were most positively oriented towards the use and maintenance of Gujerati, they also emphasized most strongly the function of Gujerati for maintaining links with their Indian homeland and cultural heritage. Those choosing a British identity showed the least positive attitude towards Gujerati, and the 'mixed' group also in this respect had an in-between attitude.

Guboglo (1979) reports on language and ethnic identity in the Udmurt Autonomous Soviet Socialist Republic. According to him, language has an integrating function with regard to ethnic identity. The relation between language and certain aspects of Udmurt culture is shown in the following data: in Udmurtia, 33 per cent of the Udmurt-speaking people in the cities and 46.3 per cent of the villagers have opted for the traditional Udmurt childbirth ritual, however, the respective figures for the people with another mother tongue are 13.4 and 21.2 per cent. Of course, these data cannot be interpreted causally. It is impossible to say whether speaking Udmurt 'causes' the choice for the traditional childbirth ritual, or the other way round. It can also be the case that there is another factor which causes both.

The use of creole by black (and white!) British adolescents was studied by Hewitt (1982). A 16-year-old black young man gave the following answer when Hewitt asked if he enjoyed speaking creole, i.e. the London variety of Jamaican creole: 'Yes. 'Cos I feel . . . sounds funny. I feel black and I am proud of it, to speak like that. That's why, when I talk it, I feel better than when I'm talking like now. You know what I mean? . . . When I speak more dread I feel more lively and more aware. In a way I feel I am more happier' (Hewitt, 1982:220). The word 'dread' is a key concept in black youth culture, and, according to Hewitt, close involvement with white society contradicts the ideal definition of 'dread'.

Lowley *et al.* (1983) interviewed representatives of three American ethnolinguistic groups: French, Spanish and Yiddish. They concluded that all three groups wanted to maintain their specific ethnic identity alongside their American identity, and that they considered their ethnic mother tongue to be its most vital and visible expression. The minority language or ethnic mother tongue turns out not to be an indispensable aspect of ethnicity, however. Ross (1979) notes that in some cases, e.g. among American Indians, a feeling of ethnicity is developed when individuals or groups give up their own language in favour of a common lingua franca. In the view of Edwards (1981), language, as one of the most noticeable manifestations of identity, is most susceptible to shift and decay. Just because language is so public people have often wrongly assumed that it is *the* most important component of identity. Particularly where minority groups want to integrate into mainstream society the regular, daily function of the mother tongue decreases. The language can maintain a ritual function, and other markers of identity can be preserved as well, if they have a function in the private life of individuals. Edwards assumes that these remaining aspects do not hinder participation in mainstream culture, and are not an obstacle to getting ahead in society.

Apte (1979) shows that there is not always a one-to-one relationship between language and ethnic identity by describing the language situation of the Marathi-speaking community of Tamil Nadu, a state in the southern part of India, where Tamil is the official language of the state (see also the introduction to chapter 5). The community of Marathi speakers consists of approximately 50,000 people. Marathi is the official language of the state of Maharashtra on the west coast of India, where it is spoken by 41 million people. The present-day speakers of Marathi in Tamil Nadu are nearly all descendants of Marathi speakers who immigrated approximately 200 years ago. According to Apte, three major caste groups can be distinguished in the Marathi community in Tamil Nadu. Deshasta Brahmins, who were closely associated with the Tanjore kings as administrators and priests; tailors, who appear to be later immigrants; and Marathas who are Kshatriyas (warriors) and were the ruling caste of the Tanjore kingdom.

The major distinction is between the Brahmins and the non-Brahmins. For ideological reasons, the Marathi-speaking Brahmins are linked to their counterparts in the dominant population, the Tamil Brahmins. The tailors stress their caste identity within the framework of the pan-Indian social structure. They also show association with their homeland in terms of their religious behaviour. Apte argues that the two groups, with the same mother tongue, have different ethnic identities, and that there is very little communication between them. This Indian example makes clear that there may be other factors than language, such as caste, social class or political affiliation, which mark the demarcation line between ethnic groups.

So far we have discussed the relation between language and identity on the basis of the (false) assumption that languages are homogeneous. However, many varieties of a language can be distinguished. Ethnic groups may develop an ethnic variety of a language that originally belonged to another group, gradually dispense with their own minority tongue, and consider the ethnic variety as one of the carriers of ethnic identity. An example of this is the English spoken by Italian Americans, a group that has more or less successfully integrated itself into mainstream American society, and has overwhelmingly switched to English. Nonetheless, particularly inside the Italian community, Italo-Americans will sometime speak with a special intonation pattern, pronounce certain vowels and consonants in a way reminiscent of the early immigrants, use certain cultural content words (e.g. *mozzarella*), and show certain syntactic characteristics in their speech, for instance the omission of pronominal agent, as in (1)

(1) Go to a Scorsese movie (instead of: I go to . . .)

Another example of ethnic marking concerns utterances like (2) and (3) in the speech of Jewish Americans, and of Jewish New Yorkers in particular:

(2) A cadillac he drives
(3) Some milk he wants

For most speakers of English these sentences are unacceptable, because a constituent that is topicalized, i.e. moved to the front to receive emphasis, must be definite, as in (4)

(4) This book he has read (but not that one)

Although the pattern of (2) and (3), according to Feinstein (1980) has also spread to non-Jewish New Yorkers, it may be assumed to mark ethnic identity. The occurrence of topicalized indefinite noun phrases can probably be ascribed to the influence of Yiddish in which topicalization is a much more generally applicable process.

Returning to the main question of this section, we can state that there exists no categorical, necessary relation between language and ethnicity. As Lieberson (1970) noted in his study of the language situation of ethnic groups in Canada, there are many instances of ethnic groups with distinct languages, but also many instances of distinct ethnic groups with a common language. Ethnic differences do not always find parallels in linguistic differences, and vice versa. Furthmore, if we apply the approach to ethnicity proposed by Fishman, it is clear that language is not an obligatory part of patrimony, although if it is, it will generally be highly valued in the dimension of phenomenology. Following Ross's distinction, we can state that in the objective view of ethnicity the relation between language and ethnicity is accidental. Language may be or may not be included in the group's cultural bag. According to the subjective view, group members more or less consciously choose to associate ethnicity with language. The relation is subjective, as in the case of the West Indian creole speakers studied by Hewitt. Various aspects of bilingualism can only be understood rightly if the (potential) language–ethnicity relation is taken into account. Therefore this issue will reappear in many of the following chapters, for example in the next one.

2.2 Language attitudes

The fact that languages are not only objective, socially neutral instruments for conveying meaning, but are linked up with the identities of social or ethnic groups has consequences for the social evaluation of, and the attitudes towards languages. Or perhaps we should put it differently: if there is a strong relation between language and identity, this relation should find its expression in the attitudes of individuals towards these languages and their users.

The underlying assumption is that in a society social (or ethnic) groups have certain attitudes towards each other, relating to their differing social positions. These attitudes affect attitudes towards cultural institutions or patterns characterizing these groups such as language, and carry over to and are reflected in attitudes towards individual members of the groups. This chain is represented in Figure 2.1.

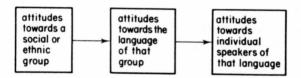

Figure 2.1 Schema representing the formation of attitudes

Generally, two theoretical approaches are distinguished to the study of language attitudes. The first one is the *behaviourist* view, according to which attitudes must be studied by observing the responses to certain languages, i.e. to their use in actual interactions. The *mentalist* view considers attitudes as an internal, mental state, which may give rise to certain forms of behaviour. It can be described as 'an intervening variable between a stimulus affecting a person and that person's response' (Fasold, 1984:147).

Nearly all researchers in the field of language attitudes adhere to this latter view, although it poses serious research problems because internal, mental states cannot be directly observed, but have to be inferred from behaviour or from self-reported data which are often of questionable validity.

In the mentalist approach, the following two methods are most commonly used for investigating language attitudes. The first one is called the *matched-guise technique*. It was developed in Canada by Lambert and his associates in the late 1950s and early 60s. In the basic set-up of a matched guise (*mg*) experiment, tape-recordings are made of a number of perfectly bilingual speakers reading the same passage of prose in both of their languages. The order of the recorded fragments is randomized, i.e. first speaker A in English, then speaker B in French, speaker C in English, speaker A in French, speaker D in French, etc.

Subjects whose language attitudes are being studied listen to these recordings under the impression that each speaker has been recorded once. The subjects (or judges) evaluate and rate the personality characteristics of the speakers, mostly on so-called semantic differential scales (Osgood, Suci and Tannenbaum, 1957). These scales have opposite extremes of certain traits at either end, and a number of blank spaces in between: the points of the scale. Examples of frequently used traits are: intelligent/dull; friendly/unfriendly; successful/unsuccessful; kind/cruel; aggressive/timid; trustworthy/unreliable. The subjects will not recognize two fragments as being read by the same speaker, and differences in reactions to the two fragments will reveal underlying language attitudes.

The second technique is that of the *questionnaire*, containing various types of questions on language and language use. Questions may be open or closed. Questionnaires with closed questions may also employ the semantic differential, or multiple-choice items. Questions like the following could be asked (in a language-attitude study in Wales):

– Rate Welsh on the following scales (e.g. beautiful/ugly; modern/old-fashioned; logical/illogical).
– Rate English on the following scales (the same scales).
– Do you agree with the following statement: more Welsh-speaking TV-programmes should be broadcast. (agree/do not agree/no opinion).
– Howard was born and raised in Cardiff, where he learned to speak Welsh. Now he lives in Manchester where he hardly ever speaks Welsh. Do you consider Howard to be a Welshman? (yes/no/no opinion).

As we stated above, most research on language attitudes follows the mentalist perspective. A central problem in this field is that mental states have to be inferred from a certain kind of behaviour. Language-attitude studies have become a central part of sociolinguistics, but we will not go further into the many theoretical and methodological issues pertaining to research in this area (see Fasold, 1984 for an excellent overview). Here we want to show what the results of language-attitude studies contribute to our understanding of the relation between language and identity.

In a first *mg*-study (Lambert *et al.*, 1960) English-speaking Canadian (EC) university students and French-speaking Canadian (FC) students rated the personalities of a series of speakers, the matched guises of fluent English/Canadian French bilinguals (EC and FC guises). The EC were strongly biased against the FC and in favour of the EC guises in their judgements. The same speakers were rated as being better looking, taller, more intelligent, more dependable, kinder, more ambitious, and as having more character in their EC-guises than in their FC-guises. In this respect, the EC-judges who spoke French as a second language did not differ from monolingual judges.

This result was not very surprising, because it could be expected that ECs would downgrade speakers of Canada's non-prestige language. But the real surprises were the evaluations by the French students. They also rated the EC-guises more favourably on a whole series of traits, except for kindness and religiousness, for which they gave more positive ratings to the FC-guises. A very striking result was that the FC students rated the FC-guises much more negatively on many traits than the EC-students had. Lambert (1967:95) considers 'this pattern of results as a reflection of a community-wide sterotype of FCs as being relatively second-rate people, a view apparently fully shared by certain sub-groups of FCs'.

This *mg*-study was replicated in many different language contact situations. For example, Lambert, Anisfeld and Yeni-Komshian (1965) investigated the attitudes of Arab-Israeli and Jewish-Israeli adolescents towards Hebrew and Arabic. The judges turned out to rate the representatives of their own group more favourably than the representatives of the other group. For instance, both the Arab and the Jewish listeners judged their own language group as more reliable, better looking, friendlier, and the like. In an *mg*-experiment on the language attitudes of black South African students towards English and Afrikaans (Vorster and Proctor, 1976) highly significant differences were found between the English and the Afrikaans guises. The English guises were expected to be much better looking, to have a higher-status job, to be more likeable, more sociable and kinder. Vorster and Proctor assume that the English stereotype is of a 'nice' person, whereas there are some indications that the Afrikaans stereotype is of a 'physically strong' person.

In studies of the language attitudes of children, it was found that at the age of 10 they generally do not yet have the cultural stereotypes prevailing among adults, and that above 10 they seem to acquire these stereotypes and begin to exhibit negative evaluations of speakers of a minority language (cf. Day, 1982).

The fact that language is often linked with specific activities or situations may cause a problem in the interpretation of results in language-attitude research. Most studies have used tape-recordings of the reading of formal prose or spontaneous speech concerning informal topics. However, certain languages do not seem appropriate for certain contexts, for example, the reading of a passage of a scientific article in a non-prestige minority language (cf. chapter 3). If this factor is not taken into account, it may influence the ratings of the speakers.

Carranza and Ryan (1975) did precisely this in their study of the language attitudes of Chicano and Anglo adolescents in Chicago. The Chicano students had learned Spanish at home, and the Anglo students in highschool foreign-language classes. Both groups had to rate the personalities of 16 speakers on a tape. Four speakers used English in a home context, four Spanish in a home context, four English in a school context, and four Spanish in a school context. The researchers did not use the matched-guise technique. Each speaker was recorded in his mother tongue, which made the passages as close to standard or 'normal' as possible. In general, English was rated higher than Spanish. But Spanish was more favourably judged in the home context than in the school context. Contrary to the expectations of the researchers, there were no differences between the two groups of students in this respect. According to Carranza and Ryan these results show that listeners take the appropriateness of the language variety for a particular situation into account in their judgements, but this conclusion seems only to be partially supported by the findings of the study.

Until now we have only discussed the attitudes towards a language in general, although especially in contact situations languages cannot be viewed as homogeneous wholes. Often in a bilingual community four linguistic varieties can be distinguished: the standard variety of language A and a non-standard contact variety of A (influenced by language B), and the standard variety of B and a non-standard contact variety of B (influenced by A). Most Mexican-Americans set a high value on standard Spanish and deprecate their own Spanish, which is often considered to be just border slang. But it is also noted that younger speakers, and especially the ones who identify themselves as Chicanos, assign positive ratings to speakers of local Spanish varieties such as Tex-Mex (see for instance Flores and Hopper, 1975). The attitudes towards local varieties of English differ from those towards Mexican-American Spanish. In the case of English, accented speech is associated with inferior status, and judges consistently show a negative attitude towards it (cf. Ryan and Carranza, 1977).

Turning now to a completely different context, Bentahila (1983) studied the attitudes among Arabic–French bilinguals in Morocco. Three language were involved: Classical Arabic, Moroccan-Arabic (the 'standard' vernacular in Morocco) and French (a compulsory subject in primary school, and used in many scientific, commercial and technical contexts). From the answers to a questionnaire Bentahila concluded that Classical Arabic was judged as the richest and most beautiful of the three languages, and French was considered the most modern and useful for studies. Bentahila furthermore conducted a matched-guise experiment in which three speakers participated: two of them spoke 'High Moroccan French' (which is very close to that of a native French speaker) and one French with a strong Moroccan accent in addition to Arabic. The first two were rated much higher than the third one in their French guises (in comparison with their Moroccan-Arabic guises) on traits related to status or education. French pronounced with a heavy Moroccan accent did not rate significantly differently from Moroccan-Arabic, i.e. accented French was not strongly associated with prestige and sophistication.

The general explanation for the results of language-attitude studies rests on the assumption that languages (or linguistic varieties) are objectively comparable, grammatically and logically, but that the differences in subjective evaluation of speech fragments is caused by the differences in social positions of ethnolinguistic groups. However, are languages comparable? This question was mainly studied in relation to two varieties of one language (standard and non-standard), but there is no reason not to extend the conclusions to languages.

Giles *et al.* (1979) report research on this issue, carried out in Canada and Wales. Two hypotheses were contrasted: the inherent value hypothesis (one variety *is* better or more beautiful than the other) and the imposed norm hypothesis (one variety is considered to be better or more beautiful because it is spoken by the group with most prestige or status). Giles and his colleagues found support for the second hypothesis: a dialect which was judged negatively by speakers from the community where it was used, in the case French Canadian in Canada, did not receive low ratings from non-users in Wales. According to Edwards (1982:21), 'we are on a fairly safe footing if we consider that evaluations of language varieties – dialects and accents – do not reflect either linguistic or aesthetic quality *per se*, but rather are expressions of social convention and preference which, in turn, reflect an awareness of the status and prestige accorded to the speakers of these varieties.'

Although speakers of non-prestige languages generally receive lower ratings in attitude studies than speakers of prestige languages, a distinction must be made between the ratings on different personality traits, especially when the rating is done by members of the non-prestige social groups themselves. For example, in the first matched-guise experiment by Lambert and his associates (Lambert *et al.*, 1960) the French Canadian judges rated the French Canadian guises more favourably than the English Canadian guises on the traits 'religiousness' and 'kindness'. In their study on the evaluation of Spanish and English, Carranza and Ryan (1975) distinguished status scales and solidarity scales. Status traits were: educated/ uneducated; intelligent/ignorant; successful/unsuccessful; wealthy/poor. Solidarity traits included: friendly/unfriendly; good/bad; kind/cruel; trustworthy/untrust-worthy. As was noted above, speakers of English were in general assigned higher ratings than speakers of Spanish, but the difference was smaller for solidarity scales than for status scales. A striking example of this differential attitude can be found in work done on Quechua–Spanish bilinguals in Peru (Wölck, 1973), where it was found that the ratings for Quechua (compared to Spanish) were higher on social or affective criteria like ugly/pretty, weak/strong and kind/unkind, while Spanish received higher ratings on traits like low class/high class and educated/uneducated.

Members of non-prestige social groups or linguistic minorities seem acutely aware of the fact that certain languages, i.e. non-prestige languages or minority languages, do not have a function in gaining upward social mobility. Spanish in America, French in Canada, Moroccan-Arabic in Morocco, or Quechua in Peru therefore are not associated with academic schooling, economic success, etc. That speakers of minority languages exhibit a negative attitude towards their own language in many respects, does not imply that they do not attach any importance to it. The language may be highly valued for social, subjective and affective reasons, especially by speakers from the younger generation in migration contexts or generally by people who feel a certain pride in minority culture. This form of *language loyalty* reflects the close relations between the language and the social identity of ethnolinguistic groups. Nevertheless there is not a one-to-one relation between identity and language. A distinct social, cultural or ethnic identity does not always have a distinct language as counterpart, while groups with distinct languages may have largely overlapping identities. Furthermore, identities and languages are not monolithic wholes but are clearly differentiated, heterogeneous and variable. This makes their relation in specific situations even more intricate.

Further reading

The two most informative collections of articles on language and ethnicity are H. Giles (ed.) *Language, ethnicity, and intergroup relations* (1977) and H. Giles and B. Saint-Jacques (eds.) *Language and ethnic relations* (1979). J.J. Gumperz (ed). *Language and social identity* (1982) contains articles on identity from the perspective of the ethnographic study of interaction. One issue of the *International Journal of the Sociology of Language* (nr. 20, 1979) is devoted to the subject 'Language planning and identity planning'. Similarly the *Journal of Multilingual and Multicultural Development* (vol. 3, no. 3, 1982) has a special issue on language and ethnicity in bilingual communities.

A well-known early source on language attitude studies is R.W. Shuy and R.W. Fasold (eds.), *Language attitudes: Current trends and prospects* (1973). For a recent collection on language attitudes, we refer the reader to E.B. Ryan and H. Giles (eds.) *Attitudes towards language variation* (1982).

3 The sociology of language choice

In many communities, not one language is spoken, but several. In these communities bilingualism is the norm, rather than the exception. The functioning of the two languages requires a particular set of norms for the speakers, and a functional specialization of the languages involved. Note that here, as elsewhere, we are talking about two languages, but in many situations more than two languages are involved. To get an idea of the complexity of the problem, take a situation such as Mauritius (Moorghen and Domingue, 1982). On an island with less than a million inhabitants, over 10 languages have sizable groups of speakers. Most of these are associated with particular ethnic groups, often descendants of migrants from South Asia, and in addition there is the colonial language, French (to some extent sharing this status with English). In between there is Creole, which on the one hand is the ethnic language of a particular group, termed General Population by Moorghen and Domingue, and on the other hand functions as a lingua franca. Thus a businessman with a Bhojpuri ethnic background may use English on the telephone when dealing with a large company, French when negotiating a building permit with a government official, joke with his colleagues in Creole, and then go home to speak Hindi with his wife and both Hindi and Creole with his children: Creole when making jokes, Hindi when telling them to do their homework.

We can approach the division of labour of the two languages involved, and hence the problem of choosing between the languages, from a number of different perspectives, which can be schematically presented as in Table 3.1:

Table 3.1: Sociological models for language choice

PERSPECTIVE	DOMINANT CONCEPT	PRINCIPAL REFERENCE
society	domain	Fishman (1965; 1972)
language	diglossia	Ferguson (1959)
speaker interaction	decision tree accomodation	Sankoff (1972) Giles (1973)
function	functional specialization	Jakobson (1960); Halliday *et al.* (1964)

We will now go on to discuss these different perspectives in turn, illustrating each of them with a characteristic example from a bilingual society. The first two perspectives, formulated in terms of the concepts of domains and diglossia, could be considered deterministic: the emphasis lies on a set of given societal norms rather than on the ways speakers construct, interpret and actively transform social reality. They will be dealt with in the first section. The second two perspectives (discussed in section 3.2) take the individual as their point of departure, and the fifth perspective, finally, attempts a more general, integrative point of view, in terms of the functions that a given language has.

3.1 Deterministic perspectives

The *domain* takes social organization as its conceptual basis. When speakers use two languages, they will obviously not use both in all circumstances: in certain situations they will use one, in others, the other. This general perception has been explored in a number of articles by Fishman, who has been studying Puerto Ricans in New York, work that has resulted in such famous research reports as 'Bilingualism in the Barrio' (Fishman *et al.*, 1968a). The point of departure for Fishman (1965) was the question: who speaks what language to whom and when?

One type of answer involves listing the various factors involved in language choice, such as group membership, situation and topic. Obviously, since language can be used to express one's identity, the identity imposed by one's group membership is a crucial factor in language choice. A West Indian in London will want to mark his or her ethnic origin in some way in speech. Similarly, the situation in which the interaction takes place has an important influence. Two Mexican Americans may find themselves speaking English at work, but when they see each other in a bar later on in the evening, Spanish is used. Finally, the topic of conversation may influence the choice of language. In most bilingual societies topics like the state of the economy and the rate of unemployment will tend to trigger a different language than kidding around or local gossip.

We will leave it to the reader to think of yet other factors influencing language choice; in the literature a number have been put forward. Language choice turns out to be subject to the same factors as all kinds of language behaviour. This approach runs the risk of fragmentation: the many interacting factors lead to an enormous number of possibilities, i.e. an enormous number of possibly differing interaction situations, and no single coherent picture emerges. The fragmentation becomes evident when we look at specific cases, such as the situation of Moroccans in the Netherlands. The general pattern of language choice (which could be given for Moroccans in Belgium and France in the same fashion, with only minor modifications) is given in Table 3.2.

Tables such as the one presented give only an incomplete picture: many situations are not mentioned, and in different situations possible interactants are not listed (such as grandparents at home). A complete list is hard to imagine, since life itself is infinite in its possibilities, and trying to describe the language choice for each situation would be an enterprise fit for Hercules, and in any case theoretically very unsatisfactory.

For this reason, Fishman conceived of the notion of domain as something more abstract, a clustering of characteristic situations or settings around a prototypical

Table 3.2 Situations in which three different languages are used.
Moroccan vernacular = Moroccan Arabic or Berber, depending on the group, and for Berber-speakers, even on the specific situation

	Moroccan vernacular	Dutch	Arabic
Home			
husband/wife	+	–	–
parent/child	+	+	–
friend (adult)	+	–	–
friends (child)	+	+	–
Shopping			
Moroccan store	+	–	–
Dutch store	–	+	–
Education			
Dutch school	+	+	–
Koran school	+	–	+
Religion	–	–	+
Work	+	+	–
Official institutions	?	+	–
Migrant organizations	+	?	?

theme that structures the speakers' perceptions of these situations. Thus a visit to a municipal housing office and an interview with a paediatrician share some features that makes them both belong to the institutional domain that generally calls for a particular language choice. Through the notion of domain, thought of as more than a convenient sociological abstraction, Fishman was able to avoid the excessive fragmentation involved in listing yet another situation that calls for a particular language.

The sociolinguist investigating bilingual communities needs to determine what the relevant domains are. This can differ from community to community. In Carribbean societies the street plays a very different role, for instance, than in urban Germany or Britain: the division home/street is much less rigid in the Caribbean, and the choices governing language behaviour at home hold for the street as well.

The notion of *diglossia* takes the characteristics of the languages involved as its point of departure. It is not only possible to look at bilingual speech behaviour from the point of view of the situation. It is also important to focus on the languages involved. This was the approach taken by Ferguson in an early article, by now a classic, in which the notion of 'diglossia' was developed (1959). In his definition, diglossia involved two varieties of a linguistic system used in a speech community: a formal variety, termed H (high), and a vernacular or popular form, termed L (low). Each variety has its own functions in the speech community, ranging from political speeches in H to informal conversations with friends in the L variety. The formal type of speech has a much higher prestige as well, often associated with its religious functions and with a literary and historical heritage. The H variety is standardized, often internationally, and relatively stable. It is not acquired by children as a first language, but later on in life. Finally, Ferguson claims that the H variety tends to be grammatically more complex than the L variety: it tends to have more obligatorily marked grammatical distinctions, a more complex morphophonemic system, less symmetrical inflection and less regular case marking.

Consider the following sentences from Classical Arabic (CA) and Moroccan Arabic (MA) illustrating the linguistic contrasts Ferguson (1959) meant:

(1) CA qāla   rabīçun   li-'abī-hi :   'urīdu   xizānatan
    MA qal   rbiç   1 -bba -h :   bġit   waḥed 1-maryu
       said   Rabi   to father-**3** want-**1** a cupboard

    CA 'aḥuṭṭu   fī-hā   kutub-ī   wa-' adawāt-ī
    MA baš ndir   fi-h   le-ktub dyal-i u-l-'adawa
       for put-**1** in-**3**   the books of-**1** and the things
    Rabi said to his father: I want a cupboard to put my books and things in.

In example (1) a number of contrasts between the varieties can be seen as characteristic of diglossia. In CA there are case endings: *rabiçun* and *xizānatan*, and these are absent in MA. Furthermore in MA it is possible to put person markers only on certain nouns, such as *bba-h* 'father-3', but not with most nouns. For example, the CA form *kutub-ī* 'my books' is replaced by the MA periphrastic form *le-ktub dyal-i* 'the books of-me'. Finally the CA synthetic purposive infinitive *'aḥuṭṭu* is replaced by a periphrastic form in MA. It is also striking to observe the basic grammatical parallelism between the two varieties, coupled with lexical and morphological differences.

The classical case of a diglossic system is the Arabic-speaking world, where in each country there are local vernacular forms of Arabic spoken alongside the traditional and international Classical Arabic, which approaches Quranic Arabic. Here Ferguson's concept applies rather well in most countries: Morocco would be a good example. Classical Arabic and Moroccan Arabic are separate as regards the functions they fulfil. Classical Arabic has a rich tradition of grammatical commentaries and treatises, a great literature, high prestige as a religious and a cultural language. Not all Moroccans learn it, and those who learn Arabic learn it much later than their own vernacular. (Berber-speaking Moroccans learn Classical Arabic always after they have learned Moroccan Arabic.) Moroccan Arabic, on the other hand, is barely recognized as a separate language, it does not have an officially recognized written form, and has less complex verbal paradigms, as can be seen from the example given above.

There are also lots of cases, however, where the concept of diglossia is less adequate in describing stable bilingual situations. We will briefly mention a number of divergences. In Paraguay, for example, there appears to be a classic division between Spanish and the original Amerindian language Guarani in terms of Ferguson's (1959) L and H varieties:

Table 3.3 Different characteristics of Spanish and Guarani

GUARANI (L.)	SPANISH (H)
private life	public life
low prestige 'Indian'	high prestige 'international'
mostly oral literature	rich literary tradition
acquired at home	acquired outside the house by most speakers
little standardization	clear standard norm

Even though Guarani is clearly viewed as the indigenous language and Spanish as the colonial language, many Paraguayans, including non-Indians, are bilingual between Spanish and Guarani (Rubin, 1968). As for the linguistic characteristics, however, the situation is unlike the one sketched by Ferguson. Not only are the L and the H forms unrelated, but using Ferguson's criteria Guarani is grammatically much more complex than Spanish.

A second type of situation where Ferguson's concept loses its usefulness lies in the centre of the Arabic world: urban Egypt. Here the description given above for Morocco used to apply as well, but now a whole range of varieties intermediate between vernacular Egyptian Arabic and international Arabic is emerging, leading to a blurring of the distinctions between H and L forms, and to a redefinition of linguistic norms (cf. e.g. Meiseles, 1980; Diem, 1974). In fact, the situation may be changing now even in Morocco itself, where it is becoming more and more clear that there are H and L varieties within Moroccan Arabic itself, and the distinction between Classical Arabic and Moroccan Arabic may become blurred as well.

In the third place, consider regional minority languages in contemporary Western Europe. An example is Provençal. In the Middle Ages, Provençal was a standard language with a flourishing literary tradition, but the formation of the French national state caused the hegemony of the Langue d'oil (the French from the North) over the Langue d'oc (Provençal). For many years this led to a diglossic situation in Provence, where French was the H variety and Provençal the L variety, conforming in every way to Ferguson's typology. As Provençal disappeared from the home, however, due to a general decline in its use, a new situation arose: Provençal remains in some ways the L variety, but mostly in terms of being a language of local identification. It is not learned at home any more, but outside, perhaps as late as adolescence, and is reacquiring some of its H functions, but only on the strictly regional level (Kremnitz, 1981). The situation of Provençal, in this respect, may well be characteristic of more traditional minority languages in Western Europe that have been losing ground.

Finally, the criterion of relatedness used by Ferguson is not unproblematic in another respect as well. We have seen in the case of Paraguay two totally unrelated languages, but consider a situation such as Haiti, cited by Ferguson. In Haiti, of course, we find Haitian Creole spoken by the people in addition to French, spoken by the urban elite. Sociologically French functions as a classic example of an H variety, and Haitian as a prototypical L variety, but scholars working on creole languages agree that Haitian Creole and French are only related in the very superficial sense that the vocabulary of Haitian is mostly derived from some form of French. Structurally, the two languages have very little in common. In chapter 15 we return to the question of what structures languages such as Haitian possess and how they are related to the European colonial languages.

Studies such as Rubin's analysis of Paraguayan bilingualism and the careful analysis of the situations in Egypt, Haiti and Western Europe have led, in fact, to a gradual redefinition of the term diglossia: it is now used to refer to bilingual communities in which a large portion of the speakers commands both languages, and in which the two languages are functionally distinguished in terms of H and L.

3.2 Person-oriented approaches

Both the analysis in terms of domains proposed by Fishman and the notion of diglossia suggested by Ferguson require a very large perspective: overall social norms. How do individual speakers and listeners deal with these norms? Are they strict, or fluctuating? We will now look at ways of dealing with language choice that take a more microscopic perspective.

One more person-oriented way to approach the problem of language choice is through the model of the *decision tree*. In this model the speaker is faced with a hierarchical set of binary choices, which can be represented formally as a tree. Taking again an adult Berber-speaking Moroccan in the Netherlands as an example, the tree might be as in Figure 3.1.

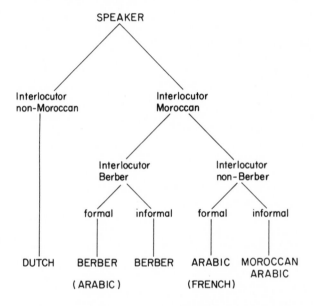

Figure 3.1 The Decision Tree model for the language choices of Moroccans in the Netherlands

Factors such as the ethnicity of the interlocutor, the style, the topic of conversation determine which language is finally chosen. The great advantage of the decision tree model is its descriptive clarity, but it suffers from a certain rigidity. In many situations more than one language is possible, often speakers are observed to make choices that are not exactly predicted by the tree model, and the model seems to exclude the use of two languages at the same time in one situation (code switching).

For this reason Sankoff (1972) has proposed combining the deterministic tree model with a more interpretive model, along the lines developed by Gumperz and Hernández-Chavez (1971). Suppose that the tree model only gives the ordinary, expected or unmarked choice for each situation. In many cases, however, there is the option for the speaker of introducing a marked choice, to indicate a special intention, irony, a change of style, or what have you. Sankoff (1972) at the same time shows scepticism towards the categorical use of the interpretive approach, however, on the basis of her own research in New Guinea. She studied a community in which three languages were spoken: Buang, the language of the tribe, Tok Pisin, the lingua franca, and Yabem, a language introduced by the missionaries. In many cases it was simply not possible to determine the unmarked choice, for instance in political speeches, in which all three languages were used systematically. In chapter 10 we return to the cases where more than one language at the same time seems to be called for.

Within social psychology there has been an attempt, primarily by Howard Giles and his colleagues, to develop a model of language choice called the Interpersonal Speech Accomodation Theory (cf. Giles, 1973; Giles *et al.*, 1973). The main idea behind it is that language choice cannot be explained adequately by referring to situational factors only. Aspects of the interpersonal relation have to be taken into account. The model, which was initially developed to explain accent change within one language, stresses the relation between the participants. The essence of Giles's theory is derived from social psychological research on similarity–attraction, which claims that an individual can induce someone else to evaluate her or him more favourably by reducing the number of dissimilarities between her or himself and the other. Speakers will automatically adjust themselves to each other, both in gestures and often positioning of the body and in the type of speech. This may carry over to bilingual settings, and one way of interpreting the choice of a particular language is in terms of the other speaker's language and identity.

The process of adjustment is called *accommodation*. In fact, accommodation may work in two opposite ways. The first way is convergence: the speaker uses the language that the hearer knows or likes best. A bilingual inhabitant of Brussels, for instance, addresses somebody from Flanders in Dutch, even though the latter may know some French in addition to Dutch. The second form of accommodation is divergence: the speaker tries to create distance between himself and the hearer by maximizing differences in language use.

Giles *et al.* (1973) illustrate the process of speech accommodation with an example provided by Dell Hymes. Consider a Westerner speaking to a Tanzanian official. When this Westerner starts using Swahili this form of accommodation does not induce the approval the speaker expects, because the official will think that the Westerner considers him not proficient in English, which is an insult. Accommodation should proceed in the following sequence: the Westerner uses English first, so that the Tanzanian can show his skills in this language, and after that the Westerner switches to Swahili to express solidarity.

Roughly along the same lines, but from a different perspective, Gumperz and his colleagues have worked on language choice in terms of the common understanding of speaker and hearer. Language forms do not have a social meaning by themselves, but only in so far as the participants in the interaction agree on this meaning. The latter is crucial; the social meaning of language does not depend on the speaker alone, not on the hearer alone but on an agreement, the result of negotiation as it were, between speaker and hearer. There is no fixing of the situation at one point of time, but rather the participants' on-going process of interpretation of the situation. Particularly in multilingual communities the conventions by which the social meaning of the forms of language used is interpreted are not automatically shared by the participants in interactions, rather they need to be established and reinterpreted in the course of each conversation. Blom and Gumperz (1972), in research directed at language use in Norway, distinguish three levels in the interpretive process. First, the *setting* is determined: the locale for the interaction, the socially recognized chunk of the environment. An example of such a setting may be the down-town post office. Within a given setting, different *social situations* are possible; which one is valid at a particular moment is determined by the interactants on the basis of the constellation of particular people, in a particular setting, at a particular moment of time. Within the setting of the post office, different social situations are possible. One would be a stamp-buying interaction, another one a chance encounter with an acquaintance. Finally, given a specific social situation, speaker and hearer need to come to terms with the question in which *social event* they find themselves. Events have clearly defined and socially recognized sequencings, centre around a limited range in topics, etc. To continue with the post office example, the notion social event may refer to the way the participants in the chance encounter choose to keep their distance, use the encounter as a way of renewing old ties, etc. Each of these options requires a specific set of routine remarks and gestures, confronts the speaker with complex choices, in other words. The three notions setting, situation and event are not given, once again, but need to be interpreted and recreated by speaker and hearer in each interaction.

Working within this paradigm, Heller has written a number of papers on the choice between English and French in present-day Montreal, both in the workplace and in public places. The following is an example from a restaurant interaction (1984):

Waiter: Je reviens dans une minute.
        I'LL BE BACK IN A MINUTE.
        (Pause. Second look.)
        Anglais ou français, English or French?
Patron: Ben, les deux. WELL, BOTH.
Waiter: Non, mais, anglais ou français? NO, BUT, . . .
Patron: It doesn't matter,
        c'est comme vous voulez. . . . AS YOU LIKE
Waiter: (Sighs)
        Okay, okay, I'll be back in a minute

Language choice, according to Heller's enthnographic observation, is a very complex process, not just the reflection of the changing sociolinguistic realities of Montreal but part of that reality.

3.3 Function specialization

A model which has the potential to integrate the various approaches given above is one in terms of functional specialization. Language use involves various functions of the language system; following research by Jakobson and Halliday, Mühlhäusler (1981) distinguishes six functions – six uses to which a language may be put:

1 the *referential* function: by referring to extralinguistic reality information is transferred. This function is often thought to be the only function of language, and any knowledge of a language implies command of this function;
2 the *directive* and *integrative* function: by using standard greetings, conventional

modes of address, imperatives, exclamations, and questions contacts are made with others and enough of an interactive structure is created to ensure cooperation;

3 the *expressive* function: by making one's feelings known one can present oneself to others as a unique individual. Many non-fluent speakers have great difficulty with this function;

4 the *phatic* function: in order to create a channel of communication and to keep the channel open speakers make use of conventionalized openings, closings, and ways to signal turn taking, and if necessary, also of language forms that identify the in-group within which interaction is taking place;

5 the *metalinguistic* function: by using language the speaker's attitude towards and awareness of language use and linguistic norms are made known;

6 the *poetic* function: by means of jokes, puns and other word play, and conscious style and register shifts language is played with, so that the use of language becomes a goal and source of joy in itself.

Now what do these different functions have to do with language choice and bilingualism? Simply that different languages may fulfil different functions in the lives of bilingual speakers, and in bilingual conversations a choice for one particular language may signal the primary functions appealed to at that moment. The functions listed here encompass the approaches that we have briefly described above.

We all know how hard it is to make puns, let alone write poems, in a foreign language even if we feel perfectly comfortable making an airline reservation in it. The same holds for the metalinguistic function: many English-speakers will remember the time they were in a shop in Paris trying to ask, in French, how something they wanted to buy is called in French.

Not only can (as the attentive reader will undoubtedly have noted) the different functions of language be hierarchically arranged from 1 to 6 with respect to the differing demands they make on our command of a language, but they also differ in the domain in which they are most frequently called upon. Something like the parallel in Figure 3.2 is not entirely far-fetched:

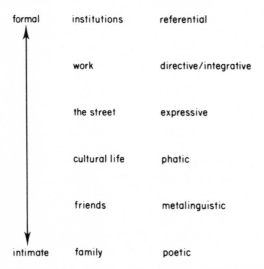

Figure 3.2   An integration of the domain and the functional perspective

The parallel is not perfect because the functions are much more abstract than the domains, but it may be safely said that the more one moves towards the lower end of the domain column the more the functions at the lower end of the right-hand column play a role.

The integrative potential of the functional model can be illustrated, perhaps, in Figure 3.3:

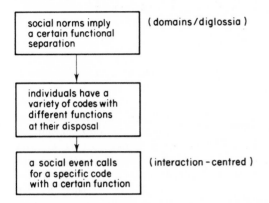

Figure 3.3 Abstract representation of the way in which language choices are made

The notion of function links the deterministic with the interaction-centred approaches.

Before concluding this chapter we should note that not all cases of bilingualism can be discussed satisfactorily in terms of the notion of functional specialization adopted here. In chapter 11 on strategies of neutrality, an alternative approach will be explored: There may be situations in which two languages are used which do *not* have clearly separate functions.

Further reading

Two volumes of articles give a good overview of the classical approaches to the problem of language choice: J.A. Fishman (ed.) *Readings in the Sociology of Language* (1968) and J.J. Gumperz and D. Hymes (eds.), *Directions in Sociolinguistics* (1972). More recent studies focus on language choice in relation to other topics, and further reading on these is provided in chapters 2, 4, 10 and 11.

4   Language maintenance and shift

When Dolly Pentreath died in December 1777, the last native speaker of Cornish passed away. Cornish was formerly spoken by thousands of people in Cornwall, but the community of Cornish speakers did not succeed in maintaining its language under the pressure of English, the prestigious majority language and national language. To put it differently: the Cornish community shifted from Cornish to English (cf. Pool, 1982). Such a process seems to be going on in many bilingual communities. More and more speakers use the majority language in domains where they formerly spoke the minority tongue. They adopt the majority language as their regular vehicle of communication, often mainly because they expect that speaking that language gives better chances for upward social mobility and economic success. As Dressler and Wodak-Leodolter (1977:35) point out in an article on language preservation and death in Brittany (France): 'it is necessary to present oneself as a member of the national majority to acquire positions (like jobs, official functions and educational facilities)'. In such cases the minority language is in danger of becoming obsolescent.

When a community stops speaking a minority language, of course this language will not always be extinguished. For example, if the Gujerati-speaking people in England shifted to English completely, Gujerati would not become a dead language. There are millions of speakers of Gujerati in other parts of the world, especially in India. For the (erstwhile) Gujerati community in England it would be a dead language.

Sometimes it seems that 'shift' can be equated with 'shift towards the majority or prestigious language', but in fact 'shift' is a neutral concept, and also shift towards the extended use of the minority language can be observed. For example, in the last decades French has strengthened its position in Quebec at the expense of English. After a period of shift towards the majority language, there is often a tendency to reverse the process, because some people come to realize that the minority language is disappearing, and they try to promote its use. These defenders of the minority language are often young, active members of cultural and political organizations that stand up for the social, economic and cultural interests of the minority group.

Why does one language survive and another one disappear? In section 4.1. we will give an overview of the factors that govern language maintenance and shift. Knowledge of these factors does not guarantee insight into the process of language shift, since people bring this about in their daily speech, and it is on this level that explanations for shift must be found. This approach will be outlined in section 4.2.

When a language is reduced in its function, which happens in the case of shift towards the majority language, generally speakers will become less proficient in it, i.e. *language loss* is taking place. Language shift linked up with loss will finally result in *language death*. In section 4.3. we will further discuss these issues.

4.1 Factors influencing language maintenance

In various publications, for instance Glazer (1978), Gaarder (1979) and Clyne (1982) factors influencing language maintenance are discussed. Giles, Bourhis and Taylor (1977) have constructed a model to systematize the many factors operating. They propose a combination of three main factors (status, demographic and institutional support) into one factor which they call 'ethnolinguistic vitality'. According to Giles *et al.* (1977:308), '[the] vitality of an ethnolinguistic group is that which makes a group likely to behave as a distinctive and active collective entity in intergroup situations. From this, it is argued that ethnolinguistic minorities that have little or no group vitality would eventually cease to exist as distinctive groups. Conversely, the more vitality a linguistic group has, the more likely it will survive and thrive as a collective entity in an intergroup context.' With respect to the minority language, this implies that high vitality will lead to maintenance (or even shift towards extended use) and low vitality will result in shift towards the majority language, or, in some cases towards another more prestigious vernacular. In this section, we will largely follow the model presented in Giles *et al.* (1977), although it must be noted that the terminology in that model partly seems somewhat circular, and therefore trivial: the more *vitality* a group has, the more likely it will *survive*.

The first main category of factors distinguished by Giles *et al.* concerns *status*.

Economic status is a prominent factor in nearly all studies on language maintenance and shift. Where groups of minority language speakers have a relatively low economic status, there is a strong tendency to shift towards the majority language. For example, most speakers of Spanish in the USA find themselves in the low-income groups. They associate speaking English with academic achievement and economic progress. Spanish gets the stigma of the language of poor people, and parents who themselves sometimes have a poor command of English try to urge their children to speak English, because they have internalized the societal attitudes towards Spanish. Immigrant workers in Western Europe are also more or less forced to believe that their low economic status is mainly caused by the fact that they speak a minority language, for example Turkish, Serbo-Croatian or Greek. Immigrants who want to get ahead in society place a high value on speaking the majority language. This will negatively affect the use of their own language. According to Li (1982), Chinese Americans of lower socioeconomic status tend to be more easily assimilated than are those of higher status. The low-income Chinese Americans show the highest propensity for shift away from the Chinese mother tongue.

Economic changes, i.e. modernization, industrialization and urbanization, are important variables in the description of language maintenance and shift. Rindler Schjerve (1981) in an article on Sardinian notes that this type of economic change has led to a trend to use more Italian, which is associated with 'modern life' and higher standards of living. In periods of modernization minority languages often suffer a double stigma: they are spoken by poor and traditional, old-fashioned people who cannot fully cope with the reality of modern economic life. However, economic changes might also affect language maintenance positively. Paulsen (1981) writes about the Ferring language, a Germanic language spoken on the islands Föhr and Amrun off the North Sea coast of Germany in the North Sea, and describes economic developments in the sixteenth century. After a strong reduction of the income from the fishing of herring, a school to teach young boys the craft of navigation was founded. The islands were thus able to offer the new Dutch overseas companies many well-trained sailors and officers, mainly for whaling in the Arctic and for the Far East shipping. This resulted in nearly three centuries of economic independence which was a safeguard to the position of Ferring.

Social status is very closely aligned to economic status, and it is probably equally important with respect to language maintenance. A group's social status, which here refers to the group's self-esteem, depends largely upon its economic status. Speakers of Quechua in Peru, Ecuador and Bolivia will generally consider themselves to have low social status, and tend to shift towards Spanish, which has the connotations of higher social status.

Sociohistorical status is derived from the ethnolinguistic group's history. Many groups can refer to periods in which they had to defend their ethnic identity or their independence. These historical instances can be viewed as mobilizing symbols which inspire individuals to struggle for their common interests as members of an ethnolinguistic group, as group members in the past did. The Flemish people, for example, can draw inspiration from their struggle against French domination. The 'Guldensporenslag' (Battle of the Golden Spurs) in 1302 when Flemish troops held their own against French-speaking nobles, still has mobilizing power. Tupac Amaru, the eighteenth-century Peruvian rebel against the Spanish colonial regime, stressed Quechua as a symbol of the glorious Inca past, and gained a large following as a messianic leader.

Language status can be an important variable in bilingual communities. For instance, French, Russian, English and Spanish have a high status as languages of international communication. Therefore it would be easier to preserve French in Quebec than Ukrainian, Vietnamese or Dutch. However, it should be noted that status within a community should be distinguished from status outside the community. French has high status outside Canada, but in Canada English has higher credits. Also, in the Arabic world Arabic has very high status, because it is the language of the Koran, i.e. the language of God. In Belgium, France and the Netherlands, however, Arabic is not held in high esteem by most people.

Language and social status are closely related in the sense that the latter influences the former. The self-ascribed language status will be low especially if the minority group speaks a dialect of the language in question. Many speakers of Spanish in the South-West of the USA have negative attitudes towards their variety of Spanish; they view it as 'only a dialect', or a kind of 'border slang', and not as a real language. This feeling of linguistic inferiority is particularly strong in cases of a minority language which is not standardized and/or modernized (see chapter 5). For this reason, a creole language like Haitian will have a low status in New York where there is a large community of Haitian immigrants and refugees. Languages with low status are in danger of becoming obsolescent. Whether this will happen also depends on the status of the 'competing language', which will often be the majority language. Immigrants in Denmark will have a weaker tendency to shift towards Danish than immigrants in England towards English, because of the higher status of English compared to Danish generally.

Demographic factors constitute the second main category in the model of Giles *et al.* (1977). They concern the number of members of a linguistic minority group and their geographical distribution. The absolute number of speakers of a certain language becomes important when it decreases. Such a development implies decreasing usefulness of the language in question, which in turn will give rise to language shift away from the minority language. Clyne (1982) studied language maintenance among immigrants in Australia, and he concludes that there is no general correspondence between numerical strength and language maintenance. For one group, the Maltese community, however, such a correspondence could be found when comparing data on language shift in various Australian states. The two states with relatively large Maltese populations turned out to have the lowest rates of shift towards English, and those with very few Maltese immigrants had very high rates of shift (see Table 4.1.).

Table 4.1 Maltese population ratio in four Australian states and language shift towards English in first generation immigrants, i.e. immigrants born outside of Australia (table adapted from Clyne, 1982)

State or territory	% of Maltese born to total population	language shift (%) in first generation
Victoria	0.81	29.29
New South Wales	0.52	28.31
Northern Territory	0.06	66.67
Tasmania	0.02	67.95

The percentage of speakers maintaining a minority language can be strongly influenced by the occurrence of mixed or inter-ethnic marriages. In these marriages, the most prestigious language generally has the best chance to survive as the language of the home, and hence as the first language of the child. Pulte (1979) conducted a household survey in several Oklahoma Cherokee communities in an attempt to obtain data on language maintenance and shift in Cherokee families. Although Pulte concludes that Cherokee is still flourishing in a few communities, he also notes that in every family where a Cherokee-speaker was married to a non-Cherokee-speaker, the children were found to be monolingual speakers of English.

Clyne (1982) also provides data on the effects of marriage between native speakers of English and speakers of other languages, so-called Anglo-ethnic marriages. Table 4.2. (compiled on the basis of two tables in Clyne's study) presents the rate of language shift in the second-generation children of intra-ethnic and Anglo-ethnic marriages.

Table 4.2 shows that shift towards English is nearly complete for children from Anglo-German, Anglo-Maltese and Anglo-Dutch marriages. With respect to other inter-ethnic marriages (with no native English-speaking parent) Clyne states that the number of children born from these is too small to generalize, but it appears that most of them adopt English as their main language, except in cases where one of the parents, particularly when it is the father, is of Italian or Greek origin.

Table 4.2 Rate of language shift in the second-generation children of intra-ethnic and Anglo-ethnic marriages in Australia

Birthplace of both parents or one parent	% language shift of 2nd generation children of intra-ethnic marriages	% language shift of 2nd generation children of Anglo-ethnic marriages
Germany	62.3	96.2
Greece	10.1	68.4
Italy	18.6	78.5
Malta	53.7	94.6
Netherlands	80.0	99.1

The geographical distribution of minority group members generally affects language maintenance and shift considerably. As long as they live concentrated in a certain area, minority groups have better chances of maintaining their language. The importance of this factor can be illustrated with examples from all over the world. Especially in Quebec where many French-speaking Canadians are concentrated, French is a vital language, while in other parts of Canada, where the speakers of French live more dispersed, there is a tendency to shift away from French (cf. Lieberson, 1967). Li (1982), in his study on language shift of Chinese Americans, found that third-generation Chinese-Americans residing in Chinatowns shifted substantially less often towards English than their agemates living outside Chinatowns. For example, less than 30 per cent of the third-generation Chinatown residents aged 20–39 had adopted English as their mother tongue, while this was the case for 50 per cent of the group living outside Chinatowns. In the same way the distribution of minority language speakers can change because of immigration and emigration patterns. Jones (1981) shows that Welsh, which was in Wales unquestionably dominant at the end of the nineteenth century, has been forced back in areas where large-scale immigration of workers from outside Wales took place in the first decades of this century. Emigration during the depression in the 1930s from mining valleys where Welsh was widely spoken has had the same result. With respect to the more recent period, Jones points to tourism and the in-migration of English-speaking retired people and second-home ownership. The consequences were (and are) that the concentration of Welsh speakers is becoming lower, and mixed Welsh–English communities arise with a shift towards English.

Urban–rural differences are important in the analysis of patterns of language shift as well. Generally, rural groups tend to preserve a minority language much longer than urban groups. Hill and Hill (1977) studied language shift in Nahuatl-speaking communities in Central Mexico (Nahuatl is also known as 'Mexicano' or 'Aztec'). They found that the settlement of rural people in cities and industrial suburbs fostered shift towards Spanish. In an article on the survival of ethnolinguistic minorities in Canada, Anderson (1979) concludes that research in Saskatchewan has indicated that members of ethnic groups (such as Ukrainians) living on farms have maintained their language better than those living in small towns and villages, who in turn have resisted shift towards English more strongly than those in large urban centres.

Probably, the geographical distribution in itself is not the causal factor in language maintenance and shift, but related communication patterns and the absence or presence of daily social pressure to use the prestigious language. When residing on a farm, where perhaps the neighbours are members of the same linguistic minority group, there is not much need to use the majority language. The home is the most important domain of language use, and this domain is reserved for the minority language. On the contrary, people living in urban centres will be forced in various situations to use the majority language daily, which will weaken the position of the minority tongue.

The third main cluster of factors proposed by Giles *et al.* (1977) is that of the *institutional support factors*, which refer to the extent to which the language of a minority group is represented in the various institutions of a nation, a region or a community. Maintenance is supported when the minority language is used in various institutions of the government, church, cultural organizations, etc. In politically well-organized minority groups (such as the Chicanos in the USA) minority languages are often a vehicle of expression.

Mass media can affect language shift considerably. In the above-mentioned study by Hill and Hill (1977), it is argued that the shift from Nahuatl towards Spanish is also brought about by the introduction of electricity and radios in the early 1940s. Nowadays, many ordinary dwellings in the area studied in Central Mexico have high-fidelity stereo consoles, television and radio which will further promote the use of Spanish. Broadcasting in minority languages, on the other hand, can boost these languages, just like the publishing of newspapers, books, etc. in minority languages.

When the minority language is also the language of the *religion* this will be an impetus for its maintenance. For example, German has held a rather strong position in the United States for a long time, compared with immigrant languages like Dutch and Swedish, because it was the language of the Lutheran church. Religion can also be a general divisive force, which among other things affects language maintenance. Kloss (1966) studied the language situation of the Old Order Amish and Old Order Mennonites of German descent living in Pennsylvania, who speak Pennsylvania Dutch (from *Deutsch* = German) as their mother tongue. According to Kloss, the point of departure for these Old Order groups is their religion rather than nationality or language. 'They maintain their language in order to more fully exclude worldly influences and, perhaps, because change in itself is considered sinful. Neither language nor nationality is valued for its own sake, (Kloss, 1966:206).

Providing *governmental or administrative services* in the mother tongue can stimulate maintenance. In modern societies every individual has to interact frequently with representatives of local or national authorities. If the medium of communication is always the majority language, this will diminish the usefulness of the minority language.

Education is very important with respect to language maintenance. If children's proficiency in the minority language is fostered at school, and they learn to read and write in it, this will contribute to maintenance.

Government activities concerning languages in multilingual communities will be further dealt with in chapter 5, *Language Planning*. One of these activities might concern education, for example establishing facilities for education in the minority language in addition to the majority language. It will be discussed in chapter, 6, *Bilingual Education*.

Besides the main factors distinguished by Giles *et al.* (1977), we further mention *cultural (dis-)similarity* as an important variable in the analysis of language maintenance/shift. On the basis of data on language shift of immigrants in Australia, Clyne

(1982) concludes that when the cultures involved are similar there is a greater tendency for shift than when they are less similar. German and Dutch immigrants, who have culturally much in common with the English-speaking Australian community, show a greater shift towards English than Italian and Greek immigrants, who will experience a greater cultural distance.

Before we turn to the next section, in which the process of language shift itself will be discussed, three things must be said about the factors presented thus far.

1 The various factors and sub-factors are presented separately, but they may correlate strongly. For example, a group with a low economic status will often have a low sociohistorical status as well; it will not have control over mass media and it will not be able to fight for educational programmes in the minory language.

2 Since so many factors (probably interrelated) play a part, it is impossible to predict language maintenance or shift for certain groups. Most research on this issue is purely *post-hoc* and descriptive, and a fully-fledged theory of language maintenance is not available.

3 The factors considered do not influence language maintenance and shift directly, but only indirectly via intervening variables, as is represented in Figure 4.1.

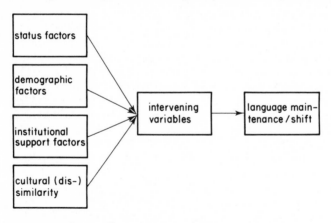

Figure 4.1   Factors affecting language maintenance

The crucial question is of course: what are these intervening variables? How do the large-scale sociological factors influence individual behaviour, and thereby language maintenance/shift? To answer this question, a different type of research is necessary. To this we will turn in the next section.

4.2 The process of language shift

To study language maintenance or shift a researcher can collect data on the factors discussed in the previous section and on the distribution and use of languages in a multilingual community by asking people questions like: Which language do you speak regularly in your home? Which language do you speak regularly at work? Then the researcher can try to relate information about social factors to the data on language use. This type of research is usually large-scale, and the actual language behaviour and language attitudes of the members of the community are not studied. In another approach the focus of the investigation is on the language behaviour and attitudes of individuals, because it is assumed that only in this way can researchers gain real insight into the process of language shift. (Because multi-lingual situations are never stable, there will always be some kind of *shift*, therefore, we will restrict ourselves in this and the next section to this process; see also chapter 2.) Such studies have to be conducted on a smaller scale, because the researcher must become aquainted with the social life of individuals in the community. Participant observation, i.e. living in the community to be studied and participating in its daily activities like an anthropologist in an African village, is the best method of reaching this goal.

Susan Gal's study of language shift in Oberwart (Austria) is a magnificent example of research along these lines (Gal, 1979). Oberwart (Felsöör in Hungarian) is a village in Burgenland, a province in the east of Austria, bordering Hungary. Oberwart was a peasant village, and the peasants generally spoke Hungarian. German was only used with outsiders and strangers. However, in the last 50 to 70 years, especially after the Second World War, German has been replacing Hungarian in many instances of everyday interaction. In the 1920s children spoke only Hungarian with each other, while at the time of Gal's stay in Oberwart (she lived there for a year), the use of German between age-mates was quite common for children under 15. Young parents address their children not in Hungarian – like their parents did – but in German, and they switch to Hungarian only occasionally.

The language shift in Oberwart can be related to economic changes. The former more or less 'pure' peasant economy of Oberwart does not exist any more. Since about 1950 industrialization has become important. Agricultural work came to be associated with the past and with a lack of social mobility and economic opportunities. If an Oberwarter did not want to stay on the farm, a good proficiency in German was indispensable. German began to intrude in domains, e.g. the local inn, which were formerly nearly completely reserved for Hungarian. Gal notes that language shift is related, of course, to social-economic change. The real question, however, is '[by] what intervening processes does industrialization, or any other social change, effect changes in the uses to which speakers put their languages in everyday interaction?' (Gal, 1979:3). In answering this question Gal takes two sociolinguistic phenomena into account. The first one concerns the relation between language and identity (see also chapter 2). In post-war Oberwart Hungarian has lost prestige, it has become the language associated with traditional, elderly people, while German has come to be seen as the language of economic progress and modern life. Generally, speakers want to express their social status in their linguistic behaviour, and try to assert their identity by choosing a certain language. Most of the younger people in Oberwart, who had no knowledge of speakers of Hungarian outside the village, therefore adopted German. Hungarian was associated strongly with a stigmatized social group.

The second sociolinguistic phenomenon Gal considers is the importance of social networks, i.e.'the networks of informal social interaction in which speakers are enmeshed and through which, by pressure and inducements, participants impose linguistic norms on each other' (Gal, 1979:14). It is not only the frequency of social contact which is important, but also the nature of the relationship between the speakers, the social character of the contacts and the purpose of the interaction. In

Oberwart one cannot simply say: that person belongs to the social group of peasants, therefore he or she speaks Hungarian, and that person belongs to the group of non-peasants, therefore he or she speaks German. Again, there is no direct relation between social factors and language use, because the networks in which people participate have a stronger and more direct influence. For example, an industrial worker with a largely peasant network will use more Hungarian than one with a non-peasant network. Figure 4.2. indicates the proportion of German – (G + GH)/(G + GH + H) – used by speakers in three age groups. In each generation the informants are grouped according to the proportion of peasants in their networks. The proportion of German used is computed on the basis of information provided by the speakers on domains in which they spoke German (G), German and Hungarian (GH) and Hungarian (H).

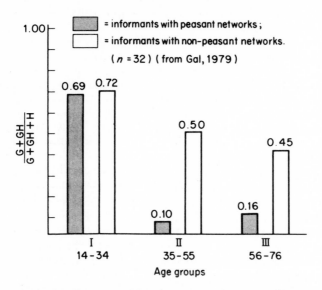

Figure 4.2 Proportion of German used by informants in Oberwart with peasant and non-peasant networks in three age groups

Figure 4.2. shows that speakers in the younger generation in general use more German, irrespective of network, but the people of the middle and the older generation vary their language according to the network they are participating in.

The processes described by Gal are not exclusive to multilingual societies. They can also be observed in monolingual communities, where different linguistic varieties are in use. The form of linguistic change in Oberwart, where Hungarian is gradually being replaced by German, has a direct parallel in a monolingual community where one linguistic variant takes the place of another. The social meaning of the variants considered, the status speakers want to claim in choosing certain variants, and the social networks these speakers are part of, are important factors in explaining linguistic change in this situation as well.

Linguistic change takes place by the gradual spread of the 'new form' in a certain domain. Language A (or variant A) is never replaced suddenly by language B (or variant B), but language use becomes variable, i.e. A and B are both used in the same social context. After this stage of variable use, the use of B will become categorical. In Oberwart, Gal has observed this variable use of German and Hungarian in social contexts where formerly the use of Hungarian was categorical, and she predicts categorical use of German in the future. Linguistic change, within a language, or in the form of language shift, as in Oberwart, has its source in the synchronic heterogeneity in the speech community. Linguistic diversity is at the same time the reflection of and the impetus for this change.

In many minority communities the ethnic language has had a strong position in informal domains, particularly in family interaction. However, here, the majority language often intrudes, with variable language use as its result. Lieberson and McCabe (1982) studied the relation between domains of language use and mother-tongue shift in Nairobi in the Gujerati-speaking population. They found that many parents used both Gujerati and English in addressing their children, and that much of the shift from Gujerati towards English can be explained by this fact. In interactions in the homes of immigrant workers' families in Western Europe the same pattern can be observed, but there especially the children introduce the majority language.

Language shift is in fact the redistribution of varieties of language over certain domains. If the shift is towards the majority language, this language seems to conquer domain after domain via the intermediate stage of bilingual language use. When the minority language is spoken in fewer domains, its value decreases. This in turn will lessen the motivation of younger people to learn and use it.

In addition to 'domain', an important notion in the analysis of language shift is *generation*. Figure 4.2. already showed clear generational differences in Oberwart related to different social perspectives of the younger group: they often want to claim social status different from that of their parents' generation. Therefore, younger people choose another language as their regular medium of communication. Rindler Schjerve (1981), in an article on bilingualism and language shift in Sardinia, gives an example of a household with family members belonging to four generations. 'An 80-year-old grandmother was illiterate and monolingually Sardinian, the 50-year-old mother, due to insufficient education, had a rather limited proficiency in Italian, the 30-year-old daughter having been to school for eight years spoke Italian well, though not perfectly, and used it when talking to their children, while she used Sardinian with her husband. Her reason for using Italian with her children is to avoid their being discriminated against in school; this, of course, resulted in the 12-year-old schoolboy's having only a limited command of Sardinian and speaking a rather mono-stylistic and Sardicized Italian' (Rindler Schjerver, 1981:212).

Language shift may come about slowly and go on for several generations, but especially in changing social situations it may be a rather fast process. This is often the case for immigrant groups. Tosi (1984) studied bilingualism and language shift among Italian immigrants in Bedford (Great Britain). The first-generation immigrants generally use a local Italian dialect as the principal medium of communication within the family. Until school age, their children mostly speak this dialect, only occasionally switching to English, and when there are several children in the household they often speak English among themselves. But English really gains influence when the children go to school and become more proficient in it. English will then inevitably be brought into the household: initially for use mainly with other siblings, but later also in interactions with the parents. A younger person will gradually learn to understand that the two languages are associated with two different value systems, and that these systems often collide with each other. This results in personal and emotional conflicts. Tosi points to the linguistic and cultural conflict between generations. The 'regular' conflict between two generations is accentuated because of differences in values, outlook and aspirations. These differences are symbolized in the language behaviour of the generations, i.e. the preference for Italian (dialect) vs English.

The general pattern for language shift in immigrant groups is as follows. The first generation (born in the country of origin) is bilingual, but the minority language is clearly dominant, the second generation is bilingual and either of the two languages might be strongest, the third generation is bilingual with the majority language dominating, and the fourth generation only has command of the majority language. This is only a general pattern, and the picture for specific immigrant groups is different, largely depending on the factors discussed in section 4.1.

To conclude this section, we want to emphasize one important issue: the literature on language shift sometimes suggests that a whole minority group is in the process of shifting from one language to the other, and differences between individuals are not noticed. However, minority groups are not undifferentiated, monolithic wholes, but comprise different sub-groups with different cultural attitudes and political opinions. These differences may come to surface as differences in language behaviour. Language shift is not inevitable, and (groups of) individuals may promote the use of the minority language in the home environment, aiming at bilingualism. Tosi (1984) witnessed this attitude among a few young people of Italian descent in Bedford.

4.3 Language loss

As a language loses territory in a given community, speakers will become less proficient in it. In linguistic minority groups children will often speak the language of the group less well than their parents. In a study of bilingualism among children of Italian background in South Australia, Smolicz (1983) concludes that their command of Italian and Italian dialect is generally inferior to their command of English. The same holds for the language proficiency of Yugoslavian children in Germany, analysed by Stölting (1980). The children, from Serbo-Croatian speaking families, were born in Yugoslavia, and had been living in Germany for at least two years. Stölting found that the children had only a limited command of Serbo-Croatian, especially the ones who had come to Germany at an early age. Many children spoke German better than Serbo-Croatian, particularly as far as vocabulary was concerned.

Many members from minority groups seem to have word-finding problems. Appel (1983:164) quotes a Moroccan boy of 14 years who had lived in the Netherlands for four years. The boy admitted that with other Moroccan boys he generally used a mix of Dutch and Moroccan-Arabic: 'You have forgotten a few words and then you just say it in Dutch'. Kiers (1982) interviewed Moroccan young men who complained about the fact that the words in their mother tongue seemed 'to fly away'.

The loss of lexical skills in the minority language goes hand in hand with another phenomenon, i.e. the process of relexification: words from the dominant language are replacing words in the minority language. In their analysis of language shift in

Nahuatl-speaking communities in Central Mexico, Hill and Hill (1977) identify massive relexification from Spanish. This influences the attitudes of the people towards Nahuatl negatively. They feel that it is no longer pure and this probably contributes to its decline in use. Jones (1981) also points to the fact that the English relexification of Welsh 'has the effect of undermining attitudes towards the language and encouraging a feeling of Welsh linguistic inadequacy' (p. 49). Furthermore, Jones sees the code-switching and code-mixing he has observed in Wales as a negative phenomenon; it might be an intermediate stage between the usage of Welsh only and English only (see also section 4.2.). However, code-switching can also have other connotations, as we will illustrate in chapters 10 and 11.

Another frequently observed aspect of language loss is the reduction of the morphological system by less proficient speakers. The morphology of the minority language is often simplified, and fluent speakers only apply general rules without knowing the exceptions. Nancy Dorian investigated extensively what she calls a 'dying Scottish Gaelic dialect', East Sutherland Gaelic (ESG) spoken by fewer than 150 people at the time of the study (in the 1970s) (all of them also English-speaking) on the east coast of the county of Sutherland, in the extreme north of mainland Scotland. In addition to other aspects of bilingualism, Dorian analysed the application of morphological rules in three groups of speakers: older fluent speakers of ESG, younger fluent speakers and semi-speakers. The Gaelic of the semi-speakers is imperfect in many ways, in terms of the older group. She asked informants from the three groups to translate sentences from English into ESG, in order to determine whether changes were appearing in the complex morphology of noun plurals and noun gerunds of ESG.

Dorian (1978) distinguishes 11 morphological devices in the formation of the noun plural, simple suffixation being the most simple one; examples of other, more complex devices are changes in vowel length plus suffixation and vowel alternation plus suffixation. She also distinguishes 11 morphological devices in the formation of the gerund, again simple suffixation being the simplest one in addition to more complex devices comparable to the pluralization devices. Table 4.3. presents part of Dorian's results with respect to realization of noun plurals and gerunds.

Table 4.3 Realization of noun plurals and gerunds by three groups of speakers of East Sutherland Gaelic (adapted from Dorian, 1978)

	Speaker group		
	old fluent speakers	young fluent speakers	semi-speakers
% of plurals formed by simple suffixation	50	44	63.5
% of zero plurals	–	0.5	9
% of gerunds formed by simple suffixation	49	46	63.5

The table shows that the less proficient speakers use the device of simple suffixation (for forming plurals as well as gerunds) considerably more than the two other groups who employ more complex devices. Strikingly, the data on plurals and gerunds almost match one another. Furthermore, zero plurals (i.e. no change in the root noun, where it should be changed) are in fact only present in the language of the semi-speakers. In the title of her article, Dorian uses the expression 'the fate of morphological complexity': there is a clear tendency in less proficient speakers of ESG to drop complex morphological devices, and to restrict themselves to simple rules.

Next to lexical reduction and replacement, and morphological simplification, monostylism is a third aspect of language loss. In general, languages are heterogeneous: different variants of one language can express the same meaning, and the actual choice of a certain variant depends on characteristics of the speech situation. One could also say that a language consists of different styles (although it is impossible clearly to divide a language into them) and that styles are related to situations, i.e. a certain style is considered appropriate in a certain situation. However, in cases of language shift, the language shifted away from will be used in fewer situations. This will entail a reduction of the number of stylistic variants. As Dressler and Wodak-Leodolter (1977) have noted with regard to Breton, the styles will merge with one another, and monostylism is the result. 'The young non-nationalistic speakers of Breton especially cope with formal situations in French; Breton remains restricted to informal events. If such monostylistic Bretons are forced by a nationalist to speak Breton in other situations, they do not have command of a suitable style' (p. 37). Monostylism will further contribute to the decay of a language because it restricts its use value.

Lefebvre (1979) addresses the issue of monostylism by analysing the relation between function and form of a language. Many scholars have shown that in the process of creolization, expansion in function of a language is correlated with expansion of the linguistic structure (see also chapter 15, *Pidgins and Creoles*). Lefebvre demonstrates in her article on the spoken Quechua in the community of Cuzco (Peru) that a loss of function by a language may entail a loss of a specific linguistic distinction. Although the speech community of Cuzco is quite heterogeneous, in general, Quechua is considered as the intimate code, and Spanish the formal code, also for fluent Quechua speakers. In the last decades Spanish has gained in importance over Quechua, because Spanish is associated with formal education and social progress. Lefebvre analysed the use of the first-person plural inclusive in sentence like:

(1)   maymanta   wayqi-y   ka-n-čis
      where-from   brother-my   be-1st pers. pl.incl.
      Literally: 'where are we (incl.) from my brother?' – 'Where are you from, brother?'

The first-person plural inclusive is used to indicate respect towards the addressee, it marks distance between the interlocutors, but also tenderness or affection. The alternate form, the second person singular, has no connotations. According to Lefebvre, it is the neutral or unmarked form. In (1a) the speaker does not express his or her relation to the addressee.

(1a) maymanta   wayqi-y   ka-nki
      where-from   brother-my   be-2nd pers. sg.

In the data Lefebvre recorded, the first-person plural inclusive used for addressing a second-person singular only occurred in the speech of the older speakers, and not in the speech of anybody under 30 years old, except for two radio announcers (who used Quechua in their announcements). A correlation could be observed between use of the first-person plural inclusive and poor Spanish skills. Lefebvre argues that Quechua monolinguals or quasi-monolinguals use the first-person plural inclusive in contexts where bilingual speakers would switch to Spanish. This means that the expanding use of Spanish in formal domains entails the loss of a morphological marker in Quechua; the loss of a function for Quechua correlates with the loss of a form. The fact that the radio announcers still use the 'old form' can even be considered as further evidence supporting this conclusion. On the air, a formal code is used.

Language shift and language loss go hand in hand. The two processes reinforce each other with the ultimate result of language death, when no other community speaks the language in question. But also if the language does not die, because it is still in use somewhere else, for a certain community it may become a dead language. The community loses a strong symbol of identity which will influence the social-psychological conditions and the social life considerably.

Language shift and loss are not inevitable processes, however. Minority groups can experience that shift towards the majority language does not always imply better chances for educational achievement and upward social mobility. A group may 'give away' its language without getting social-economic advantages in return. It is no longer discriminated against because of language, but because of colour, culture, etc. On the basis of such experiences minority group members may develop strategies to foster use of the minority language and to improve proficiency in the minority language, which is then revitalized. That such strategies may succeed is shown by the fact that French has regained a rather strong position in Canada.

Further reading

Fishman's *Language loyalty in the United States* (1966) is an early and classic study on language maintenance and shift of linguistic minorities in the USA. It has found a more recent counterpart or follow-up in Veltman's book *Language shift in the United States.* (1983) Collections of articles on the subject of language maintenance with case studies from different parts of the world can be found in J. Fishman (ed.) *Advances in the study of societal multilingualism* (1978) and the *International Journal of the Sociology of Language*, no. 25 (1980). In Clyne's *Multilingual Australia* (1982) much information on an extensive study of language maintenance and use of Australian immigrants is presented. Cooper has edited a book with articles on the subject of language spread, i.e. the increasing use of certain languages: *Language spread; Studies in diffusion and social change* (1982). Finally, we want to mention again Susan Gal's excellent study *Language shift; Social determinants of linguistic change in bilingual Austria* (1979) which contains a discussion of various theoretical sociolinguistic issues related to the subject of language shift.

5   Language planning

India is linguistically one of the most heterogeneous nations of the world: the number of languages spoken is at least 800. It would be much higher if many dialects are considered not as varieties of the same language, but as separate languages. The languages spoken in India belong to four language families: Indo-Aryan, Dravidian, Austro-Asiatic, and Tibeto-Burman. Languages from the first two families have by far the most mother-tongue speakers (about 70 per cent and about 25 per cent of the population, respectively).

After gaining independence in 1947, the federal government established the following language policy. English should be replaced by Hindi as the official language of the federation, one of the most widely used languages especially in North India. Furthermore, regional languages should be used as the official languages of the states of India; in fact, the states were more or less reorganized along linguistic lines. In order to stimulate the spread of Hindi, books were translated into it, dictionaries and encyclopaedias in Hindi were compiled, keyboards for typewriters and teleprinters were standardized, etc. Also many states paid considerable attention to the further development of their respective major languages: for instance, special committees devised new technical, legal and administrative vocabularies. The dual-language policy of India failed partly because of the politically, religiously and practically motivated opposition against Hindi. As a result, in 1967 English was again adopted as the second official language. The educational consequence is that many children have to learn two languages (English and Hindi) next to their mother tongue in school. Other children, speaking a non-official minority language, are taught three languages: English, Hindi and the official language of the state they live in.

This example provides a first illustration of what governments can or must do in multilingual countries, particularly in Third World or recently independent countries. They often have to choose a national language, they have to further develop or cultivate it to make it more useful for various communicative needs, they have to foster its spread, they have to make decisions with regard to the position of the minority languages, etc. This chapter discusses various aspects of such language planning processes.

Government institutions often get or take on the task of language planning, but individuals can be active in it as well, for instance by creating and consistently using a new word. In section 5.1 we will deal with national vs individual language planning, and language planning as part of language policy reflecting general government policy. There we will also discuss two conflicting theories of language planning; this discussion is focused on the following question: are there linguistic, objective norms for clarity, economy and redundancy which must be used in language planning? Section 5.2 contains a description of the activities and stages in language planning. In the final section of this chapter we will go further into the question of which factors influence the language planning process although some socio-political factors already appear in 5.2, because of the impossibility of considering language planning as a process taking place in a socio-political vacuum.

5.1 Types and theories of language planning

Language *planning* is in fact a part of, or the factual realization of, language *policy*: a government adopts a certain policy with regard to the language(s) spoken in the nation, and will try to carry it out in a form of language planning. Any case of language planning is based on a certain language policy, and this will often reflect a more general government policy. For instance, in Spain, when it was ruled by the dictator Franco, the use of Catalan in schools, and the printing of Catalan books or newspapers was forbidden, because the Catalan language was considered to be an important symbol of the Catalan Movement. This movement was seen as a threat to the unity of Spain with its hegemony of Castilians. Therefore the government tried to suppress the use of Catalan; it planned to extinguish the language as part of a policy directed at the strengthening of the unified state. In this chapter we will employ the term *language planning* in a relatively wide, general sense, i.e. including the underlying language policy.

Two examples have already been given in which governments were active in language planning. However, this activity is not reserved for governments or government institutions only. Individuals or groups of individuals can also be involved in it. They can try to unite people on the language question in multilingual settings, particularly in cases where a minority language is in danger of becoming obsolete. They can publish books in the language they want to revive or maintain, organize cultural events in the language concerned, edit a newspaper, organize language courses, etc. A unique example of such an individual language planner was Eliezer Ben-Yehuda (1852–1922), who lived in Palestine and, with a handful of followers, tried to restore Hebrew as a spoken language. For a period of nearly 1700 years, Hebrew had not been used orally in daily life, but only as a liturgical language, i.e. for saying prayers, and reading and studying sacred texts. Ben-Yehuda tried to set an example for others by establishing the first Hebrew-speaking household in Palestine. Perhaps one can imagine the potential communication problems in the family, considering that at that time Hebrew vocabulary lacked such everyday words as the equivalents of *kitchen* or *stamp* (Morag, 1959). Of the many language planning activities Ben-Yehuda was engaged in, we further mention the publishing of a modern Hebrew newspaper and the compiling of a dictionary of modern and ancient Hebrew (Fellman, 1974). The Norwegian teacher Ivar Aasen is another famous 'individual language planner'. He was the initiator of and the stimulus behind the group that finally devised one of the two Norwegian languages, Landsmål, on the basis of an extensive study of Norwegian dialects (see p. 52 for information on Norwegian language planning).

Official or government language planning takes place via Language Agencies, Academies or Departments. The task of such a Department might be to devise an orthography for an unwritten language, to revise a spelling system, to coin new words, etc. Although governments may be powerful, it is still difficult for them to force people to speak a certain way. Often the (unconscious) choices of individuals, exhibited in their daily speech, will conflict with the official, deliberate language planning as put down in proposals by a Language Academy. Frequently, language – in any case spoken language – goes its own way (i.e. the way speakers want it to go). For example, the Spanish Academies in Latin-American countries and Spain have made frequent proposals to replace English loanwords by new Spanish words, but the speakers generally persist in using the loanwords (Guitarte and Quintero, 1974). The French government even went so far in 1975 as to pass a law stating that people can be fined for using a loanword where a French equivalent exists (e.g. *ticket* instead of *billet*). In most cases language planning has more success with regard to written language than spoken language. In this way a literary standard may be created which differs considerably from the vernacular.

Depending on the situation in a country or in a speech community language planning may take different forms. In developing nations, often the first task is to determine which language (or languages) should fulfil the role of national language. Many countries which have recently become independent went through this process of selecting a national tongue. For example, Indonesia adopted Bahasa Indonesia as its national language, and Mozambique chose Portuguese. This type of language planning we will call *language selection*.

In all countries minority languages are in use next to the national one(s). Language planning is concerned with the position of these minority languages: are they to be tolerated, stimulated or oppressed, are they to be used in education and in administration? Even if a government does not not have a publicly stated policy with regard to minority languages, it might have a covert one, because, for instance, not supporting minority languages might result in language decay or even loss, which could be the ultimate, hidden goal of the government. Language planning dealing with the position of minority languages we will call *minority language treatment*.

Language planning can also be directed at the (further) development of languages, both national ones and minority ones. This further development can affect any aspect of the spoken and written language, like the revision of the spelling system, the choice of a particular variety of the newly selected national language as the standard variety, etc. Where the language only exists in a spoken form an orthography can be devised. This type of planning we will call *language development*, not to be confused with ontogenetic language development, i.e. the acquisition of its native language by a child. Language development as a type of language planning occurs in all kinds of countries and speech communities, in developing as well as developed countries, although in differing degrees: in industrialized, developed countries with a long tradition of one or more national languages, language development generally is a relatively marginal enterprise, but in developing nations many language development activities must be carried out. In the next section we will deal more extensively with these activities.

An important question is: how can the direction of language planning best be determined? If one claims that any case of planning (from the planning of household activities to economic planning) aims at improving the situation, the problem lies in the definition of 'improvement' (apart of course from the problem of how to attain this improved situation). Translated to language planning the question can be formulated as: is there an 'optimal language', a particular code to be selected and developed further so as to serve the communicative needs of the speech community optimally? In the literature on language planning two answers to this question can be found, answers based on different theoretical views of the social nature of language and the scope of linguistics.

The first is often called the *theory of instrumentalism* (cf. Haugen, 1971). It is not very popular among (socio-)linguists, but it probably has many lay adherents. Tauli (1968) is one of its most forceful advocates. He sees language as a tool or an instrument, which implies that it can be evaluated, changed, regulated and improved, and even that new languages can be created. According to Tauli, it is possible to evaluate languages with regard to their efficiency, since linguists are quite able to make value judgements, to point to illogical constructions or unclear structures. Tauli also notes, however, that we do not need primarily the evaluation of languages as wholes 'but evaluation of concrete linguistic features from the point of economy, clarity, elasticity, etc. It is essential to stress that such an evaluation is possible and is objectively verifiable, in many cases quantitatively measurable. Thus we can say that a certain linguistic feature or language is better than another from a certain point of view' (Tauli, 1968:11). From one of the first examples Tauli discusses, it is clear that his approach runs into serious problems. The 'certain point of view' he mentions is often a quite limited one which conflicts with other perspectives. Tauli states that languages differ with regard to economy and redundancy in grammatical structure. He gives the example of the German expression *du kommst* ('you come'), in which the meaning 'second person singular' is expressed twice: by *du* and the suffix *-st*. In the corresponding English utterance *you come* this meaning is only expressed once, so in this respect English is more economical. However, how must this conclusion be weighed if the same expression is evaluated from another perspective, e.g. the meaning of *you* in English which in many languages is expressed by two or more pronouns? German has *du* (second person, singular, informal) and *Sie* (second person, singular, formal; and second person, plural, formal and informal). A fuller comparison of the English and the German pronoun system will yield more differences, but this limited comparison shows that in German it is possible to express a distinction (formal vs informal, singular pronouns) which can not be marked in English by pronoun choice. Therefore, from the point of view of linguistic economy in establishing and confirming social relations in verbal interaction, German is more economical than English. In addition, we should note that redundancy in languages is functional. If one meaning cue is not understood or noticed by the listener, he will hear a second one which makes it easier to arrive at the proper interpretation.

In the example above we have illustrated the technical problems in comparing two languages or structures from two languages with the aim of defining 'the best structure'. The second theory of language planning claims that such an undertaking is theoretically impossible. This theory, which is often called the *sociolinguistic theory of language planning*, is based on two principles:

(a) all known languages are symbolic systems of equal native value;
(b) language planning should not only deal with the technical aspects of language, but also with its social aspects.

Principle (a) is in agreement with a generally accepted assumption in modern linguistics, supported by research on many languages. The normative, prescriptive linguistics from before the nineteenth century has evolved into a science with descriptive and theoretical aims in which value statements with regard to the superiority of languages or linguistic structures have no place. Haugen, who adheres to this position, further states that 'when judged by strictly logical standards, natural languages are both redundant and ambiguous. Familiarity with more than one language makes one painfully aware of the inadequacies of each. This is indeed the reason for the development of logic and mathematics: these allow one to escape from the logical imperfections of natural languages. But who should wish to replace language with mathematics in our social life? The rich diversity of human languages and dialects is part of the human condition. To iron them out so that all languages would either be uniformly logical or identical in reference is not only a labour of Sisyphus, but a monstrous goal unworthy of a humanist' (Haugen, 1971:288). In this view, 'primitive languages' do not exist either. Of course, some languages lack a vocabulary necessary for talking about certain aspects of modern life in industrialized societies, but that does not make them primitive. In fact, they often have very complex grammars. Furthermore, vocabularies turn out to be easily expandable.

In the second principle of the sociolinguistic theory of language planning, already touched upon in the quotation from Haugen, the social nature of language is stressed. Languages are produced by people in their daily, social interactions. They have different social values, and peoples' identities are strongly linked to the language they speak (cf. chapter 2). Therefore, languages can not simply be considered as tools like a hammer or a saw. Language planning must be regarded as a form of social planning, in which an account of the social status of a language, its use in varying social contexts, its relation to the identity of various groups of speakers, etc. must play a primary role. This view does not deny the feasibility of planned language development, but it claims that the possibilities are limited and subject to social conditions.

Generally, linguists of the present generation have not paid much attention to language planning. There are two reasons for this apparent lack of interest. (1) Most linguists hold the view that language is an 'autonomous system' that can not be deliberately changed by variables outside the system (cf. Rubin and Jernudd, 1971a). (2) In most cases language planning is concerned with the written language, and speech is considered secondary. As Haugen (1966b:53) says, for linguists this 'turns things upside down. It considers as primary what linguists regard as secondary and assigns value to something which the linguist considers only a shadow of reality.'

5.2 Stages and activities in language planning

Initial fact-finding is the first stage in language planning processes. An overview of the language situation must be obtained before any further steps can be taken. In such a background study information must be gathered on, for example, the number of mother-tongue and second-language speakers of each language, its social distribution, its sociolinguistic status, the existence of written forms, the elaborateness of the vocabulary, etc.

Which facts are studied will depend on the actual sociolinguistic situation in the speech community. For instance, in developing countries more facts will be unknown, especially when the language situation is very complex, as in many African nations. In such cases even the number of speakers of the national language must be ascertained by a survey, as well as the number of languages actually spoken. An example is the linguistic survey of Ethiopia, which was a four-year project done by a number of scholars. Seventy languages were involved from four different language families. The number of speakers ranged from 7,800,400 for Amharic, an Ethio-Semitic language, to 250 for Kwega, a Nilo-Saharan language (cf. Bender *et al.*, 1976). However, it must also be noted that recently in many Western countries multilingualism has increased because of immigration from former colonies and the settlement of immigrant workers. This was one of the reasons for establishing the Linguistic Minorities Project in Great Britain (see Linguistic Minorities Project, 1985). One of its goals was to conduct a survey of the number of languages spoken, and the number of speakers of each language. It was found, for instance, that in the London Borough of Haringey, school children spoke 87 languages, Greek and Turkish having the most mother-tongue speakers.

In the second stage, the actual planning takes place. *Procedures*, constituting a programme of action, will be devised in which the specific objectives of the language planning process are determined. Because they can be considered as the heart of the process, we will deal more extensively with these procedures than with other stages in language planning, illustrating them with actual planning activities carried out in different countries.

The first two were already mentioned in the first section of this chapter, *language selection* and *minority language treatment*. Language selection implies the choice of a (new) national language. As stated before, many developing countries faced this problem after gaining independence. Often the national language in use was too strongly associated with the former colonial power. Therefore, for instance, Tanzania opted for Swahili instead of English. However, in many cases social, political or linguistic factors made the choice of a native language undesirable (see also the next section) with the outcome that the former colonial language maintained its position, as for instance English in Kenya.

Minority language treatment refers to the decisions on the (planned) use of minority languages in education, administration and public life. For example, in some South American countries minority languages are used to some extent in primary education: Guarani in Paraguay and Quechua in Ecuador. In Friesland, in the northern part of the Netherlands, Frisian is permitted alongside Dutch in administration. Such forms of minority language treatment are often devised for the sake of minority language maintenance.

The third procedure is that of *codification*, which is an explicit statement of the code via dictionaries, grammars, spellers, punctuation and pronunciation guides, etc. Codification is a prerequisite for the *standardization* of a language. If a speech community does not have a standard language, or wants to adopt a new standard language, this sometimes does not exist in a standardized form. The central problem in codification is, of course, that of heterogeneity. For example, codification of the grammar of a language is not simply writing down the grammatical rules of the language, but generally means that one of two or more rules from different dialects will have to be chosen as the 'standard' one. Codification implies then that a standard variety is established, and generally this will be based on one of the varieties or dialects of the language in question. In Tanzania, for instance, many dialects of Swahili were spoken. The dialect to be codified had already been selected before independence. In 1930, the Inter-Territorial Language (Swahili) Committee, later called the East African Swahili Committee, was established to select the form of Swahili to be used in education in Kenya, Uganda and Tanganyika (now Tanzania). They choose Kiungaja, the dialect spoken in Zanzibar Town, to form the base for the standard language. Therefore, Kiungaja grammar and vocabulary were codified (cf. Whiteley, 1969).

Norway faced interesting long-term planning problems. In 1814 it gained independence from Denmark. Due to the centuries-long hegemony of Denmark, Danish had a strong influence on language use. The varieties spoken in Norway ranged from more or less pure Danish to local Norwegian dialects without any Danish influence. In the middle of the nineteenth century two codification efforts were made in the direction of a Norwegian standard language. The first effort, lead by the language reformer Knud Knudsen, was directed at a gradual revision of written Danish in the direction of the so-called Colloquial Standard, which can be characterized as a variety of Danish with strong Norwegian influence. The outcome of this effort was called *Riksmål* ('state language') and later *Bokmål* ('book language'). A competing standard was devised by a group led and inspired by Ivar Aasen. However, they did not take one variety as a base for codification, but tried to reconstruct Norwegian from all the Norwegian dialects in order to find the 'real' or the 'pure' Norwegian language. The language they proposed was called Landsmål ('national language'), and the name was later changed into *Nynorsk* ('new Norwegian'). Since then Norwegian has had two codified national languages which the government is trying to bring closer together or to converge linguistically via new codification efforts (cf. Haugen, 1966a).

Codification is not only necessary when a (new) national language is adopted, but can also be part of minority language treatment. Particularly, when minority languages acquire an educational or administrative status, the need arises for a codified form. For instance, since 1957 vernacular teaching has been possible in the Philippine public school system. However, instructional materials were hardly available or not at all, and most vernaculars did not exist in a codified form. Since then, many linguists have been engaged in studying and scientifically describing dozens of Philippine languages. Such a description necessarily comes down to codification. In this sense also dialectologists aiming to describe a dialect are working on its codification.

Where languages do not exist in a written form, codification will imply *graphization*: the reduction of spoken language to writing, or the devising of graphic symbols to represent the spoken form. The first decision in the process of graphization, of course, concerns the choice of alphabet or script. Subsequently the important question will be: what is the relation between phonemes and graphemes, or how should words be spelled? We will illustrate the technical problems involved in orthography development with an example from the debate about the spelling of Quechua, an Amerindian language, in countries such as Ecuador. Like many other languages, Quechua has velar stops and labial glides. A linguistic spelling convention would lead to such words as:

kasa ('frost') and *kiru* ('tooth')
wasi ('house') and *wira* ('fat')

In fact, both national and foreign linguists have suggested an official spelling along these lines. The problem is, however, that both the *k* and *w* are felt as English, by the majority of (literate) Ecuadorians, and carry the connotation of American imperialism, extended in this case to 'innocent' Indian peasants. The alternative of Spanish conventions is not so attractive, either:

casa and *quiru*
huasi/guasi and *huira*

This spelling raises two difficulties. On the technical side, Spanish conventions give a result for velar stops that maps one phoneme into two graphemes, depending on the following vowel, and for labial glides the option of either *gu* or *hu*, which may lead to confusion and inconsistency. On the ideological side, using the Spanish conventions stresses the dependence of Quechua on Spanish, and of the Indians on the Mestizos.

Where languages already exist in a codified form, re-codification may be attempted. For example, in the USSR after the Revolution many languages in the Central Asian area were given a Latin alphabet instead of their Arabic script or other, rather less-known or idiosyncratic scripts. After about 1935, the policy of the central government changed in the direction of introducing the Cyrillic script, in which Russian is written. By 1940 Cyrillic had spread to most Republics (Lewis, 1972).

Norway, again, offers a typical example of re-codification. In 1934, the Norwegian parliament appointed a commission for spelling reform which aimed at a rapprochement of the two national languages (which are phonologically and syntactically very much alike). The government hoped (or expected) that new forms, promoted officially through sanctioned spelling lists, would be adopted by users of the two languages, finally bridging the gap between *Bokmål* and *Nynorsk*.

The last planning procedure is the *modernization* of language (also often called *cultivation* or *elaboration*). Codification and modernization together make up the activity of language development (see section 5.1). According to Ferguson (1968:32), '[the] modernization of a language may be thought of as the process of its becoming the equal of other developed languages as a medium of communication; it is in a sense the process of joining the world community of increasingly intertranslatable languages as appropriate vehicles of modern forms of discourse'. Two processes are involved: (a) the expansion of the lexicon, and (b) the development of new styles and forms of discourse. Till now, the second aspect has received far less attention than the first one. Nevertheless, when a language has always functioned only in informal contexts, people will lack the skills of using it appropriately if it is selected as a national langue or as a medium of instruction in the schools. In such cases language planning could include the development of style manuals, writing books, etc.

Lexical expansion is one of the issues in language planning most discussed. Newly promoted national languages and officially recognized minority languages often lack the vocabulary to talk about many aspects of the modern, scientific and industrialized world. Hebrew offers a striking example. During the revival of Hebrew (section 5.1), words had to be 'invented' for many aspects of daily life: for parts of the car, for military concepts, for many tools, etc. Generally, three main processes in the creation of a (new) technical vocabulary can be distinguished: compounding of existing words, forming of new words by native-language derivational processes, and the adoption of words from a foreign language. We will illustrate these processes with a few examples from Pilipino, the national language of the Philippines which is based on Tagalog. After 1964, the *Lupon sa Agham* (Science Committee) in the Philippines prepared an integrated vocabulary of basic scientific and technical words and expressions adequate for modern living but consistent with the morphology of Tagalog. Examples of proposed new words are given in Table 5.1.

Table 5.1

Compounding	*buumbilang* ◄———————	*buo* plus *bilang*
	'integer'	'whole' 'number'
	bahagimbilang ◄———	*bahagi* plus *bilang*
	'fraction'	'part' 'number'
Derivation	*pamahiga* ◄———————	*pang-* plus *bahagi*
	'denominator'	instrument prefix 'part'
	sabansain ◄———————	*sa-* plus *bansa* plus *-in*
	'nationalize'	action prefix 'nation' action suffix
Compounding and	*balikhaan* ◄———————	*balik* plus *likha* plus *-an*
derivation	'regeneration'	'return' 'create' process suffix
combined	*dalubwikaan* ◄———	*dalub* plus *wika* plus *-an*
	'linguistics'	'expert' 'language' process suffix

Borrowing of foreign words in a phonologically adapted form is also proposed by the *Lupon*, e.g. *eruplano* ('airplane'), *Merkuryo* ('Mercury') and *ampir* ('ampere'). Other processes applied in addition to these three are the expansion of meaning of an existing word (in Pilipino *mikmik*, in Tagalog meaning 'very small' for 'microscope'), and the use of words from dialects: 'earth' as a synonym for 'soil' is *lupa* in Tagalog, so the Science Committee took the equivalent for *lupa* from the Visayan dialect, which is *duta*, to denote 'Earth' as a planet (cf. for more examples Del Rosario, 1968).

Comparable to lexical expansion is the procedure of deliberately proposed lexical change. This language planning procedure is carried out when it is felt that too many foreign words have intruded in the language. Particularly, the influence of American technology and entertainment is reflected in the languages of many countries. Mainly for that reason, the Congress of the Spanish Academies of the Latin-American countries and Spain in Bogotá (1960) approved a resolution in which it was recommended that each Academy should create a commission on technical vocabulary. The commission of the Colombian Academy has proposed many Spanish terms to replace English loans which has been approved by the other Academies (Guitarte and Quintero, 1974).

It must be emphasized that all the procedures in a language planning programme are also (unconsciously) applied by individual speakers of a language. For example, modernization of languages has always occurred and will always occur, because people adapt their language to their communicative needs. As Ferguson points out, the process of modernization is not really new or 'modern': 'it is essentially the same process that English went through in the fifteenth century or Hungarian in the nineteenth when the language was extended to cover topics and to appear in a range of forms of discourse for which it was not previously used, including non-literary prose and oral communication such as lectures and professional consultations' (Ferguson, 1968:32).

The similarity between planned and unplanned language change can also be illustrated with the example of the 'spontaneous' formation of new words. O'Grady (1960) gives examples of the various ways in which new Western concepts are expressed in Nyaŋumada, an Australian Aboriginal language. In derivational processes, they use the suffix *-pinti* for example, 'complement of', denoting an element of the material culture which is associated with a particular object or action, as in ŋaṇkapinti ('razor', from ŋaṇka, 'beard' plus *-pinti*), or waŋalpinti ('electric fan', from waŋal, 'wind' plus *-pinti*). Or existing words were given a new meaning: *kitakita*, 'head-rest' got also the meaning 'pillow', and *mapan*, 'clever man', came to stand for 'European doctor'.

Implementation is the third stage of the language planning process. Language Committees or Academies can have far-reaching plans for a language, but these mean nothing if they do not affect ordinary language use. Common implementation techniques are the publication of word lists and grammars, the funding of language maintenance efforts (in the case of minority languages), the publication of text books for schools, the vocational training of teachers in a (new) language, the publication of governmental decisions in a certain language, the passing of laws concerning language use, etc.

The fourth and last stage of the language planning process is that of *evaluation*: are the goals attained? Many evaluation studies show that language planning can be successful. For example, Swahili has become a real, multi-purpose national language in Tanzania; it is even used in secondary education where it has to compete with English, which occupies a strong position. The two Norwegian standard languages seem to be merging gradually (in their written forms) as a result of the planning efforts of the government. The introduction of new orthographies in the USSR has been successful.

On the other hand, language planning can also fail, because the individual speakers do not change their language habits, or they change them in a direction different from the one planned. This becomes particularly clear for expansion or innovation of the lexicon. Language Committees nearly always try to reduce the number of borrowed words, but the purist forms they propose are often not adopted by the speech community. Speakers are obstinate, and language goes its own way. Furthermore, in many cases language planning only affects the written form of the language, but the spoken varieties remain unchanged, even when change of the oral language was aimed at. In fact, language planning is a circular process, because evaluation implies discovering and interpreting facts about languages and language use, which is the first stage in a new process of language planning.

5.3 Factors influencing language planning

As we noted earlier, language planning does not take place in a social vacuum. Instead, it is affected by many factors. In this section, we will deal with social-demographic, linguistic, social-psychological, political and religious factors. They will be discussed separately, since on the abstract level they can be studied in isolation. It will be clear that in social reality they have strong mutual interactions.

Social-demographic factors include the number of languages spoken, the numbers of their speakers, and their geographical distribution. An example is East Africa, particularly the contrast Tanzania–Kenya. Tanzania has many languages (about a hundred) with comparable numbers of speakers. The fact that these ethnolinguistic units were numerically small clearly favoured the selection of Swahili as a national language (cf. Whiteley, 1971). In contrast to Tanzania, Kenya has a relatively small number of languages. They were able to compete with Swahili, and therefore English could strengthen its position.

Social and demographic factors can also indirectly influence language planning. For instance, Indonesia and Malaysia consist of thousands of islands. There has always been the need for a lingua franca, a common language. The fact that Malay became this lingua franca was determined in good measure by the fact that native speakers of Malay lived on both sides of the Straits of Malacca, the most important sea route in this area. Being a commonly used lingua franca, Malay was selected as a national language in Malaysia and as the base for the national language Bahasa Indonesia in Indonesia, although it was culturally and quantitatively (with regard to numbers of mother-tongue speakers) not the most important language of the Malay-Polynesian group (cf. Alisjahbana, 1974).

Linguistic factors mainly have to do with the status and the character of a language, and the (dis-)similarities between languages. With the concept 'status of a language' we refer to the degree of (modernized) development as well as literary tradition. Many native languages in developing African nations could never be considered as candidates for a national language because of their low degree of modernized development, especially where fully developed colonial languages were in use. In South India most people would have welcomed the continuation of English as the official language. According to Apte (1976), it was claimed that Hindi was not as well developed as some other Indian languages, particularly Tamil and Bengali, which have long literary histories.

Similarities and dissimilarities between languages can be very important in language planning. For example, the strong position of Swahili in Tanzania was fostered by the fact that Swahili is a Bantu language, and that more than 90 per cent of the population speak Bantu languages; Swahili is closely related to several of these languages and therefore not difficult to learn. The 'character of a language' is a notion used by Alisjahbana (1974). He states that because of its character Malay, in comparison with Javanese, is relatively easy to learn. Malay does not have social dialects as Javanese has, where different words are used to express the same idea depending on the age, rank and social position of the addressee. In the view of Alisjahbana, this is one of the reasons why Javanese, numerically and perhaps also cutlturally the most important language, did not become the national language of Indonesia. It would not have been impossible, of course, to develop a Javanese with simplified registers as found in the Javanese speech community in Surinam.

However, this was not done. Also, we stressed before that in fact a language must develop stylistic variants in order to function as a national standard.

Social-psychological factors, in their broadest sense, concern the attitudes of people towards a language. These attitudes are related to the social distribution of languages in the speech community, and the social meanings attached to the various languages (see also chapter 2). Many languages in developing African countries are closely identified with a single ethnic group. Other ethnic groups might develop negative attitudes towards them, especially if one such language were to become the national one. The national hegemony of one (ethnic) language seems to imply domination by the original speakers of that language, i.e. by one specific ethnolinguistic group.

Political factors are of considerable importance in language planning. Here the direct relation between general policy and language policy becomes visible. In section 5.2 we gave the example of the introduction of the Cyrillic script for Central Asian languages in the USSR as part of a policy of russification. In 1984 and 1985 Bulgaria made efforts to 'bulgarize' the ethnic Turks, living in Bulgaria. They were forced to choose between either adopting a new Bulgarian name instead of their Turkish one, or returning to Turkey. The changing of names is a typical example of language policy.

The strong relation between general political aims and language planning can also be demonstrated with the case of Irish. Somewhere between 1750 and 1850 the majority of the Irish people seem to have shifted from Irish to English. Irish gradually became the language of an impoverished and disinherited peasantry. In 1893, the Gaelic League was founded, which tried to foster the revival of Irish. It became closely connected to the independence movement. Strangely enough, the success of that movement, culminating in the establishment of the Irish Free State in 1922, weakened the League, and with it, the language movement (cf. Macnamara, 1971). However, the many efforts of the Irish government, trying to spread the use of Irish, reflect the general policy of establishing an Irish identity; language is considered to be an important part of that identity.

The general policy of the former colonial powers was also expressed in language planning. For example, Belgium and Great Britain promoted the use and standardization of local languages in their African territories. This form of planning, which had a 'paternalistic flavour' (Spencer, 1974:168), derived from a colonial policy which emphasized 'separate development' for the different races in contact in Africa. By contrast, the Portuguese authorities pursued a policy of restricted assimilation, and discouraged the use of local languages; nothing was allowed to appear in print in an African language without concurrent translation in Portuguese (Spencer, 1974).

The strong influence of political factors on language planning can also be illustrated with cases of bilingual education or minority language education. This subject is taken up in chapter 6.

Religious factors are the last we will discuss here. They concern the relation between language and religion, and, more specifically, the use of local languages in the spread of religion. With regard to the former, an example can be given from Sudan. This country inherited English as an official language, although it was only used by a very small, but important élite (cf. Whiteley, 1974). English has been replaced by Arabic, however, which was already a first language for more than half of the population. The government has successfully promoted the use of Arabic in connection with the Islamization of the country.

The work of Christian missionaries has strongly favoured the use and standardization of local or vernacular languages instead of national or colonial ones. Because of their evangelical interests, these missionaries studied local languages, wrote grammars, orthographies, school books and religious books, and translated the Bible in many of these languages. It was their contention that evangelization would be most successful if it was undertaken by means of the mother tongues of the people. The Summer Institute of Linguistics still offers facilities for this type of work, for example in Papua New Guinea (cf. Welmers, 1974).

Further reading

The book *Language planning processes*, edited by Joan Rubin and others (1977) contains mainly case studies of language planning and some more theoretically oriented contributions. The same goes for two other collections of articles: W.M. O'Barr and J.F. O'Barr (eds.), *Language and politics* (1976), which gives much information on Tanzania and Papua New Guinea, and J. Cobarrubias and J.A. Fishman (eds.), *Progress in language planning* (1983). Carol Eastman's *Language planning* (1983) is the only introductory textbook available on this subject.

6   Bilingual education

It would seem only natural that children in bilingual communities should have the opportunity to be educated in two languages: the language of the home and the language of other groups in the community. But the reality is different. In most bilingual communities the two (or more) languages do not have equal status. Side by side with majority languages, which have prestige and positive social-economic connotations, there are the minority languages, often associated with low social-economic status and lack of educational achievement. They are more or less stigmatized, and not considered as suitable vehicles for communication in school or subjects to be taught. Therefore, all over the world examples can be found of children who are confronted with a language in school that they do not speak as well as native speakers of their age, or not at all: Sarnami-Hindi speaking children in Surinam where Dutch is the language of the classroom, Mozambican children who speak Shona at home while only Portuguese is used in school, Finnish children in completely Swedish-medium classes, Sardinian children in Italian-speaking classrooms, etc., etc.

In all these cases there is what is often called a *home–school language mismatch* or *switch*, and this mismatch can have several negative consequences, for example, poor educational achievement. There is in fact a vicious circle, because the minority language is seen as a main cause for this failure, and its negative connotations are reinforced once again. Many writers have argued that this situation can only be changed if the minority language is introduced into the school, and facilities for minority-language teaching provided. In section 6.1 the arguments will be analysed that have been thrown back and forth, both for and against schooling in the minority language.

If minority languages are introduced into the school, this can be done in different ways, depending, among other things, on the sociolinguistic and the political situation in the community concerned. In section 6.2 we describe different types of bilingual education. There we will also discuss an educational model for majority children (or children speaking a prestige language) that stimulates them to learn the minority language: the so-called immersion model.

Section 6.3 presents results of research on bilingual education: does it or does it not promote the educational success of minority children, and what are the consequences for proficiency in the minority and the majority language?

This chapter should be read in conjunction with chapters 4 and 5. In chapter 4 we dealt with the issue of language maintenance and shift. Institutional support factors were discussed as important variables influencing the maintenance and shift of minority languages. Institutional support is partly, or in some cases largely, determined by the government, via its language policy (chapter 5). The school is a central institution in modern societies, and government decisions on the status of minority languages in schools can have considerable effects.

6.1 Minority languages in the school

Traditionally, minority languages on the whole have had only a marginal place in the education system, but there are various exceptions. For example, in the nineteenth century and in the first decades of the twentieth century, many immigrant groups in the United States organized mother-tongue education. In the Soviet Union educational innovations were introduced immediately after the Revolution to promote the use of various national languages besides Russian in the schools. After gaining independence the federal government of India undermined the strong position of English in the Indian education system. According to the new official policy, children should receive primary education in their mother tongue, which in most cases was not English or Hindi, the newly chosen national language.

Since about 1950 the education of children from minority groups has been discussed more widely than before, and an interest in minority languages has increased. 1951 is an important year in this context, because in that year the UNESCO meeting of specialists on the use of vernacular languages in education was held. The meeting's main concern was language education in the Third World, but it also had an impact on discussions about the educational status of minority languages in other countries. A famous, often cited statement in the report of the meeting is 'It is axiomatic that the best medium for teaching a child is his mother tongue' (UNESCO, 1953:11).

In the United States the educational rehabilitation of minority languages started in the early 1960s. In 1963 the Dade County public schools in Florida established the Coral Way School with a Spanish–English programme to meet the needs of an increasing number of Cuban children. It is striking that provisions were made for use of Spanish in schools by immigrant children and *not* by children from Spanish-speaking families who had already lived in the USA for generations. In 1967 the Bilingual Education Act (Title VII of the Elementary and Secondary Education Act) was passed, which allocated funds for bilingual programmes, in principle for all children speaking a minority language.

In Western Europe similar developments took place. The position of minority languages in the education system improved in the 70s, which found expression also in directives and resolutions of the EEC (1977) and the Council of Europe (1976). In many African countries, for example Sudan and Nigeria, an attempt was made to develop some form of minority language education. In 1957 the Philippine government decided that the local vernacular could be used as the medium of instruction in the first two years of schooling.

In the 30 years since the UNESCO meeting in 1951 there has been a growing trend, worldwide, to enhance the role of minority languages in the school curriculum. In the discussions on this issue the following, partially overlapping arguments were (and still are) given in favour of the minority language. The first five arguments, (a)–(e), concern the educational situation and the future of minority children.

(a) The first language of the child must be used as the initial medium of instruction to ensure that *academic progress* is not hindered, while the majority language can be learned as a subject. Educators agree that a child's first language is normally the best instrument for learning, especially in the early stages, and that reading and writing in the first language should precede literacy in the second. Larson *et al.* (1981) present a clear description of the negative effects of the completely Spanish curriculum of Amuesha-speaking children living in the Peruvian jungle. 'The Amuesha children entered knowing little or no Spanish and sometimes spent years in school before finishing first grade because they first had to try to understand what the teacher was saying. As a result of the communication problem the situation seemed so hopeless that the Amuesha children in one such school were sent out to work the teacher's garden most of the day, while the Spanish-speaking children had classes' (p. 39).

(b) The minority child's general cognitive development will be retarded if he or she does not receive education in the mother tongue, and if the mother tongue is not further developed in the school. Cummins has developed the threshold hypothesis (Cummins, 1978) to account for the results of studies on bilingual education. According to this hypothesis, minority children must attain a certain level of competence (the threshold level) in their first language (and in their second language as well) to avoid cognitive disadvantages. When the children's first language has low prestige, as is generally the case with minority languages, language development is not stimulated outside the school, so this is a task for the education system. Cummins's ideas will be further discussed in chapter 9.

(c) Minority language teaching is a requirement for a healthy development of the child's personality and the development of a positive self-image. If schools do not provide any minority language teaching, then the school becomes for minority children 'a place where neither their language nor culture exists, possibly where they are not even accepted, a place where their social identity is questioned and undermined' (Toukomaa and Skutnabb-Kangas, 1977:20). It is also stated that the self-image of minority children will be harmed if, in the school, literacy in the minority language is not developed. When minority children only learn to read and write in the majority language, then the minority language 'must almost inevitably be considered a second-rate means of communication. It is not far from that conclusion to the conclusion that those who speak the home language are second-rate people' (Christian, 1976:28)

(d) As an extension of argument (c) it can be claimed that the use of the minority language as a medium of instruction will relieve the cultural shock which minority children can experience at the transition from the home to the school. It is the minority language that is the link between child and his/her community. This argument can also be related to argument (c) concerning the development of the child's self-image.

(e) Minority language education is necessary to develop the child's first language and this in its turn, is a necessary prerequisite for the successful acquisition of the majority language. Cummins (1978) has formulated the developmental inter-dependence hypothesis to explain this relation. We will return to this hypothesis in section 9.1 where the linguistic effects of bilingualism are discussed.

The following three arguments ((f)–(h)) have to do more with general aims concerning minority groups and societies as a whole than with individual minority children and their academic careers. The division between the two types of argument is only made for reasons of clarity, given the close interrelation between social and individual development.

(f) Minority language teaching will help to prevent the forced linguistic and cultural assimilation of minority groups. Cultural pluralism can be seen as an enrichment of society as a whole. Minority languages are often a fundamental part of a minority group's cultural identity (cf. chapter 2), and many minority groups derive their strength from this identity, especially when they are discriminated against in the larger society. Furthermore, a country can profit from the fact that many languages are spoken in it, and that therefore it has many bilingual citizens within its borders. An example of this is Switzerland, but the same would be true for Spanish in the USA.

(g) Recognition of the language (and culture) of minority groups will improve the social and cultural relations between these groups and the rest of society. The reinforcement of the cultural identity of minority groups (through minority language teaching) will help reduce the likelihood of polarization and socio-political friction.

(h) Especially in Third World countries minority language teaching seems to be the best way to reach isolated groups who do not participate in mainstream society. Members of such groups can gain literacy both in their native language and the majority language, and learn something about the country as a whole. On the government side, this has the advantage that it will be easier to influence these groups and to direct their social development. Of course, this same argument was used by missionaries who educated indigenous tribes via their native tongue, in order to promote their development *and* to convert them to Christianity.

In the 1980s the tide seems to have turned, which might partly have been brought about by the world-wide economic recession. Minority language teaching is considered a luxury. The sharpening ethnic conflicts in many (Western) countries can also be held responsible. The following, partially overlapping, arguments against minority language teaching have been articulated.

(a) The cultural identity of a country will be promoted when everybody is educated in the same (majority) language. According to Edwards (1981) one can question whether cultural pluralism should be aimed at, and ethnic diversity – especially as this is manifested through language maintenance – should be encouraged. Edwards argues for 'pluralistic integration' which implies only a marginal role for the minority language in the school.

(b) The political unity of a country will be fostered if everybody is educated in the same national language. In the USA the slogan 'one nation, one flag, one language' was used in this context. The minority language is thought to have an important cultural and political meaning for minority groups. The use of minority languages will strengthen the political identity of these groups, and this could endanger political unity, especially in the case of regional or ethnic independence movements (e.g. the Basques in Spain).

(c) The social unity of a country will be promoted if everyone is educated in the same language. When different groups are educated in different languages the social gulf between groups will become greater, leading to segregation.

(d) To ensure a positive socio-economic future, minority children should receive majority language education. This is the best way to guarantee good proficiency in the majority language, which is needed to promote academic achievement and academic success. According to various authors (e.g. Skutnabb-Kangas, 1983), the fear that minority language teaching will lead to social fragmentation and separatist movements lies behind this argument.

(e) The linguistic situation is too complex, and there are not enough resources, financial and other, for organizing minority language teaching for a variety of minority groups. This purely pragmatic and economic argument can often be heard in countries where many languages are used that only exist in a spoken form. In such cases no books are available, and the languages must be codified (cf. chapter 5). Some countries, especially in the Third World, have opted for schooling in the national language, preferring to spend their funds on agricultural and medical development, the training of more teachers, etc.

(f) Many parents from minority groups are opposed to minority language teaching because of their negative attitudes towards the minority language. In chapter 2 we have already shown that negative social attitudes towards minority languages are often adopted by the minority groups themselves. Thus, the parents mainly reinforce the general prejudice against them: the minority language, being the language of a stigmatized group, can not be the right medium of instruction in school or a valuable school subject.

(g) Minority children often speak a variety of the minority language different from the standard variety that is being used in school, for example, Moroccan children speaking Moroccan Arabic at home while in school classical Arabic is used.

Skutnabb-Kangas (1978) points to a possible eighth argument. This argument is never clearly expressed by the people or institutions (e.g. governments) who plead for majority language education for minority children. The content of this 'hidden' argument, which runs counter to argument (d), is:

(h) Majority language education keeps minority children in their disadvantaged or oppressed position; this is favourable for certain societies and economic systems that are in need of cheap labour forces. According to Skutnabb-Kangas (1978) exclusive majority language education is not effective for minority children. Competence in both the minority and the majority language will not fully develop: the result of this is called semilingualism (for this concept, see also chapter 9). 'Because of their semilingualism minority children will under-achieve in school, and therefore they are more or less predestined to get low-status and low-income jobs, for instance unskilled labour' (p 119).

Here we will not go into the question of the desirability or necessity of minority language education any deeper, returning to this issue at the end of the chapter.

6.2 Types of bilingual education

In 6.1 we used expressions such as 'the introduction of minority languages into the school' and 'minority language education' without explaining what this may actually involve. A system in which a minority language has a certain role alongside the majority language is generally called bilingual education. This type of education generally only exists at the elementary school level. Using the following criteria, a number of different types of bilingual education can be distinguished.

1 Are both languages used during the whole curriculum or only in certain stages?
2 Do both languages function as media of communication in the classroom?
3 Is there a one-to-one relation between subject (like arithmetic or geography) and language, or are both languages used alternately as media of instruction for all subjects except when the languages themselves are subjects?
4 Are both languages taught as subjects, and is the aim of the bilingual programme literacy in both languages?
5 Do only minority children participate in the bilingual programme, or majority language speaking children as well?

With regard to question (3) it must be noted that in most bilingual programmes the 'one language for one subject' approach is used. The Redwood City Project (California) is an exception to this general trend (Cohen, 1975). It is difficult to give a short overview of this Spanish/English experiment, since each year changes have been introduced. However, in the third year of the project, the alternate-day approach to bilingual schooling was initiated: a subject was taught in Spanish on Monday, in English on Tuesday, in Spanish on Wednesday, and so forth. That year other innovations were brought in as well, the so-called Preview-Review technique. This teaching technique implies that the teacher previews the lesson in one language, presents it in the other, and then reviews it in the first. In this way, no student loses out in concept acquisition as a result of limited second-language proficiency, when his or her second language is the language on a given day.

The Redwood City Project is also an example of a programme in which both minority and majority students participated in the same classes. Mexican American and Anglo children attended the bilingual programme. In most cases, however, such programmes are only organized for minority children. Bilingual programmes do not appear to have been devised to stimulate societal bilingualism in general. We will return to a special form of bilingual schooling for majority children later in this section.

With regard to criteria (1), (2) and (4) above, it is possible to distinguish two general models of bilingual education, schematically reproduced in Figure 6.1. In both models, the amounts of time reserved for the two languages may differ. For example in Model I a programme may not have facilities for prolonged minority language teaching as a subject after Grade 3. In another programme the majority language may be introduced as a medium of classroom interaction as early as the first grade. A version of Model I often applied is the programme which offers minority language only as a subject matter. In such cases the regular curriculum is followed in the majority language, and for a few hours minority children study their own language. In our opinion, such a programme can not be labelled bilingual.

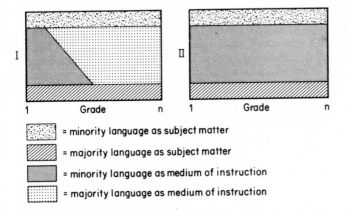

Figure 6.1 Models of bilingual education

Model I is mostly called the *transitional* or the *assimilationist* model. The minority language is mainly used in the early grades, since its most important function is to bridge the gap between the home and the school. In fact, the minority language is only used in school to make it easier for the child to adjust to existing educational demands. Using Macnamara's (1974) phrasing, the minority language is seen as a disease from which the child must be cured. Such programmes do not affect the school as an institution representing a society which considers itself monolingual. Bilingualism is not really encouraged, especially as in most cases facilities for prolonged minority language teaching as a subject are lacking. Cziko and Troike (1984:10) claim that most transitional programmes accomplish assimilation through 'humane linguicide' of minority languages. They can be contrasted with monolingual majority programmes which lead to 'brutal assimilation' of minority children.

Model II is the *pluralistic* or *maintenance* model, promoting linguistic pluralism. The minority language in itself is not considered a problem, but rather societal attitudes towards the minority language, related to the oppressed socio-economic position of the minority group. In this view, the minority language has a value of its own and is as important as the majority language. Therefore it is not only used as an initial medium of instruction for the minority group but also in later classes. The minority language occupies a more important position in the curriculum than the majority language, because the weakest language, which has only low prestige outside school, must be supported most strongly. Therefore, the model is sometimes also called a 'language shelter model'. It is expected to contribute considerably to maintenance of the minority language by promoting more favourable attitudes towards it, and higher oral and written proficiency.

Although most proponents of bilingual education adhere to the maintenance view, the transitional model is most frequently applied, at least in the Western world, probably as a result of the strong assimilative pressure of mainstream society. In some developing countries the situation is different. For example, the general practice in India is that children receive initial education through their native language, while Hindi and English are studied in secondary education. However, when their native tongue is not a regional language of wider use, then this regional language also has to be introduced in secondary education.

The situation is even more complex when the native language does not exist in a written form, because in such cases elementary education will take place in the regional language which the child may know only slightly. Spanish–English bilingualism and bilingual education in the United States or Finnish–Swedish bilingualism in Sweden offer a much simpler field for research than does the situation in India.

As we noted above, a special bilingual education model for speakers of the dominant or the most prestigious language exists as well: the *immersion model*. Initially, immersion programmes were organized for English-speaking students in Montreal (Lambert and Tucker, 1972). Later on, they were also set up in the United States, for instance, the Spanish programme for English-speaking children in Culver City (California). Cohen (1976) gives a list of 17 characteristics of immersion education. The most important of which are:

- All instruction is initially (i.e. in Kindergarten and Grade 1) in the second language (French in the Canadian immersion programmes).
- In second, third or fourth classes first language skills (reading, writing and so on) are introduced in the children's first language.
- By the fifth year, content subjects such as geography or history may be taught in the children's first language.
- The teachers are bilingual, although they only speak the second language in the classroom (with exceptions for points two and three above).
- In kindergarten, the children are permitted to use their mother tongue until they are proficient enough in the second language. The teacher shows that he/she understands the children's first language by reacting appropriately.
- In first year and beyond, the teacher requests that only the second language be spoken in class, except during classes in which the children's first language is the subject.
- In the early years there are no structured classes for second language learning such as pattern drills or grammatical instruction. Guided second language acquisition of the majority language (grammar, pronunciation) can be introduced in the later grades.
- Students participate in the immersion programme voluntarily and only with the consent of their parents.

These characteristics can be considered the basic ones, but immersion education may also be organized in another way. Particularly, the starting point of the full-time classes in the second language may be later, and the extent to which the children are allowed to use their first language may vary. Generally, early and late immersion programmes are distinguished. Early immersion has the basic characteristics described above, while in late immersion programmes the second language is introduced in a later stage of elementary education. In addition to early vs late, also total vs partial immersion can be distinguished. The features listed above apply to total immersion. In partial immersion programmes, the second language is not used during the whole day or the whole week. The first and the second language function alternately as the medium of communication in the classroom.

Immersion education has been organized virtually only for children speaking a prestigious language, such as English-speaking students in Quebec. An English immersion programme for French-speaking children does not exist, and is even forbidden by Quebec state laws, since it may strengthen the position of English at the expense of French. The idea behind immersion education is that it should only be organized when the child's mother tongue is already supported substantially outside the school.

Immersion education should be clearly distinguished from *submersion education*, i.e. the type of education in which minority children are schooled completely through the majority language, and where no 'immersion facilities' like a bilingual teacher are provided. In submersion education the children's first language is neglected totally, and the only provisions made consist of extra second language courses in the majority language.

6.3 Results of bilingual programmes

First we will give some examples of bilingual programmes both from the industrialized West and from the Third World. After that we will present a more general conclusion about the effectiveness of bilingual education, and comment on the methodological problems in evaluation studies. At the end of the chapter we will formulate our own views on the desirability of bilingual education, taking into account the evidence available thus far.

On first inspection, different programmes of bilingual education have produced rather different results, as the following case-by-case account will demonstrate. Cohen (1975) reports on the Redwood City Project. Redwood City is located approximately 30 miles south of San Francisco. The Project began in September 1969 with a a pilot first-grade group. In the year 1970-71 a Follow Up I group of first graders and a Follow Up II kindergarten were added. Mexican-American and Anglo children participated in the programme, which provided for teaching in Spanish and English, both as subjects and as media of instruction (see also section 6.2). The content of the curriculum, i.e. the 'treatment' in methodological terms, varied from year to year and from group level to group level. The longitudinal study on the effects of the programme was conducted during the fall of 1970 and the spring of 1972. The bilingually schooled Mexican children generally were as proficient in English as comparable Mexican children from another school in Redwood City taught only in English (the Comparison Group); the Mexican children from the bilingual school lagged behind in English vocabulary development, however. The bilingually schooled children were slightly better in Spanish than the students from the Comparison Group, and the bilingual programme seemed to promote greater use of Spanish. With respect to non-language subjects the students from the two groups performed about the same. The Mexican American students who had been in the Bilingual Project for three years were more positive towards Mexican culture than their Mexican age-mates from the monolingual school. Finally, the school attendance of the children from the Redwood City Project was much better than that of the students in the Comparison Group.

While English had been the language of instruction in Philippine schools for many years, the government decided in 1957 that Pilipino, the prevailing local vernacular, derived from Tagalog, the general vernacular in the Philippines, or another local language – should be used as the only medium of instruction in Grades 1 and 2, with English being used as the primary medium of instruction in Grade 3. In the Rizal Experiments varying the introduction of English was studied by comparing three groups: one group received instruction, in English, from Grade 1 to 6 with Pilipino as a subject, another group was initially taught in Pilipino and switched to English in Grade 3, and a third group was taught in Pilipino in the first four grades and in English after that.

The results of the Rizal Experiments, as reported by Davis (1967) and Revil *et al.* (1968) were not very favourable for the vernacular language approach. By Grade 6, the students educated in English from the beginning performed better on all tests, even Pilipino reading tests, than those who were taught initially in Pilipino. The second group (switch to English in the third year) outperformed the third group, who only switched in the fifth year. In the second year of High School the group taught monolingually in English still had the best test results.

Appel (1984, 1987) reports on an educational experiment in Leyden (the Netherlands), where Turkish and Moroccan immigrant workers' children followed a transitional bilingual programme with a considerable amount of minority language teaching: 75 per cent in the first year and 40 per cent in the second year. After that they went to regular schools with an average of 10 per cent minority language teaching, the minority language being taught only as a subject. The children came directly from Turkey or Morocco, so they did not speak any Dutch on entering the school. A number of aspects of their linguistic, social, emotional, and educational development was compared with that of a group of Turkish and Moroccan children who went to regular schools with hardly any, or only a minimal amount of, minority language teaching (a mean of 13.3 per cent over three years; the minority language only as a subject).

At the end of the first school year the oral Dutch proficiency of the two groups was highly comparable. At the end of the second year the group from the bilingual programme performed somewhat better than the dominantly monolingually schooled children with respect to oral Dutch skills; the written proficiency of the two groups was approximately the same. At the end of the third year, the group from the bilingual programme surpassed the other group in oral as well as written Dutch proficiency. Children from the Comparison Group exhibited more problems of aggressive behaviour, apathy, isolation, strong fear of failure or exaggerated nationalism than children from the experimental bilingual school. Also more children from the Comparison Group seemed to develop a growing feeling of resistance towards the dominant (Dutch) school culture. With respect to arithmetic as well, the children from the experimental group outperformed the children from the dominant Dutch schools.

In 1952 the Peruvian government together with the Summer Institute of Linguistics created a bilingual education programme for non-Spanish speaking children in the Peruvian jungle. In 1953 11 bilingual teachers were working in 11 communities, in six language groups, teaching approximately 270 children (Larson and Davis, 1981). In 1977 the programme had grown to 320 teachers in 210 communities in 24 language groups, teaching approximately 12,000 children. The teachers in the programme are bilingual Indians who speak the native language of the students fluently. The children are first taught in their native language, and later on Spanish is introduced. It is the aim of the programme to develop literacy in Spanish as well as in the native language.

Hard empirical evidence is lacking, and the only evaluative papers available are written by the organizers of the bilingual programme from the Summer Institute of Linguistics. They state that it has many benefits, for instance:

- the children learn more effectively in all areas (reading and writing, arithmetic);
- the culture shock, dramatically experienced by children attending an all-Spanish school, is reduced;
- ethnic pride is promoted, particularly because of the fact that the community sees its language in written form being used for educational purposes (Larson and Davis, 1981).

As in most former British colonies, English has been maintained in sub-Saharan Africa as the official language. It is used as the principal medium of education and for government functions. Nigeria is linguistically a very diverse country, but there are large regions in which one of the three 'big' African languages – Hausa, Igbo and Yoruba – are widely spoken. In these regions it has become standard practice to use the vernacular language as the medium of instruction in elementary education and to make a transition to English after the third grade. Cziko and Troike (1984) summarize the results of an experimental project undertaken at Ile-Ife in the former western state of Nigeria where Yoruba was the *sole* medium of instruction throughout primary school.

The evaluation carried out at the end of Grades 3 and 4 found that the pupils from the experimental Yoruba programme generally performed as well as or better than an English-instructed comparison group in all of the subject areas tested. The students from the experimental group also seemed to have fewer problems in school. Further, the proportions of students entering secondary school after completing primary school were the same in the experimental and comparison group.

Swain and Lapkin (1982) give an overview of research results with regard to various types of French immersion programmes for English speaking children in Canada (for a characterization of these programmes see the preceding section). In general, the outcomes are positive. Here, we present only the most striking conclusions.

- Despite a temporary lag in the first grades, at the end of all types of immersion programmes students perform as well as or better than students from regular English programmes in the area of English language skills related to literacy.
- Students from early total immersion programmes attain near-native proficiency in receptive French language skills. Their productive skills remain non-native, although they can express themselves adequately in their second language.
- Students from early immersion groups perform better in French than students from late immersion programmes.
- Immersion education has not had negative effects on the students' general intellectual development. Early French immersion even favours it.
- Students from early total immersion groups achieved as well in mathematics, science, and social studies as students from regular schools where English was the language of instruction. Early partial and late immersion students lagged somewhat behind.

We have now looked at results of some bilingual education programmes in California, the Philippines, the Netherlands, the Peruvian Amazon, Nigeria and Canada. It is difficult to give a definite answer to the question of the desirability or necessity of bilingual education because of conflicting findings and very different circumstances. Before giving at least a *tentative* answer to this question, we must say something about the problems in evaluating such programmes.

In the first place, the educational, social, linguistic, economic and political situations in different countries are not comparable at all. There are more differences than similarities between second-generation immigrant Italian children in Great Britain and Nahuatl-speaking children in Mexico, or between Shona-speaking children in Mozambique and Finnish children in Sweden. William Mackey, one of the most important writers on the subject of bilingual education, said therefore 'We can only evaluate specific types of bilingual schooling one at a time for a particular group in an attempt to answer such specific questions as: to what extent do the modifications in the language behaviour of this school population in these classes enable this group of learners to achieve this particular linguistic or educational objective?' (Mackey, 1977:227).

Secondly, it is extremely difficult to carry out methodologically flawless evaluation studies in this area. Problems arise in finding a control group of monolingually educated students who are in all respects similar to the students from the experimental bilingual programme, especially where students (or their parents) have volunteered for the programme. They may have an exceptionally positive attitude towards the programme which may positively influence their achievement. The so-called Hawthorne-effect also constitutes a methodological problem. According to this effect, the results of an evaluation study in which two groups are compared – one experimental and one standard group – cannot be attributed to the independent variable, e.g. the amount of minority language teaching, but is due to the fact that it is an experiment. This makes it special, and makes the students and their teachers think they are special, which stimulates them to perform better. Furthermore, the educational material used in bilingual and monolingual schools is often not comparable. In many bilingual programmes new educational material in the minority language must be developed and tested, while in regular monolingual programmes teachers work with existing books and exercises. With respect to this issue, the monolingual programmes are in an advantageous position.

Third, and here the first two points come together, the effects of bilingual programmes can only be understood in relation to the educational, social, linguistic, economic and political context of the programme. To put this in methodological terms: these factors are the causal variables, while the educational programme is only a mediating variable. The factors mentioned above exert their influence via the educational programme. However, in most evaluation studies of bilingual experiments the educational programme is considered to be the causal variable. We can again refer to Mackey's statement: a certain programme in a certain context has a certain outcome.

With these restrictions in mind we can try to give the tentative answer promised. Although there are some exceptions, such as the experiment in the Philippines, the general trend in the research literature is that bilingual education for children from linguistic minority groups has positive outcomes in all areas: first and second language skills, other subjects, and social and emotional aspects. It is especially striking that minority language teaching – the use of the first language as the medium of instruction – does not seem to hamper or hinder second language acquisition. Some authors, for instance Skutnabb-Kangas (1983), hold that prolonged minority language teaching in bilingual maintenance programmes is necessary to attain positive results.

In sharp contrast to this conclusion stand the results of evaluation studies on immersion education. These studies show that initial and prolonged education in the *second* language has positive outcomes. However, this type of education is organized for children who speak a high-status language and who come from families with relatively high social-economic status. They are not forced to learn the second language as is the case with children from low-status minority groups. Summarizing, children from disadvantaged or oppressed linguistic minority groups generally profit from bilingual programmes in which their first language plays an important role, while children from dominant social groups or higher social classes benefit from bilingual programmes in which the second language is used most frequently. In this chapter we will not present the theoretical explanations for this conclusion, since they have to do with the effects of bilingualism on individual speakers, and we will leave these explanations for chapter 9.

To end this chapter we want to emphasize that research results indicate that bilingual education for children from low-status linguistic minorities *can* be profitable, but no *predictions* can be derived from these results, because of the many varying social situations. A point of considerable interest is the social and political attitude of the majority towards minority groups. If this attitude is too negative and too many segregative trends exist in society, it may not be advisable to organize separate bilingual education for children from linguistic minorities. Probably it is always a good idea to integrate bilingual programmes into regular schools in order to further the relations between minority and majority students. Bilingual programmes should not be organized to bring about a kind of 'splendid isolation' for minority groups, which will often turn out to be dangerous isolation as well, but should guarantee that students from minority groups gain better educational and social opportunities, while at the same time maintenance of the minority language is fostered.

Further reading

J. Cummins and T. Skutnabb-Kangas (eds.), *Education of linguistic minority children*, 2 vols. (1987) contains articles providing arguments for and against bilingual education as well as descriptions of bilingual programmes. Various theoretical and more practical educational topics are discussed in the following two books: J.E. Alatis (ed.), *Georgetown University round table on languages and linguistics (Current Issues in Bilingual Education)*, 1980, and B. Hartford, A. Valdman and C.R. Foster (eds.), *Issues in international bilingual education*, 1982. Bilingual programmes from all over the world are described in B. Spolsky and R.L. Cooper (eds.), *Case studies in bilingual education*, 1978. Vernacular language teaching in a Third World country, i.e. in India, is dealt with in Pattanayak's book *Multilingualism and mother-tongue education*, 1981. M. Swain and S. Lapkin, *Evaluating bilingual education* (1982) present an overview of results of immersion programmes in Canada.

II   The bilingual speaker

7   Psychological dimensions of bilingualism

In this book we are mainly concerned with individual or collective language beha-viour in bilingual communities. However, language behaviour is possible because of some sort of underlying competence. People possess implicit knowledge of the language(s) they speak and/or understand, or to put it differently: they have more or less internalized the language. An interesting question, the focus of this chapter, is how are the two languages of bilingual individuals internalized? Do bilinguals differ from monolinguals in this respect? In the first section we will discuss the problem of neural representation of the two languages. Are they localized in the same area or in different areas of the brain? Section 7.2 deals with the mental representation of two languages. In keeping with research in this field of study, we present information about the mental lexicon, connected with each language. Here again, the question is, whether the two languages are mentally or psychologically discrete, with two discrete lexicons, or whether the bilingual individual operates on the basis of one unified mental lexicon. Generally, bilinguals keep their languages separate in language pro-cessing, i.e. in speaking and understanding. Does a special mental faculty develop which enables them to do this adequately, to process the languages without mixing them up? In section 7.3 we will pursue this problem.

There is still little information on the issues dealt with in this chapter. Grosjean (1982: 267) says 'the bilingual brain is still very much *terra incognita*'. Researchers do not have direct access to the brain or the bilingual mind. The question, for example, whether there is one lexicon or two, cannot be answered directly. Possible answers must be inferred from observable phenomena. Furthermore, research results often are not unambiguous, and there is much disagreement between different authors. It is difficult therefore to give a coherent picture of the state of the art in this field of research.

7.1 The bilingual brain

It is generally assumed that the left hemisphere of the brain is mainly responsible for language processing. This dominance of the left hemisphere is particularly strong in right-handed males. The question now is whether this also holds for bilinguals, and whether the two languages are localized in the same area of the brain, and share the same neural mechanisms. Answers to this question are mainly based on two sources of information: reports on the linguistic effects of brain injuries, and psycholinguistic experiments which measure the involvement of the left and the right hemisphere.

Aphasia is the name for all types of disturbances of language and speech resulting from brain damage. This damage can be caused by accidents, shot wounds, a stroke or a brain tumour. Paradis (1977) gives an extensive overview of case studies of bilingual aphasic patients, analysed to gain information about the bilingual brain. In about half of the cases reported, patients followed a synergistic pattern of recovery, i.e. a pattern in which progress in one language is accompanied by progress in another. Paradis further distinguishes a parallel and a differential pattern within the synergistic pattern. It is parallel when the impairment of the languages involved is identical and recovery proceeds at the same rate. The pattern is differential when the languages are impaired to a different degree and are restored at the same or a different rate. Out of 67 synergistic cases surveyed by Paradis 56 were found to follow a parallel synergistic pattern of recovery.

Another frequent pattern is that of selective recovery: in nearly 30 per cent of the cases analysed the patient did not regain one or more of his languages. Paradis cites some of the cases reported by Pitres (1895), one of the first articles on polyglot aphasia. One patient of Pitres recovered French and Spanish, but lost the ability even to comprehend Italian. Another patient regained some of his proficency in French but not in German, Basque, English, Spanish or Arabic, all of which he spoke fluently before the injury. Other modes of recovery, for example the successive pattern – one language begins to reappear after another has been restored – are even more infrequent. The parallel synergistic pattern is obviously the most frequent one. Nair and Virmani (1973; cited in Paradis, 1977) report that 90 per cent of 33 randomly selected patients showed the parallel pattern. It should also be noted that non-parallel patterns of recovery could be influenced by many factors, including, for example, degree of proficiency and the affective value attached to each language. Futhermore, authors of case studies tend to stress the exceptional cases. Therefore, the regular parallel pattern probably occurs more frequently in reality than is reported in the literature. A tentative conclusion based on studies of polyglot aphasia is that different languages are generally represented in the same area of the brain.

The left hemisphere is generally dominant in language processing by monolinguals, although the right hemisphere also seems to be involved to a certain extent. It had long been thought that bilinguals use the right hemisphere more than monolinguals, especially bilinguals who acquired a second language after childhood. However, recent studies have made clear that this is probably not the case. For example, Soares and Grosjean (1981) did a study on the left vs right hemisphere language processing of English monolinguals and Portuguese–English bilinguals. They were asked to read a set of isolated English and Portuguese words presented to the right or to the left visual field by means of a tachistoscope, a device used in psychological research which presents visual stimuli for very short periods of time, in this case separately (and randomly) to the right or the left eye. As Soares and Grosjean expected, for monolinguals the reaction time was shorter for words presented in the right visual field, because this is connected to the left hemisphere, where the language centre is located. The bilinguals turned out to behave exactly like the monolinguals, for both English and Portuguese. Futhermore, in both groups the number of exceptions was identical: two out of ten subjects in each group did not show left-hemisphere dominance.

Even if one concludes that languages are not located in completely different regions of the bilingual brain, one can differ with regard to the neural aspects of language organization. Paradis (1981) distinguishes two views. In the first one, the 'extended system hypothesis', it is stated that two languages form one system, and the elements of the two languages are supported by the same neural mechanisms. The proponents of the second view, the 'dual system hypothesis', hold that the two languages are located in the same area, but that different neural mechanisms support each language. According to this view, the two languages are separately represented in the human brain. Paradis (1981) has proposed some kind of compromise hypothesis: the languages are stored in a single extended system, but the elements of each language form separate subsystems within the larger system. This sub-set hypothesis can explain parallel as well as non-parallel recovery patterns.

Since there is probably one extended system for the neural processing of two languages, the bilingual brain does not suffer an extra neurological burden compared to the monolingual brain. According to Segalowitz (1977) a brain can process two languages as easily as one. However, these are still mere hypotheses, in need of further empirical support.

7.2 The mental representation of two languages

Every student of bilingualism probably knows at least one Russian word: *kníga* ('book'). Weinreich used this word in his famous typology of bilingualism, distinguishing three types: coordinate, compound and subordinate bilingualism. According to Weinreich (1953) for coordinate bilinguals equivalent words in the two languages have (slightly) different meanings or refer to different concepts (A). For compound bilinguals, the two forms – /buk/ and /ˈkn'iga/ – have an identical meaning: 'book' ≡ 'kníga' (B).

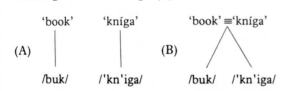

In this example the concepts are expressed by means of words, but they could also be represented in a picture (in case (A) a typical English, respectively Russian book, and in case (B) a general book), or they could be described more elaborately, for instance as is done in dictionaries. In our example the words between inverted commas are in fact abbreviations for the more elaborate concepts.

The coordinate bilingual functions as two monolinguals, and the compound bilingual merges the two languages at the conceptual level. In the subordinate type of bilingualism (C) one language is dominant, and the words in the non-dominant language are interpreted through the words in the dominant language. A subordinate bilingual has learned a second language with the help of his or her first language or dominant language.

(C) $\left\{ \dfrac{\text{'book'}}{\text{/buk/}} \right\}$

/ˈkn'iga/

Ervin and Osgood (1954) revised Weinreich's typology, by distinguishing only between coordinate and compound bilingualism, the latter also comprising Weinreich's subordinate type. Furthermore, they gave the coordinate–compound distinction a theoretical basis in stimulus–response theory. We will not elaborate on this theory here, because it has generally been rejected as a useful approach in psycholinguistic research (see for instance Cairns and Cairns, 1976). Ervin and Osgood suggested also that coordinate and compound bilingualism will arise in different acquisition settings. When people acquire languages in separate contexts, they become coordinate bilinguals. The compound system is developed when the two languages are acquired and used in the same setting. Lambert *et al.* (1958) tried to test this idea empirically. They ran three experiments with two English–French bilingual groups, one group of coordinate bilinguals and one of compound bilinguals according to the theoretical predictions. In the first task the subjects had to rate English words and their French equivalents on a so-called semantic differential, a method of placing stimulus words on a standard scale. For example, the subjects had to rate the word *house* along a seven-point scale as 'ugly – beautiful' or 'pleasant – unpleasant'. Taking the scores on the semantic differential as an indication of the meaning ascribed to the stimulus words, Lambert and his colleagues concluded that the coordinate bilinguals showed a difference in meaning of translated equivalents significantly greater than the compound bilinguals. When, however, a comparison was made between coordinate bilinguals who acquired their languages in geographically distinct cultures and those who acquired them in separate settings within one geographical region, it became clear that bicultural experience accounted for the overall difference between the coordinate and compound groups. Cultural experience seems to be more important, therefore, than acquisition context in establishing bilingual meaning systems.

In the second task Lambert *et al.* made use of a technique called 'retroactive inhibition design'. The basic procedure in this technique is that a subject learns list A, then list B, and then relearns list A. If the interpolation of list B has no effect on the previously memorized material, then the two can be considered functionally independent. By presenting subjects with a list of 20 English words and a list of their exact translations in French, and asking them to reproduce the words of the first list, the functional separation of the two languages was studied. The coordinate group turned out not to profit from the interpolated French list, while for the compound group the French list supported the retention of the English list. According to the researchers, the translated equivalents were semantically more similar and functionally more dependent for this last group. A difference between the 'bicultural' and the 'unicultural' coordinate group did not appear in this task.

The third part of the experiment was a translation task. It was predicted that compound bilinguals would show greater translation facility (measured by speed of translation), because they would not have to 'translate' the concepts, but could follow a direct path from word in language (A) through general concept to word in language (B). However, the two groups did not differ in translation facility.

Although Lambert and his associates (1958:243) concluded that '[the] theory of coordinate and compound language systems has been given empirical support', many questions about its usefulness remain, since the results do not support the distinction unambiguously. In addition, other studies failed to substantiate Ervin and Osgood's distinction empirically. Kolers (1963) did a study on word associations by bilinguals.

Compound bilinguals gave associative responses to stimulus words in English that differed considerably from responses to the translated equivalents in their native language. This cast serious doubts on the assumption that for people who acquire two languages in fused settings, two equivalent words have the same meaning. Kolers found that there was no relation between history of bilingual acquisition and response.

The compound–coordinate distinction has also fallen into disuse, because various methodological and theoretical objections were raised against it. The way 'meaning' was studied in experiments, was severely criticized, for instance (cf. Segalowitz, 1977). The semantic differential technique used by Lambert and his associates only deals with the affective or emotive aspects of meaning, and does not cover its most important aspect, i.e. denotation. Another criticism is that the experiments deal only with isolated words, while Weinreich's original distinction was directed at the complete language system. Furthermore Macnamara (1970) has pointed out that many words in two languages do not have completely overlapping meanings or semantic contents. He gives the example of the French word *couper* which has two equivalents in English: *to cut* (with, for instance, *hair* as direct object) and *to carve* (*the meat*). Inspection of any bilingual dictionary yields numerous examples of only partially overlapping meanings, and, of course, these incongruous meanings always trouble translators. The question is now: what could be the one general meaning for compound bilinguals in such cases? What is, for instance, the general concept for English–Turkish compound bilinguals which underly the following words in thier two languages (see Table 7.1.)

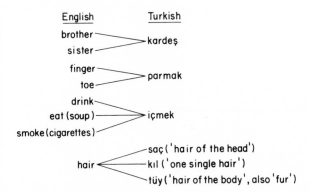

Table 7.1 Words with partially overlapping meanings in English and Turkish

Although many researchers have thrown the coordinate–compound distinction in the scientific garbage can, some students of bilingualism still see some value in it, adding Weinreich's subordinate type of bilingualism again (e.g. Skutnabb-Kangas, 1983). It seems to describe adequately the type of bilingualism that arises in the initial stages of second-language learning through instruction in the first. With regard to the compound–coordinate distinction also two revisions are made: (a) completely compound and completely coordinate bilingualism are the end points of a continuum on which a bilingual individual can be rated, and (b) the language system of a bilingual may be partly more compound (e.g. the lexicon) and partly more coordinate (the grammar). It must be emphasized that these are still rather intuitive ideas which again need empirical verification.

After abandoning the compound–coordinate distinction, many researchers in the field of bilingualism directed their attention to another but not dissimilar issue: the mental lexicon or the semantic memory of bilinguals, notions which were often incorrectly equated. The mental lexicon is a kind of internal dictionary containing 'entries' for each word that a speaker 'knows'. Each entry contains all the linguistic information about the word: its semantic content, syntactic properties, phonological shape, etc. An example would be:

DECEIVE – an English transitive verb
– pronounced /disi:v/
– weak past tense
– related to *deceit, deceitful,* etc.
– means: 'to mislead by concealing or distorting the truth'
– etc.

(We will not elaborate on technical details; see Clark and Clark (1977), especially for a discussion of the representation of the semantic content.)

The semantic memory is not strictly linguistic, containing as it does the mental representation of the individual's knowledge of the world. This knowledge is represented in concepts and relations between these concepts (cf. Lindsay and Norman, 1977).

The question researchers have wanted to tackle was: do bilinguals store information centrally and do they have equal access to it with both languages, or is information storage linked to separate languages, i.e. in two separate mental lexicons. The above-mentioned study by Kolers (1963) supported the two-store position. The low degree of similarity between the associations given to equivalent stimulus words in two languages suggested that the two languages involve two separate semantic systems.

Other studies support the one-store hypothesis, for example the bilingual version of a technique known as the *Stroop procedure* (after Stroop, 1935). In the original Stroop experiments words which named colours were written in coloured ink that did not match the meaning of the word, for example the word *green* written in red ink. In bilingual versions of this technique, subjects had to respond in language (A) while the coloured word was from language (B). For instance, *schwarz* ('black') in yellow ink, which had to be named in English (correct response: yellow). All studies employing this procedure found a considerable amount of cross-language interference, i.e. *schwarz* printed in yellow ink slowed down the naming of the colour by English–German bilinguals in the same way as *black* printed in yellow ink in the case of English monolinguals (cf. Segalowitz, 1977).

Essentially the same technique was used by Ehri and Ryan (1980) in a picture–word interference task. In their adapted procedure subjects had to name pictures with and without distracting names printed on the pictures. Bilingual subjects were asked to respond in one of their two languages, and the distracting words were in the response language or in their other language. For example, they had to name a picture of a house in English, and on the picture the word *church* or *église* was printed (in the case of English–French bilinguals). Bilinguals turned out to suffer substantial interference from printed words regardless of whether the picture names and the distractor words came from the same or a different language. Ehri and Ryan (1980:299) conclude that 'lexical items from different languages are closely and automatically connected in semantic memory and the bilingual cannot turn off his inactive language'.

Most studies undertaken give evidence in favour of the one-store hypothesis, but empirical support for the other position can not be neglected. Therefore, Paradis (1980) formulated a compromise hypothesis. In his view, bilinguals 'possess one and only one set of mental representations but organize them in different ways depending on whether they verbalize a thought in L1 or in L2, and to that extent function cognitively differently when speaking or decoding in L1 or in L2' (p. 421). Here, we can again refer to the difference between the notions 'semantic memory' and 'mental lexicon'. According to Paradis (1979) bilinguals have one semantic memory or conceptual system, and this is connected to two lexical stores, which can be activated at will. This view is further substantiated in a study by Potter *et al.* (1984), who asked bilingual subjects to name pictures in, and to translate first-language words into, their second language. They predicted that in the case of a separate, not language-specific conceptual system to which pictures also have access, the subjects would perform faster, i.e. in the naming task, because it requires only one step: from concept to word. The translation task would require two steps: from word via concept to word. The results were consonant with the predictions.

One further thing must be noted. In studies of the mental lexicon and semantic memory the compound–coordinate distinction was unfortunately not taken into account. Therefore the language histories of the subjects participating in the experiments were neglected, whereas these histories may be crucial to the way a bilingual has the words of his or her language stored. This means that still much remains unclear about the semantic and conceptual organization of the bilingual mind.

7.3 The use of two languages

An individual who is competent in two languages must keep them more or less separate in language production and reception. How can this be achieved in such a way that when on language is 'on' the other is 'off'? Penfield and Roberts (1959) proposed a theory which is known as the *single-switch theory* to account for this phenomenon: it assumed one mental device, a 'switch', which operated in such a way that when one language was on, the other was off. Apart from the problem of the neural status of such a device (the switch was still not more than a metaphor for an unknown device in the brain), results of experiments using the bilingual version of the Stroop procedure (see section 7.2) showed that this theory was too simple. Subjects had to respond (i.e. name colour words) in one language, so that system must be 'on', but the printed words in the other language still distracted the subjects, and therefore this system was 'on' too. These findings are in agreement with the common-sense observation that bilinguals are quite capable of speaking one language while listening to somebody else speaking another language.

These facts can be accounted for in a theory in which two switches are hypothesized: an output switch and an input switch (cf. Macnamara, 1967). The speaker is in control of the output switch, choosing a certain language deliberately. But as the results of the bilingual Stroop tests show, he cannot control the input switch in the same way: subjects were not able to filter out the language of the distracting word. The input switch is therefore said to be 'data driven': the language signal from the outside operates the switch, whether the bilingual individual wants it or not.

If these input and output switches really exist, their operation should require time, like any other mental operation. Various studies were undertaken to see whether this is so. For example, Kolers (1966) asked French–English bilinguals to read aloud monolingual and mixed French–English passages. The subjects answered comprehension questions equally well for monolingual and bilingual texts, but the reading aloud of mixed passages took considerably more time: Kolers computed that each switch took them between 0.3 and 0.5 seconds. Reacting critically to this early study, other researchers suggested that Kolers had not differentiated between the input and the output switch. Reading aloud requires both receptive and productive language processing. Macnamara *et al.* (1968) isolated the output switch in an experiment in which bilinguals had to write numerals, i.e. linguistically neutral stimuli, first in one language, then in another, and then alternating between the two languages. It was found that the task required more time in the last condition, when the output switch was involved. Each switch took about 0.2 seconds.

In a subsequent study, Macnamara and Kushnir (1971) looked at the input switch separately, in a relatively simple experiment. They asked bilinguals to read monolingual and bilingual passages silently. The subjects read the monolingual passages faster than the bilingual passages, and each switch took about 0.17 seconds.

The two-switch model appeared to find rather strong support in the various studies. Even the computation times corresponded neatly. Kolers's 0.3 to 0.5 seconds for input plus output switch was approximately the same as the 0.2 seconds for the output switch and the 0.17 seconds for the input switch found by Macnamara and his colleagues. The value of the two-switch model was later seriously questioned, however, on the basis of observations of natural code-switching in bilinguals and new research results.

Many bilinguals switch from one language to the other in their daily interactions. This form of code-switching takes place between sentences as well as within sentences (see chapter 10 on bilingual code-switching). Code-switching is an extremely natural strategy of language production for bilinguals, while the experiments reported above seem rather artificial. The results in the laboratory only bear a weak relation perhaps to the natural process of language comprehension and production. The language material in the experiments does not really compare with natural speech. Many of the sentences used by Kolers and Macnamara and his associates turn out to be quite unnatural for people who regularly switch between codes. Many of the switches occurred at randomly selected places in the sentences in the experiments, while analyses of the 'mixed' speech of bilinguals has shown that code-switching tends to take place at natural breaking points in the sentence, not just anywhere. There appear to be a number of structural constraints on code-switching. It is hard to switch between an article and a noun, for instance.

Studies which took the structural constraints on switching into account yielded quite different results. For instance, Chan *et al.* (1983) asked Chinese–English bilinguals to read a passage with spontaneous or natural switches, and compared the reading speed with that of a monolingual Chinese passage. They found no differences between the reading speed for the two conditions. This result supported Paradis's contention that bilinguals do not use a special switching mechanism different from the mechanism monolinguals employ in language processing. According to Paradis (1977:114), there 'is no need to hypothesize any special anatomical structure or function in the brain of the bilingual as differential from the monolingual. The same general neural mechanism that makes a speaker select /k/ and not /t/ in a given context can account for the selection of *Käse* instead of *fromage*.' With regard to input, bilinguals have no problem with switches when they can anticipate them. If not, it takes some time to adjust to the 'new' code, but this is the same for the monolingual who needs some extra time for processing a sentence, if he is not expecting that he will be addressed and suddenly somebody asks him a question. Everybody is familiar with this experience.

One aspect of bilingual language usage that we will touch upon only briefly is *translation ability*. Contrary to expectation, it turns out that bilinguals who are very proficient in both languages are not always good translators. Lambert, Havelka and Gardner (1959) asked English–French bilinguals to translate lists of English and French words. Speed of translation did not correlate with the subjects' degree of bilingualism. Probably, bilinguals use their two languages in different domains of their life (cf. chapter 3). They are connected to different cultural experiences. If a bilingual speaker always uses language (A) in informal and language (B) in formal settings, it will be difficult to translate a passage referring to experiences in informal settings from language (A) into language (B). It might take some extra time to find 'the right words', for these words generally do not come up in the situations in which (B) is spoken.

Further reading

There are not many books available which can be recommended for further reading on the subjects discussed in this chapter. Albert and Obler's book *The bilingual brain; Neuropsychological and neurolinguistic aspects of bilingualism* (1970) gives much detailed and technical information on the issues dealt with in the first section. *The Journal of Verbal Learning and Verbal Behavior* has devoted a special issue to the 'mental lexicon', especially the bilingual's mental lexicon (Vol. 23, nr. 1, 1984). It should be noted that this literature is mainly written for fellow researchers.

8 Second-language acquisition

In chapter 3 we pointed out that diglossic speech communities without (individual) bilingualism virtually do not exist. This implies that in bilingual communities many people have to learn two languages, particularly those speaking a minority language. In addition to their vernacular they acquire a second language, often the majority language or another language of wider communication: a Turkish immigrant worker in Germany learns German, a speaker of Lotuho in Sudan learns Arabic, a speaker of one of the Aboriginal languages in Australia learns English, etc. Members of minority groups must attain a certain degree of bilingualism if they want to participate in mainstream society. Speakers of a majority language are in a much more comfortable position. If they wish they can stay monolingual: Germans generally do not learn Turkish, etc.

In *Languages in contact* Weinreich (1953) claims that '[the] greater the differences between the systems, i.e. the more numerous the mutually exclusive forms and patterns in each [language], the greater is the learning problem and the potential area of interference' (p. 1). Weinreich suggests that the first language influences the acquisition of the second one. With the term *interference* he refers to the 'rearrangement of patterns that results from the introduction of foreign elements into the more highly structured domains of language, such as the bulk of the phonemic system, a large part of the morphology and syntax, and some areas of vocabulary' (p. 1). It is a common-sense notion that second language learners use elements or structures of their native language in speaking a second tongue: the stereotypic English-speaking Frenchman says 'I seank' instead of 'I think', because his French phonological system keeps intruding, and the equally stereotypic French-speaking Englishman says: 'Parlay vuw anglay?'

The influence of one language on the other is extremely important in situations of prolonged and systematic language contact. Here again a quotation from Weinreich is appropriate. 'In speech, interference is like sand carried by a stream; in language it is the sedimented sand deposited on the bottom of a lake' (Weinreich, 1953:11). However, the interlanguage of second-language learners, i.e. their version of the target language, can also be characterized by other structural features in addition to interference, for instance features due to simplification of target-language structures. These features can also become habitualized and established, or – in Weinreich's metaphor – become the sedimented sand deposited at the bottom of a lake. A language might change, or a new variety of a language might develop, because of widespread second-language acquisition by individual speakers. In chapter 13 we will deal with language change in situations of contact. In the first section of this chapter, features of the interlanguage of second-language learners will be discussed.

Individuals can differ considerably with regard to their progress in second-language acquisition: some learners are very successful, others seem to acquire the language very slowly, or they reach only a low level of proficiency. Many factors influence the rate of second-language development, e.g. intelligence, age and language aptitude. In the context of this book, the most important factors seem to be socio-psychological factors which are often summarized as attitude and motivation. A frequently expressed assumption is that the attitude of a second-language learner from a minority community towards the majority or second-language community affects second-language acquisition considerably, because it directs his or her motivation for language learning. In section 8.2 we will discuss this relation between socio-psychological factors and second-language acquisition. People can learn a second language when they have already mastered a first one to a certain extent, but children can also learn two languages more or less at the same time. This 'simultaneous acquisition of two languages' (as it was called in McLaughlin (1978)) will often occur in bilingual families. In the last section of this chapter we will present information on this topic. There we will pursue questions like: how does the simultaneous acquisition of two languages proceed, how do the two languages influence each other via (mutual) interference, do these bilingual children lag behind compared to monolingually raised children, and how can parents influence the bilingual acquisition process positively? Before dealing with these questions, we will briefly discuss the problem of age: what is the optimal age for learning a second language? We should stress that we do not intend to give a more or less complete overview of findings and theories on second language learning, but limit ourselves to discussing it in relation to language contact. This also means that we are only concerned with second-language acquisition in natural contexts, and will not deal with learning in classrooms.

8.1 Features of interlanguage

Interlanguage, a concept introduced by Selinker (1972) refers to the version or the variety of the target language which is part of the implicit linguistic knowledge or competence of the second-language learner. He or she proceeds through a series of interlanguages on the way to complete mastery of the target language. Of course, most second-language learners never reach this stage, getting stuck in one of the intermediate stages. Although the term seems to imply it, interlanguage is *not* a kind of language somewhere between the first and the second language with structural features from both, but rather an intermediate system characterized by features resulting from language-learning strategies. In this section we will discuss the following features: interference, simplification and generalization.

Since about 1970, 'interference' or 'negative transfer' has been an important issue in research on second-language acquisition. Many studies were undertaken to find out whether the first language (or source language) of second-language learners influenced their acquisition of a second (or target) language. Many researchers have tried to invalidate the common assumption that second-language learners experience difficulties in learning the second language mainly because of differences between the first and the second language, or that the learning process is determined by the degree of (dis-)similarity between the first and the second language. This assumption, which was developed in foreign-language classrooms but also generalized to natural language learning contexts, was called the *Contrastive Analysis (CA) Hypothesis*. The CA hypothesis was not often tested empirically; anecdotal observations were frequently used to support it.

In the literature on the CA hypothesis there is much misunderstanding and confusion about the nature of interference. Weinreich (1953), as will be clear from the first quote in the introduction to this chapter, implicitly distinguished two types of influence: *difficulties* caused by the differences between the source and the target language, and *interference*, the use of elements, structures and rules from the source language in the production of the target language, a phenomenon which is also often called 'negative transfer'. This distinction was adopted by Lado in his famous book on second-language learning, *Linguistics across cultures* (1957). Lado states that 'the student who comes into contact with a foreign language will find some features of it quite easy and others extremely difficult. Those elements that are similar to his native language will be simple for him (positive transfer will take place, RA, PM), and those elements that are different will be difficult' (p. 2). On the same page it is claimed that 'individuals tend to transfer the forms and meanings, and the distributions of forms and meanings of their native language and culture to the foreign language and culture'.

Perhaps because Weinreich and Lado were not very explicit about it, many other authors blurred the distinction between difficulties and interference. The 'difficulties' from the CA hypothesis came to be more or less synonymous with 'errors caused by interference'. Another reason for the equation of 'difficulty' and 'interference error' probably lies in the fact that the CA hypothesis was developed in a kind of symbiosis with behaviourist learning theory, in which 'transfer' is a central notion (Ellis, 1965). Errors in second-language performance were believed to be mainly the result of transfer of first-language skills or habits. Or to put it another way: old habits (the source language) interfere with the learning of new habits (the target language).

Research on this issue was mainly conducted in foreign-language classrooms. Duškova (1969), to name but one example, investigated the grammatical and lexical errors in the written English of Czech adult second-language learners. She found many interference errors: the direct object was frequently placed behind an adverbial modifier, as in Czech (* 'I met there some Germans'; Czech: Potkal jsem tam nejake Nemce) and articles were often omitted (* 'I should like to learn foreign language'), according to Duškova because Czech has no articles. She also notes that many errors seem to have little, if any, connection with the mother tongue of the students. Dalbor (1959) writes about the problems Spanish speakers experience in hearing and pronouncing the English phonemes / š/ and / č/ which have no exact parallels in their first language. Spanish-speaking learners of English may produce utterances like 'While shaving John cut his *shin*'.

Evidence for interference remained largely anecdotal in these studies. Its impact and frequency were more or less taken for granted, and many scholars aimed at writing parts of contrastive analyses of two languages in order to serve the development of teaching material in foreign-language courses.

In research on language contact, i.e. when second languages are acquired in natural settings, first-language influence has never been systematically investigated.

Weinreich (1953) even discusses interference from first to second and interference from second to first language indiscriminately. In his examples he fails to indicate whether they are taken from native speakers (influenced by a second language) or from second-language speakers. Weinreich only notes the influence from one language to another, for instance when he writes that *-en* replaces *-∅* (no marking) for the plural in a Swiss Italian dialect. Probably this is an example of influence from the second (Swiss German) on the first language. In another example, Weinreich notes that *ge-* replaces ∅- (no marking) for the passive participle in Yiddish-affected English: a clear instance of interference from the first language.

In a few other studies attention is specifically given to first-language influence. For instance, Muysken (1981) shows that Quechua has influenced Spanish in Ecuador via the process of second-language acquisition: structural features of Quechua have entered the Spanish dialect used by bilingual speakers. This type of interference in language contact situations will be further dealt with in chapter 13.

In the 1970s, the CA hypothesis was heavily attacked by proponents of mentalist theories of language and of the mind. They particularly opposed the view that first-language skills influenced second-language acquisition strongly, and that this influence should be visible in the copious occurrence of interference errors. An alternative hypothesis was proposed: the *identity hypothesis*, also called the L1 = L2 hypothesis, the universalistic or creative construction hypothesis. In brief, the identity hypothesis claims that second-language learners actively organize the target language speech they hear, and make generalizations about its structure in the same way as children learning a first language. The course of the acquisition process is determined by the structural properties of the target language and of the learning system, not by the differences or similarities between the source and the target language. The errors second-language learners make are not due to source/target differences but to characteristics of target language structures. According to the identity hypothesis, the errors of second-language learners are largely identical to those made by children learning that same language as their first language. In most cases errors are due to (wrong) generalizations and simplification, strategies to which we return below. It was thought that 'interference/transfer was of no importance whatsoever' (Hatch, 1977:17).

Two studies by Dulay and Burt were often cited to support the identity hypothesis. In the first one (Dulay and Burt, 1974a), they analysed the spoken English of children who had Spanish as their native language. Three types of errors were distinguished:

- intralingual or developmental errors (comparable to the 'errors', i.e. deviations from the adult norm, of first-language learners) e.g. 'They hungry' instead of 'They are hungry';
- interlingual or interference errors, e.g. 'They have hunger' ('Ellos tienen hambre');
- unique errors, e.g. 'Them hunger'.

The results indicated that first-language influence could account for only 4.7 per cent of the children's errors, while 87.1 per cent of the errors were developmental.

In another study, Dulay and Burt (1974b) compared the proficiency in producing correct English grammatical morphemes of Spanish- and Chinese-speaking children. They studied morphemes like plural *-s*, third person singular *-s*, *be -ing* for progressive form, copular *be*, etc. Because Spanish and Chinese differ considerably from each other with respect to the notions associated with these morphemes, the CA hypothesis would predict that the order in which the morphemes are acquired would be different for the two language groups. After computing a proficiency score for all children, and rank ordering the morphemes, Dulay and Burt found, however, that the rank order for the two groups was nearly the same: morphemes easy for the Spanish group were also easy for the Chinese group, morphemes difficult for the Spanish-speaking children were also difficult for the children with Chinese as their mother tongue. Dulay and Burt concluded that the children's first language had no substantial influence, and that the results supported the identity hypothesis.

Dulay and Burt's study is well known, but it is also quite controversial, especially because of the methodology employed. For instance, the cross-sectional data were interpreted longitudinally. In Dulay and Burt (1974b) it is assumed that the proficiency order for a *group* of children which is studied at a certain point in time can be equated with the acquisition order for each individual child, which applies to a certain period of time, and therefore, in fact, requires a longitudinal research design. We will not go into the methodological issues, but point to one interesting aspect of the results of Dulay and Burt which they themselves seem to ignore: the rank orders of the Chinese and the Spanish group are approximately the same, but the Chinese-speaking children have lower proficiency scores for each morpheme than the Spanish group, although they did not have lesser opportunities for learning English. This result may be brought about by the fact that Chinese differs considerably more from English than Spanish does. Perhaps English is more difficult for the Chinese-speaking children, as the CA hypothesis predicts.

The distance between the two languages involved seems to affect the process of second-language acquisition, as Weinreich (1953) had already indicated. When language (A) differs from language (B) with respect to structure (X), this structure will be difficult to acquire for native speakers of (A) learning (B), and the greater the difference, the greater the learning problem will be, *without* transfer taking place. We can illustrate this form of *indirect first-language influence* with the example of Turkish and Moroccan children acquiring Dutch prepositions. Dutch uses prepositions to introduce phrases, while some locative prepositions have a postpositional 'alternative' expressing a directional meaning.

(1) in het gebouw
     in the building
(1a) het gebouw in
     the building into ('into the building')

Turkish does not have prepositions. Case suffixes are used where Dutch has prepositions if the relation expressed is general and does not demand any further specification. For example, the dative suffix *(y)e* generally denotes 'direction', and can be used with any verb expressing 'direction'. In Turkish separate postpositions are only used in specific instances. These postpositions have a fixed form, and they govern one or more cases, i.e. they are bound to a preceding suffix modifying the suffix's meaning. For example *ev* ('house') with the dative suffix renders *ev-e* ('to the house'). Modification with a postposition gives *ev-e kadar* ('just to the house'). Differently from Turkish, in Moroccan-Arabic and in Berber (the mother tongue of many of the Moroccan children studied) only prepositions occur.

Appel (1984) gives data on the Dutch interlanguage of Turkish and Moroccan children after about one, two and three years in the Netherlands. With respect to the realization of the preposition, transfer did not occur: Turkish children hardly produced any postpositions where Dutch requires prepositions. However, indirect first-language influence seemed to play a major role: in all three years of the study, the Turkish children deleted Dutch prepositions significantly more often than Moroccan children did. Here, first-language influence seems to lead to *simplification*, which we will further discuss later in this section.

Schachter (1974) points to another form of indirect first language influence: the avoidance of structures in the second language that diverge from structures in the first. She compared the production of relative clauses in English by speakers of Persian, Arabic, Chinese and Japanese, and found that the written compositions of the latter two groups contained significantly fewer relative clauses than those of the Persian and Arabic speaking subjects. According to Schachter, one of the plausible explanations for this finding is that Persian and Arabic are similar to English with regard to the head noun–relative clause order, while Chinese and Japanese have relative clauses which precede the head noun or the antecedent. Schachter assumed that the Chinese and Japanese students tried to avoid relative clauses in English, and only used them when they were relatively sure that they were correct. This interpretation was supported by the fact that these Chinese and Japanese students made relatively fewer errors than the students speaking Persian or Arabic.

Hakuta (1976) reported a comparable result: a child with Japanese as her first language produced far fewer relative clauses in English than a Spanish-speaking girl. Recall that in Spanish relative clauses follow the head noun, as in English. It seems that structures in the target language differing from those in the first language are learned relatively late in the acquisition process, and they are avoided in the initial stages when possible.

At the end of the 1970s and in the early 80s interference (or negative transfer) was recognized again as a major component of second-language acquisition. This reappraisal was mainly due to methodological improvements in the study of interlanguage systems. The new approach to transfer was manifest in many articles and books. Wode (1981:52) wrote for instance that 'L1 transfer must be regarded as an integrated part of man's natural linguo-cognitive processing apparatus that allows him to learn languages', and according to Meisel (1982:6), transfer 'must be interpreted as a mental activity, similar to what must be involved in the often cited "creative construction" process'. Transfer was given a place in the mentalist view of language acquisition, in which the individual mentally organizes the target language structures heard and develops hypotheses about these. One of the erroneous hypotheses may be that the target language is similar to the first language with respect to a certain structure, resulting in negative transfer.

Detailed, longitudinal studies of second-language acquisition have shown that interference certainly does occur, but mainly in certain developmental stages. Second-language learners use the strategy of transfer when they are 'ready' for it, i.e. have arrived at a level of complexity in their interlanguage that resembles the corresponding structure in their first language. This implies that a long-standing assumption from the Contrastive Analysis Hypothesis does not hold any more: 'smaller differences lead to more transfer' must be substituted for 'greater differences lead to more transfer' (Zobl, 1980, 1982). Partial similarity between languages creates the opportunity for transfer.

We will illustrate this view with an example from a study by Wode (1981) of the acquisition of negation in English by German children. In the first stage the German children used sentence-initial *no*:

(1) no finish ('Not finished')
(2) no drink some milk ('I don't want to drink any milk')
(3) no good stupid, o.k.? ('The truck is no good. It is stupid. O.K.?')

In the second stage *be* was negated inside the clause:

(4) that's no good
(5) it's not raining
(6) there it's not waterski ('There is no waterskiing/water-skier')

In the next stage, sentence-internal negation was found in the interlanguage of the children:

(7) me no close the window ('I am not going to close the window')
(8) ich have not home run ('I have not made a home run')
(9) you have a not fish ('You don't have a fish')

The transitional structures given so far are also reported in studies on the acquisition of English as a first language, where no trace of influence from German can be detected. In this third stage, however, when the negation element is brought into the sentence, utterances also appear which are not found in the English of young first-language learners:

(10) Heiko like not the school
      ('Heiko doesn't like the school')
(11) You go not fishing
      ('You don't go fishing')
(12) I want not play
      ('I don't want to play')

Here the children seem to apply a rule from German: post-verbal placement of negation exemplified in the parallel structures to (10)–(12).

(13) Heiko mag die Schule nicht
      Heiko likes the school not
(14) Du gehst nicht fischen
      You go not fish (inf.)
(15) Ich will nicht spielen
      I want not play (inf.)

Wode, who gives a much fuller account, to be sure, of the developmental sequences the children go through, notes that utterances with sentence-internal *be*-negation precede sentence-internal negation in utterances with main verbs, while the children at the same time are experimenting with pre-verbal placement of negation, producing the same type of transitional structures as first-language learners.

Le Compagnon (1984) also shows when and how transfer occurs in the inter-language of second-language learners. She studied dative constructions produced by

French learners of English. For some verbs of 'telling' English has two alternative structures, e.g. (16) and (17).

(16) He told me a story
(17) He told a story to me

Other verbs, however, only permit structures like (17):

(18) I can describe the house to you
(19) * I can describe you the house

Sentences like (19) often occurred in the interlanguage of the second-language learners studied by Le Compagnon. The explanation can be found in structural properties of French, where the pronominalized indirect object always precedes the direct object, as in (20).

(20) Il m'explique la regle

It is clear that *direct* transfer does not occur, because sentences like (21) are absent.

(21) * He me explained the rule

The first language's influence is more indirect, but that French affects the English interlanguage is further corroborated by the observation that structures like (19) only occurred when the indirect object was pronominalized (when the indirect object is a noun, French has the word order direct object – indirect object).

It is evident that there must be some resemblance between the first language and (a transitional structure in) the second language before transfer can take place. When languages differ too much with respect to a certain structure, transfer even seems improbable. Speakers of Chinese and Japanese, for instance, will certainly not produce utterances in English with relative clauses preceding the head noun, as they do in their first language. The structure of English doesn't give rise anywhere to the idea that pre-noun relative clauses would be possible. The second-language learner does not have data to build such a hypothesis on. Before turning to other features of interlanguage, three issues regarding transfer will be dealt with briefly. The first one concerns age differences. It is generally assumed that older learners show more transfer in their interlanguage than younger learners. Children seem to take on the task of learning a second language more spontaneously than adults, which might result in more structural similarity with first-language learners. Dittmar (1981) gives various examples of transfer in the German of Turkish immigrant workers, for example utterances with the verb at the end which parallel a dominant pattern in Turkish, while German main clauses have the tensed verb in second position:

(22) dann Kinder Frau alles hier *kommt* (then children wife all here come; 'then my children and my wife, they all come here')

Pfaff (1984), however, in a study likewise carried out in Berlin, found this type of structure only occasionally in the German of Turkish children.

The second issue concerns transfer in the various components of the language. Above, we mainly discussed syntactic transfer. Older learners especially often show extensive transfer in their pronunciation. This type of phonetic transfer probably occurs more often than transfer on other levels, because it has neurological and physiological causes: it seems difficult to learn new pronunciation habits in addition to the existing ones. On the lexical, semantic and pragmatic levels transfer generally does not occur very frequently (lexical transfer concerns the use of a word from the source language while speaking the target language, and semantic transfer occurs when the *meaning* of a word from the source language is extended to a corresponding word in the target language). Pfaff (1984) gives a clear example of semantic transfer in the German of Greek children. Some children use *warum* ('why') to mean both 'why' and 'because', respectively *warum* and *deshalb* in German. In the German of Turkish children this double use of *warum* was not found. According to Pfaff, this can plausibly be attributed to the fact that Greek has a single lexical item for both 'why' and 'because', while Turkish distinguishes them.

Lexical transfer, i.e. transfer of the actual word, is not a widespread phenomenon, unlike transfer from the second into the first language in the form of loanwords (see chapter 14). Sometimes second-language learners use words from their first language when they do not know the word in the second. Faerch and Kasper (1983) give the following example of a Danish learner of English: 'Sometimes I take er . . . what's it called . . . er . . . *knallert' (knallert* is Danish for 'moped'). The use of a native word in a second-language context is a type of interlanguage strategy which learners follow in order to convey meaning despite a relative lack of knowledge of the second language. Schumann (1978) contains various examples of the use of Spanish words in the English interlanguage of Alberto, a 33-year-old Costa Rican living in the USA, e.g. *necesario, interesante* and *arquitectura*. It is striking that all these Spanish words resemble their English equivalents.

Pragmatic transfer will be discussed in chapter 12.

Individual second-language learners can differ enormously in the extent to which they transfer features of their first language into their interlanguage, which is the last issue to be discussed. It is not quite clear how these differences can be explained. Possibly they can be related to differences in cognitive style. Meisel *et al.* (1981) hypothesize that social-psychological variables may explain the differential occurrence of transfer, and suggest that learners who are strongly connected with their first-language community (for instance in the case of immigrant groups) and have no substantial social and cultural ties with the target language community will show most transfer in their interlanguage. It is an interesting hypothesis, but it still lacks empirical support.

Dulay and Burt (1974a, 1974b) claimed that second-language learners largely followed the same strategies as first-language learners, and that the errors in their interlanguage were mainly intralingual or developmental in nature, i.e. comparable to errors in the speech of children learning their first language. These errors or deviations from the target norm are largely due to two learning strategies: *simplification* and *generalization*. (We use the term 'strategy' rather loosely, because there is no exact information available on the conscious or unconscious processes in the mind of the language learner. In fact it is only a theoretical assumption that the learner 'simplifies' or 'generalizes', based on features of the interlanguage.)

Simplification has been stressed in many studies of second-language acquisition: the learner postulates a simpler structure in his or her interlanguage than the one truly characterizing the target language. The English interlanguage of Schumann's (1978) subject Alberto was characterized by many simplifications. For instance, he used hardly any auxiliaries, except *is* as a copula, he did not mark the possessive, the regular past-tense ending (*-ed*) was virtually absent, and only about 60 per cent of the time he supplied the progressive morpheme *-ing*.

Veronique (1984) gives many examples of simplification errors in the French of North African immigrant workers:

(23) garage a fermé (*le* missing before *garage*)
('(the) car-repair workshop is closed')
(24) cherche un travail (*je* missing as subject pronoun)
('(I) look for a job')

The second-language learners also deleted the initial syllables sometimes whenever this reduced the morpheme load. *Deposer* ('to put down'), for instance, became *poser*, which is the same form as *poser*, 'to place'.

Second-language learners, especially in the first stages of development, seem to preserve the content words from the target language as much as possible while deleting many function words and morphemes: personal pronouns, articles, auxiliaries, prepositions and tense-indicating morphemes. Speaking a simplified interlanguage made up largely of content words still makes relatively adequate communication possible.

Generalization could be viewed as a specific instance of simplification, because it also implies the reduction of the range of possible structures. In the above-mentioned study, Veronique points to many generalizations in the French interlanguage of North African immigrants: e.g. the tendency to use *avoir* also for verbs which are conjugated with *être* (both 'have' in English); (b) the reduction of the number of allophones of many verbs, such as *pouvoir* ('to be able to'), which has seven allomorphs, but is only used in one form, [pɸ], *peut*, *peux* by some learners.

Appel (1984) gives an example of the generalization of word-order rules in the Dutch of Turkish and Moroccan immigrant workers' children. In Dutch, the tensed verb occupies the second position in declarative main clauses. Therefore, the subject–verb order (as in (25)) is inverted in sentences with a preposed adverbial phrase (26).

(25) Ik *ga* morgen naar Tilburg
I go tomorrow to Tilburg ('I go to Tilburg tomorrow')
(26) Morgen *ga* ik naar Tilburg
Tomorrow go I to Tilburg

Many Turkish and Moroccan children generalized the subject-verb order to sentences beginning with an adverbial phrase, producing sentences like (27) and (28).

(27) En dan hij *gaat* weg
And then he goes away (correct target structure: En dan *gaat* hij weg)
(28) Gisteren ik *heb* gezien De Man van Atlantis
yesterday I have seen The Man from Atlantis
('Yesterday I saw The Man from Atlantis'; correct target structure: Gisteren *heb* ik De Man van Atlantis gezien)

The same type of error is often made by native speakers of French and English learning Dutch.

The third strategy, the universal grammatical one, is probably based on general language-specific or cognitive properties of the human mind (see also chapter 15 on pidgins and creoles). This strategy for instance explains the occurrence of negation in sentence-initial position in the interlanguage of beginning second-language learners.

The ideal for many second-language learners is to achieve native-like proficiency in the target language. However, many learners, especially older ones or those who remain isolated from the target-language community, never reach this goal. As we said in the introduction to this chapter, they get stuck in one of the intermediate stages. *Fossilization* of interlanguage structures takes place, resulting in a more or less stable interlanguage. All features of interlanguage can fossilize, independently of the learning strategy they result from. When the interlanguage of many learners fossilizes at the same point for a certain structure, a new variety of the target language can develop. Massive second-language learning fosters language change (cf. chapter 13).

8.2 Social-psychological factors and second-language acquisition

Especially in bilingual communities where members of minority groups are forced to learn the majority language, the social, psychological and cultural position of the second-language learner is crucial. Research on this issue, and our perception of the main problem involved, are mainly stimulated by the work of Wallace E. Lambert and Robert C. Gardner. In their view, social-psychological factors relate strongly to achievement in second-language learning (Gardner and Lambert, 1972). The learner's attitudes towards the target-language community are believed to affect his success in learning considerably because the motivation to learn the second language is determined by these attitudes (for attitudes, see also chapter 2). Learners with an integrative motivation, i.e. the aim to become a member of the target-language community, will learn the second language better than those with an instrumental motivation, i.e. learners who only want to learn the new language because of (limited) commercial, educational or other instrumental reasons.

Many studies have been conducted that support this view empirically. For instance, Gardner *et al.* (1976) found positive correlations between motivational factors and the achievement in French of English Canadians. Comparison between the scores for integrative and instrumental motivation showed that the first ones were consistently better predictors of second-language proficiency.

However, some other studies yielded more or less contrary results. Oller *et al.* (1977) found that integrative motivation was not a good predictor of success in second-language acquisition for another group of learners. A factor defined as a desire to remain in the United States permanently – on the part of Chinese-speaking graduate students – was even negatively correlated with attained skills in English. In surveying the results of other research Oller and his associates noted as well that generally only a very weak relationship was found between social-psychological variables and second-language proficiency. For instance, the study of Teitelbaum *et al.* (1975) on the Spanish achievement of American students with English as their first language indicates only very low correlations between self-reports of attitude and motivation and performance on a test of second-language proficiency.

Another point of criticism with regared to Gardner and Lambert's view is that only a (weak) relation between social and psychological factors on the one hand and second-language acquisition on the other is established, but that this relation is often interpreted *causally* in the sense that the factors studied are expected to influence or even determine success in learning a second language. This can only be an assumption, however, since researchers have not yet been able to clarify the direction of the causal link. One could state that this direction is the other way round than commonly assumed: success in second-language learning fosters a positive attitude towards the target-language community and a strong motivation to learn its language even better. Gardner (1979) also notes that second-language achievement can affect motivational factors, and that high proficiency improves possibilities of contact with native speakers of the target language, which may again contribute to higher achievement.

A third point of discussion we want to raise concerns the fact that in the views of Gardner and Lambert (and many others) the integrative motivation is given so much weight, and that it is suggested that this will necessarily lead to cultural assimilation. According to this view, a learner can only become proficient in a second language if he or she wants to adapt to the cultural values of the target-language community. For instance, according to Gardner (1979:193–4), students while learning a second language are acquiring symbolic elements of a different ethnolinguistic community; the student has 'to make them part of his own language reservoir. This involves imposing elements of another culture in one's own lifespace. As a result the student's harmony with his own cultural community and his willingness or ability to identify with other cultural communities become important considerations in the process of second-language acquisition'. Statements like this one suggest that cultural assimilation, or at least the adoption of the main cultural values of the target-language community, is an important condition for successful second-language acquisition. However, because of the rather low correlations between social and psychological variables (including cultural attitudes) and second-language proficiency this idea lacks strong supportive evidence. Furthermore, one can point to studies of societal bilingualism. Bilinguals, especially those in an additive context (see chapter 9), do not seem to be torn between two cultures associated with the respective languages. Of course, languages are related to cultures because of their habitual use in certain cultural contexts, but this does not necessarily imply that speaking a certain language also means adopting the culture and life style of the community in which the language is the dominant medium of interaction. If this were the case, proficient bilinguals should be more or less schizophrenic, forced to live with two possibly conflicting systems of norms and values. The literature on bilingualism and personality development does not warrant such a conclusion (see chapter 9). What goes for bilinguals should also apply to second-language learners: they do not have to identify with the culture of the target community to be able to acquire adequate competence in the language of that community.

Taking a social and political perspective, it should also be noted that minority groups in many (Western) countries are pushed in the direction of the abandonment of their own cultural values and cultural adaptation to mainstream society. People who advocate assimilation of these groups could use the theory of the causal relation between cultural orientation and second-language achievement to support and legitimize their stand. Researchers should therefore be very careful in formulating results and conclusions with regard to this issue.

The fourth point we want to raise concerns the fact that 'attitudes' and 'motivations' are often considered to be individual variables, i.e. personal characteristics of second-language learners. From this, the conclusion can easily be drawn that second-language learners must be blamed personally when they only reach a low level of proficiency. However, 'motivation' as a variable in naturalistic second-language acquisition (the situation in foreign-language classrooms is completely different) is *not* an individual but a socially determined variable. Second-language learners can not be held responsible for their failure because of a supposed lack of motivation. Attitudes and subsequently motivation result from certain social-political conditions. They are the result of interactions between characteristics of the individual second-language learner and the social environment, especially the target-language community. Therefore, in accounting for the relation between social and psychological variables and second-language learning it seems better to follow an approach proposed by John Schumann.

In many publications Schumann has stressed that the *social* and *psychological distance* between the second-language learner and members of the target-language community affects the learning process considerably (e.g. Schumann, 1978). When the distance is great, learning will not be successful. Distance is a neutral concept. Both parties involved can try to reduce it. This implies that lack of success in second-language acquisition is not due to the supposedly insufficient learning motivation on the part of the learner, caused by his or her negative attitudes towards the target community. In the distance approach, the negative attitudes of the members of the target community, manifested in discrimination for instance, are as important and possibly even more important. Perhaps Schumann's concept of social distance can be extended to include cultural distance, to account for the effect of cultural differences.

To conclude, there is a certain relation between social and psychological variables and second-language acquisition, but this relation should not be over-stressed. Furthermore, these variables must not be seen as expressing individual characteristics of the learner, but as indicators of the social, psychological and cultural distance between the learner and the target-language community.

8.3 The problem of age and the simultaneous acquisition of two languages

According to popular belief (young) children are faster and better second-language learners than adults. Children seem to acquire a second language more or less without any effort and they generally attain high levels of proficiency. It is therefore often recommended that children start learning a second language as soon as possible. As they grow older they will gradually lose this unique capability. Research has shown, however, that this is only a crude generalization which requires differentiation and elaboration (cf. Krashen *et al.* 1979). We will summarize research results and current views on the problem of age in the following propositions.

(1) There is no conclusive evidence for a critical period for second-language acquisition, i.e. a period lasting until, for instance, puberty in which learning must take place, and after which a second language can never be learned in (completely) the same way. Such a critical period was proposed by Lenneberg (1967) for first- and second-language acquisition. The critical period was thought to be connected with

the lateralization of the brain, i.e. the specialization of functions of different hemispheres of the brain. Lenneberg assumed that this lateralization is finished at about puberty, however, more recent research has cast serious doubts on this assumption: it has become rather uncertain when lateralization takes place (cf. Krashen, 1973). Perhaps only a sensitive or optimal period for the acquisition of certain second-language skills, especially pronunciation, can be established.

(2) A difference must be made between *rate* of acquisition and *level* of proficiency attained. Adults seem to be faster second-language learners than children (especially in the initial stages), but children overtake them at a certain point, and achieve higher levels of proficiency. Also older children (aged between 9 and 12) are faster learners than younger children (aged between 5 and 8).

(3) Many factors mediate the influence of age on second-language acquisition. Following Lenneberg, attention used to be paid mainly to the biological factor: a critical period determined by brain lateralization. In more recent publications the effects of cognitive, affective and social factors are stressed. Due to differences in their level of cognitive development, learners from different age groups may also employ different learning strategies, which may have consequences for their respective second-language skills. There may also be differences in the relation between the learner and the target-language community: the social and psychological distance between the learner and the target community may be smaller for younger learners. Social factors, finally, refer to the different ways in which native speakers adjust themselves to the learning needs of learners of different age groups. Native speakers probably adjust the level of complexity of their speech more when interacting with children than with adults, thereby providing a language input which is more stimulating for second-language acquisition (see also 12.1, *Foreigner talk*).

It must be noted that the conclusion under (2) with regard to the older children who generally outperform the younger children, only applies to children above the age of five. Very young children did not participate in the studies on this issue, mainly because the language tests used to assess language proficiency could not be administered with this age group. Furthermore, for the youngest children the social conditions are so different from those for the other age groups that a valid conclusion would be impossible to draw. It remains possible to conclude from many anecdotal observations of individual very young children acquiring a second language that they seem very fast learners.

Not only do very young children acquire a second language rapidly, they also seem to be able to acquire two languages simultaneously without special difficulties. The remainder of this chapter will be devoted to this issue. Before going on, first a terminological problem must be clarified: when are two languages *simultaneously* acquired? Of course, if the child starts his/her learning career with two languages at the same time, the situation is clear. However, what do we say when a child is initially raised in, say, French, and from about his/her second birthday on (when he/she already speaks some French) Spanish is added? In such a situation, acquisition seems to be both successive *and* simultaneous. The cut-off point, when acquisition must be considered as primarily successive can only be determined arbitrarily: at three years of age, four years of age, having reached a certain stage in the first language? We will not try to give an answer to this question, mainly because the research in this area almost exclusively bears upon children who acquire two languages from very early on. Furthermore, there is no theory on (second) language acquisition from which arguments can be derived to determine the cut-off point. It is even questionable whether such a theory is possible. Nonetheless in many immigrant communities there are a large number of children starting second-language acquisition around ages 3-4.

The first question people often ask when they want to raise their child with two languages is: does it impede or disturb the language learning process? From many observations, surveyed in Taeschner (1983) it becomes evident that children generally do not lag behind for either languages when compared to monolingual children. The double linguistic processing load does not affect the proficiency in either language.

Another frequently asked question concerns the formal separation of the two languages, and especially the influence of both systems on each other. In the first stage of bilingual development (about age 1-2) for the children the two languages constitute one 'hybrid system' (Leopold, 1939-49, Vol. III:179). In this stage, for each referrent they generally have one word, and the use of interlingual equivalents does not occur frequently. The reason for this is, of course, that equivalents function as synonyms, and the acquisition of synonyms at such an early stage would imply too much of a burden for the child. Taeschner (1983) reports on the simultaneous acquisition of German and Italian by a girl named Lisa, and gives the example of apparent equivalents which have nevertheless not quite overlapping meanings. Lisa uses both *da* (from German) and *la* (from Italian), both meaning 'there', but *la* was very probably used for things which were not present or visible when speaking, and *da* for objects which were present. However, Leopold (1939-49) in his extensive, classical study on the bilingual English-German development of his daughter Hildegard, gives examples of the avoidance of equivalents as well as of the use of them. For instance, when she was 1 year and 8 months old (1;8) Hildegard acquired [na] for the German word *nass* ('wet'), but shortly after *wet* became active as well, [we], [wɛ] and [na] was no longer heard. At 1;11 Hildegard acquired (and used) a German and an English form to refer to flower: [bu] (*Blume*) and [wau], more or less simultaneously. When children have equivalents at their disposal they sometimes use them together, one after the other. Burling (1959) studied the language development of his son Stephen who acquired English and Garo, a language spoken in the Garo Hills district of Assam, India. Stephen knew both the word *milk* and its Garo equivalent *dut*, and sometimes he said 'milk dut' or 'dut milk'. Perhaps bilingual children do this to guarantee as much as possible that their message comes through. Older bilingual children, in later stages of development, have also been reported to follow this strategy.

Equivalents become much more frequent when the child starts separating the two systems. This will happen, very much approximately, one year after the child produces his first word. In general, this formal separation will not cause a lot of problems. Bilingual children will go through the same developmental stages (see section 1 of this chapter) as monolingual children. In acquiring the negation system, for instance, English-Spanish bilingual children follow the same developmental path in their English (i.e. use the same transitional structures in the same order) as monolingual English-speaking children, and in their Spanish the same path as monolingual Spanish children. This is only a very general picture, and interference from one language to the other occurs at different developmental stages and at different linguistic levels. Burling (1959) gives an example of interference on the phonetic level. Stephen showed problems in the acquisition of *f* and *v* in his English, presumably because Garo (his other and strongest language) does not have phonemes near the same position. Rūke-Dravina (1965) reports a case of more direct first-language influence. She studied the speech of two Swedish–Latvian bilingual children and found that the Swedish uvular /R/, which was acquired earlier, replaced the Latvian rolled, apical /r/ in their Latvian.

Lexical interference occurs frequently in the speech of bilingual children. Most studies present numerous examples of this. For instance, Burling's son Stephen inserted many English words in his Garo sentences. Burling gives the curious example of the sentence 'Mami laitko tunonaha' ('Mommy turned on the light'). Stephen used English roots, but the word order, the morphology (*-ko* as direct object marker, and *-aha* indicating past tense) and phonology were Garo. However, these lexical transfers perhaps do not occur abundantly as regularly as anecdotal observations sometimes suggest. Lindholm and Padilla (1978) is one of the few more or less experimental studies in this area. They obtained speech samples of 18 bilingual English–Spanish children between the ages of 2;0 and 6;4 years, from interactions between one child and two experimenters. One experimenter spoke only Spanish to the child and the other only English, and this suggested to the child that he/she had to act as a verbal go-between. Of the total 17,864 utterances produced by the children, only 319, or 1.7 per cent, contained transferred lexical items. Examples are: 'Este es un fireman' ('This (one) is a fireman'), 'Y los kangaroos tienen plumas' ('And the kangaroos have feathers'), and 'Te miras funny' ('You look funny').

Children mainly transfer lexical items when they do not know a word in the language they are speaking, or when they cannot recall it. Saunders (1982), who studied the bilingual English–German development of his sons Frank and Thomas gives the following examples of Thomas talking to his mother, with whom he generally speaks English.

T (5;4) (showing his mother his sore tongue): What's on my tongue?
M: Show me. Is it a pimple?
T: It might be a *geschwur* (German for 'ulcer'; he hesitated slightly before 'geschwur', and gave a slightly embarrassed grin as he said it.)
M: Oh, you mean an ulcer, do you?
T: Yeah, that's the word.

According to Jaroviskij (1979) lexical transfer is also induced when the word in the one language is phonetically simpler than in the other. Hungarian–Russian speaking children will sometimes choose the Russian word therefore when speaking Hungarian. Consider the following cases:

Russian *bulavka* vs Hungarian *biztositotu* ('safety pin')
Russian *banka* vs Hungarian *konzervdoboz* ('(tin) can').

Syntactic transfer is reported very infrequently. Saunders (1982) gives a few examples. His son Thomas persistently used English word order in German subordinate clauses beginning with *weil* ('because'), e.g 'Du musst die Säcke Gold tragen, weil sie sind zu schwer' ('You have to carry the bags of gold because they are too heavy'; in the original German utterance the verb *sind* (= 'are') should be in final position).

Saunders also reports some cases of semantic transfer, which he defines as the transfer 'of the sense, but not the word form to a *cognate* (a word in one language related in origin and meaning to one in the other), *partial equivalent*, or *(near)-homophone* (a word sounding (nearly) the same in another language)' (p. 180; see also the first section of this chapter). We will give one of Saunders's examples:

Frank (4;10) (telling his mother that he and his father have bought air tickets for the summer holidays):
    Mum, we got the cards.
Mother (not understanding): What cards?
Frank: The cards so we could go to Grandma's.
(Here the meaning of English 'card' has been extended to include 'ticket'; the German word *Karte* means 'card', 'ticket' or even 'map', depending on context.)

Citing remarkable instances of interference or transfer always suggests that it is a dominant phenomenon in the simultaneous acquisition of two languages. However, as we indicated above, this is not the case, at least not when both languages are developed equally well. When one language becomes dominant it will interfere more frequently in the less-known language. This may also happen when the languages are not distinct in their social distribution (see below), although there is not much evidence supporting this view.

The third question we will deal with here concerns the social and pedagogical aspects of raising bilingual children: what is best way to foster sound bilingual development? the answer is rather simple: follow a one person – one language strategy as much as possible, for instance, one parent consistently speaks English with the child and the other parent Welsh; in the presence of the child the parents use Welsh (or consistently English) with each other. Both parents should be proficient in both languages (in their second language at least receptively), in order not to frustrate family interactions or become frustrated themselves. When this strategy is applied and the conditions of language proficiency are met, bilingual development of the children can be successful. They will probably have fewer problems in separating the two systems formally, and they will learn more easily which language is appropriate in which situation. Parents should also try to provide equal learning opportunities for both languages. This will be difficult in situations where one of the two languages is not spoken outside the home, or where it is a negatively valued minority language. Especially at a more advanced age, children may develop a negative attitude towards the non-dominant language which will certainly affect acquisition. Søndergaard (1981) states that it turned out to be impossible to raise his child bilingually in Danish and Finnish, because of the environmental pressure against Finnish. Saunders (1982) argues that such problems can be successfully overcome when the parents are persistent, and at the same time do not try to press too hard, showing understanding for the child's problems.

Children should separate their two languages not only formally, but also functionally. Do they learn to select the right language in the right context, and to switch from one language to the other? This is the fourth and last problem discussed here. From many observations it is clear that with bilingual children the formal and functional separation of languages goes hand in hand. When the formal separation of the two systems begins, the children also learn that one system is more appropriate for use with a certain person, and the second system with another person. Saunders (1982) gives a good example of how a child can solve the problem when he wants to address two parents associated with two different languages. Around his third birthday, his son Thomas adopted the following interaction strategy: he addressed one of the parents by name, established eye contact, and then began to talk in the language he regularly used with that parent.

Bilingual children, following their parents or other caretakers as examples, generally employ the one person – one language strategy, but they diverge from it now and then. De Houwer (1983) reports on a study of the bilingual development in English and Dutch of Kate, whose father always spoke Dutch with her, and her mother English. Sometimes she addressed her father in English. She probably took into account, however, that her father was proficient in English (he used it with his wife), because she never spoke English to her monolingual Dutch-speaking grandparents.

Knowing the rules for language selection implies knowing the rules for code-switching (see also chapters 3 and 10), as it relates to changes in the situation, because there is another interlocutor, another topic introduced, a change in setting, etc. In addition to this form of situational code-switching, young bilingual children also are capable of metaphorical code-switching, in which some sort of special meaning is added to the conversation. Lindholm and Padilla (1978) give the following example of a Spanish–English bilingual child trying to make fun of an experimenter who only speaks English (as the child wrongly assumes).

C(hild): Know what's wrong with your teeth?
E(experimenter): What about my teeth?
C: Look at this one
E: What about it?
C: Es chueco ('It's crooked'; giggling)
E: It's what?
C: Es chueco
E: What's that?
C: Chueco (giggles again)
E: What's the English for that? I don't understand what you are saying
C: Chueco (the child changes the subject).

Sometimes bilingual children also switch within sentences. Apart from forms of lexical transfer (which may be seen as switching at word level), these intra-sentential switches mainly occur in the speech of fluent bilingual children (for a fuller discussion of intra-sentential code switching see chapter 10).

To conclude this section, we should mention that all statements with regard to the simultaneous acquisition of two languages must be regarded as tentative. In every conclusion above we could have used the word 'general(ly)', and we also could have modified each claim with 'probably', 'possibly' or ' in some cases'. Research in this area is mainly anecdotal, and often only one or a few cases are reported. It is often unclear whether researchers are only reporting on the striking phenomena, perhaps neglecting the less striking but far more frequent ones. Most studies lack quantitative data. Furthermore, most children observed are from middle-class, academic milieus, in which the parents have sometimes chosen deliberately to raise their children bilingually. It is not certain whether the bilingual development of children growing up in a different, and perhaps less favourable, environment will also have the same positive features. However, one conclusion can be drawn: children have such language-learning capacities that they can acquire two languages simultaneously without experiencing any real problem.

Further reading

Overviews of theories of and research on second-language acquisition can be found in the following two books. H. Dulay, M. Burt and S. Krashen, *Language two* (1982) and R. Ellis, *Understanding second language acquisition* (1985). R. Andersen (ed.), *Second languages; A cross-linguistic perspective* (1984) is a collection of studies on various theoretical issues, and provides data from many other interlanguages than English. Saunders's book *Bilingual children: guidance for the family* (1982) is highly readable. Especially the information on social and pedagogical aspects of the simultaneous acquisition of two languages is interesting. Taeschner's book *The sun is feminine: A study on language acquisition in bilingual children* (1983) is more focused on linguistic issues.

9 The effects of bilingualism

'Subject 408/16 thinks that a person who is permanently in contact with two tongues does not speak either of them correctly. This leads to a feeling of insecurity and may lead to timidity or even to an inferiority complex.' These are the feelings of one of the bilingual European informants, speaking a variety of languages and from different groups and nationalities, in a questionnaire study by Vildomec (1963:213). Another subject reported that 'there is interference with concentrated and able use of one language', she is 'always hindered by *arrière-pensées* or vividness of a particular word in another tongue' (p. 213). The ideas of these two subjects, who undoubtedly will have felt negative effects from being bilingual, seem to reflect a widespread attitude towards bilingualism in the Western world. Many Western countries are viewed and view themselves as essentially monolingual, although they may actually have many speakers of other languages within their borders. For instance, French is not the only language spoken in France. There are also speakers of Breton, Basque, Dutch (Flemish), German, Arabic and many other languages. Yet France is not a country you think of when you have a multilingual society in mind. Bilingualism is seen as an old-fashioned residue from an earlier age or as a temporary phenomenon, the result of immigration. If there is bilingualism, it is expected to fade away, and develop into monolingualism.

Many people are inclined to associate bilingualism with problems: speaking two languages, and not one as 'normal people' do, will have detrimental effects on the bilingual individual. In many non-Western countries, e.g. in Africa and Asia, bilingualism is the norm, and people are surprised to hear about the negative connotations of bilingualism. They may see it as an expression of Western ethnocentrism.

It should be noted that in Vildomec's sample there were also subjects who reported positive effects of bilingualism: e.g., widening of horizon, increase of mental alertness, and improved grasp of the relativity of all things. Both the positive and the negative view on the consequences of bilingualism for the individual have been supported by research, although most recent studies have produced evidence on the positive side. In the following sections we will discuss these views further and the research connected with them.

In Section 9.1 linguistic aspects, including the measurement of bilingualism, will be dealt with. Because research is frequently focused on the academic achievement of bilingual children, linguistic aspects will often be discussed in an educational perspective. We will go into the cognitive effects of bilingualism in section 9.2, while personality development is the subject of the third section. Before turning to these sections we want to stress an important distinction between two socially defined types of bilingualism, i.e. *additive* and *subtractive* bilingualism. In cases of additive bilingualism, an individual adds 'a second, socially relevant language to [his/her] repertory of skills' (Lambert, 1978:217), while the first language is not in danger of being replaced, because it is a prestigious language and its further development is supported in many ways, for instance in the mass media. English-speaking Canadians acquiring French or English-speaking Americans adding Spanish to their verbal repertoire become additive bilinguals (see also chapter 6 on immersion education).

When second-language learning is part of a process of language shift away from the first or the 'home' language, subtractive bilingualism results, as in the case of Turkish immigrants in West Germany or Italian immigrants in Great Britain who become more or less proficient in German and English respectively, while losing skills in their mother tongue. As Lambert (1980) observes, many ethnic minority groups are forced to shift away from their ethnic language towards a national language, by national education policies and various social pressures. The minority language, as a non-prestigious language, can not be maintained adequately, and it is 'subtracted' from bilingual proficiency (cf. chapter 4).

As noted frequently before in this book, bilingualism must be analysed in its social context, and the effects of bilingualism can only be studied fruitfully and understood properly as well if social factors are taken into account. The concepts of additive and subtractive bilingualism provide a useful way of accomplishing this in explaining the effects of bilingualism.

9.1 Linguistic and educational aspects

Before dealing with the influence of bilingualism on language skills we will briefly describe the measurement of bilingualism and the problems inherent in it. Researchers or teachers may have two aims in the assessment of bilingualism: (a) they want to compare the skills of bilinguals with those of monolinguals, for both languages; (b) they want to establish the 'stronger' and the 'weaker' language, or the dominant and non-dominant language of bilinguals.

For the first aim the following techniques can be used:

- tests for different levels of language (vocabulary, syntax, etc.) are administered in both languages;
- recordings of spontaneous speech are analysed for different linguistic variables;
- recordings of spontaneous speech are rated by judges.

The fact that most bilinguals find themselves in a situation of diglossia (cf. chapter 3) implies a problem for these approaches. A vocabulary test will contain items from different social and cognitive domains, but a bilingual may not use one of his languages in a certain domain, and therefore possibly not know the words connected with it. When spontaneous speech is used, it is extremely important that recordings are made in 'fair' settings, i.e. in settings in which the language analysed is regularly used. When the spoken Turkish of a Turkish migrant child in Western Germany is recorded in a German school, where regularly only German is spoken, it is not astonishing if the child only produces very impoverished Turkish. Similarly with other important factors influencing speech production: interlocutor and topic. Elaborating on the example above, it becomes clear that making comparisons is extremely difficult: since a Turkish child in Munich and a Turkish child in Ankara live in quite different cultural situations, how can the factor 'topic (of interaction)', for instance, be held constant?

When the researcher wants to establish which of the bilingual's two languages is dominant one of the following techniques can be used:

- translation tests in two languages;
- giving instructions to the bilingual in both languages and measuring the speed of response (in a laboratory setting);
- word associations (the number of associations to translated stimulus words in both languages), for instance, how many words in both languages can a Spanish–English bilingual come up with when presented both with *cocina* and *kitchen*;
- presenting statements in two languages and asking for true–false responses;
- presenting cognates in the two languages and recording pronunciation (for example in a mixed English–French word list words like *element*, *prime* and *lingerie*; the language of pronunciation of these ambivalent items is considered to be the dominant language);
- asking bilinguals to rate their proficiency in both languages.

The last technique may not be valid because the self-ratings are presumably partly based on social prejudices regarding the two languages. The bilingual will perhaps be inclined to state that he speaks the language with the highest social status best. The other language is 'not important', so why should he be competent in it.

The results of the other experimental techniques mentioned are influenced by the domain distribution of the two languages. A statement may be quite normal in one language, while the translated version in the other language is not 'appropriate', because it refers to a situation or domain in which the language is not regularly used.

The problems in the assessment of bilingualism have not yet been solved satisfactorily, and it remains an open question whether they will be in the future. Still, researchers and educators want to know and speak about bilingual proficiency. Because really adequate measuring techniques are lacking, many statements on this issue must be viewed as tentative, including those in the remainder of this section. Also, in some sense bilingual proficiency encompasses both languages together; separating the two partial proficiencies is artificial from the perspective of the true bilingual.

In chapter 8 (section 8.3) we discussed the simultaneous acquisition of two languages. Different case studies yielded evidence in support of the conclusion that children raised bilingually were as proficient in both of their languages as monolingual children. However, the social situation of these children was rather favourable, especially when compared with the living conditions of children from ethnic minority groups. Most of the children in the case studies came from academic home environments, their parents were often interested in their bilingual development, and tried to stimulate it, because they expected it to be an enriching experience. Therefore, the results of these case studies can probably not be generalized to all children in a bilingual environment, but they still show that growing up bilingually does not *necessarily* impede the development of both languages, when compared to monolingual children.

In spite of the evidence from the case studies mentioned, the common opinion among educators and researchers before the 1960s was that child bilingualism had detrimental effects on linguistic skills. Research had pointed to a verbal deficit with regard to passive and active vocabulary, sentence length, and the use of complex and compound sentences. It was also reported that bilingual children exhibited more deviant forms in their speech, for instance, unusual word order and morphological errors. Many of these conclusions were drawn from a study by Smith (1939) on the English proficiency of Chinese–English bilingual children in Hawaii. However, it should be noted that in the Chinese community in Hawaii a kind of pidgin English (for pidgins, see chapter 15) was quite commonly used at that time. If the children tested used this pidgin English, it is rather obvious that their English was considered deficient compared to the English of monolingual children.

Another study often cited is Carrow (1957) on Spanish–English children in Texas primary schools who were compared with a group of monolingual English speaking students. Both groups were tested in silent reading, oral reading accuracy and comprehension, spelling, hearing, articulatory skills, vocabulary, and arithmetic reasoning. In a story-retelling task a sample of the children's speech was recorded and subsequently analysed for a number of variables. The monolingual children were better than the bilinguals, but only on the tests of oral reading accuracy and comprehension and receptive vocabulary. On other tests and variables the monolingual group had higher mean scores, but the differences were not significant. Two points must be noted in connection with Carrow's study. The first is that – as in most of these studies – comparisons were made only for one of the bilingual's two languages, i.e. English considered the 'main language', the language it is all about, making social prejudices regarding minority languages quite transparent.

The second point is that Carrow's results were not so negative as findings in many other studies. The reason for this is twofold. In the first place, Carrow's bilingual subjects had acquired English and Spanish simultaneously, while in most other studies children had acquired English as a second language. It simply takes time to learn a language, and the bilingual subjects in the studies with negative results might not have had enough time to learn the second language well. The second reason lies in the fact that Carrow's study was controlled better for confounding variables than many other studies. The children in the two groups were matched for age, non-verbal IQ, and socio-economic status. Many studies did not control for these variables, especially non-verbal IQ and socio-economic status, even though it is known that they affect scores on language and other tests considerably.

The idea that bilingualism has a detrimental effect on linguistic skills was formulated as the *balance hypothesis* (Macnamara, 1966). The hypothesis claims that human beings have a certain potential, or perhaps neural and physiological capacity, for language learning. If an individual learns more than one language, knowing one language restricts the possibilities for learning other languages. More proficiency in one language implies fewer skills in the other ones.

Inspired mainly by the positive results of research on bilingual and immersion education (see chapter 6) and the views of Toukomaa and Skutnabb-Kangas (1977), James Cummins developed interesting and important ideas on the linguistic (and cognitive) consequences of bilingualism which ran counter to the views expressed in the balance hypothesis. Cummins adopted Lambert's distinction between additive and subtractive bilingualism, and noticed that the studies which pointed to negative effects were all conducted in settings of subtractive bilingualism. He further observed that 'a home–school language switch results in high levels of functional bilingualism and academic achievement in middle-class majority-language children, yet leads to inadequate command of both first (L1) and second (L2) languages and poor academic achievement in many minority-language children' (Cummins, 1979:222). Here Cummins refers to the positive results of immersion education for children speaking a high-status language in Canada and the USA, and the low achievements of minority children in majority-language education. Another important empirical finding is that bilingual education for minority children generally seems to have a positive effect on both L1 and L2 (cf. chapter 6).

These data can only be explained if proficiency in the second language is partially a function of first-language proficiency at the time when second-language acquisition begins. The *developmental interdependence hypothesis* states that children can attain high levels of competence in their second language if their first-language development, especially the usage of certain functions of language relevant to schooling and the development of vocabulary and concepts, is strongly promoted by their environment outside of school. The high level of proficiency in the first language makes possible a similar level in the second language. On the other hand, when skills in the first language are not well developed, and education in the early years is completely in the second language, then the further development of the first language will be delayed. In turn, this will exert a limiting effect on second-language acquisition. Children from majority groups have a high level of first-language proficiency, especially in certain aspects relevant to the classroom, and therefore they can follow a complete second-language curriculum without negative effects. Their second-language acquisition benefits from their first-language skills. According to the hypothesis, the minority child's first language must be further developed in school as a basis for successful second-language acquisition.

In fostering first-language development of minority children most attention should be given to academically related aspects of language proficiency. Here again, Cummins follows the views of Skutnabb-Kangas and Toukomaa (1976), who introduced a distinction between two forms of language proficiency: surface fluency and conceptual-linguistic knowledge. Immigrant children can often communicate effectively in everyday situations (surface fluency), but they lack the conceptual-linguistic knowledge necessary for the development of academic language skills, especially those related to literacy.

Cummins (1980) used the terms Cognitive Academic Language Proficiency (CALP) and Basic Interpersonal Communication Skills (BICS) for Skutnabb-Kangas and Toukomaa's two categories. BICS are the phonological, syntactic and lexical skills necessary to function in everyday interpersonal contexts, while CALP is required in tasks where students have to manipulate or reflect upon surface features of language outside immediate interpersonal contexts, as in school tasks or in language tests.

In a later elaboration of his framework, Cummins (1984) proposed to conceptualize language proficiency along two continua. The first continuum represents the amount of contextual support for expressing or receiving meanings (see Figure 9.1). At the one extreme end of the continuum communication is completely context-embedded:

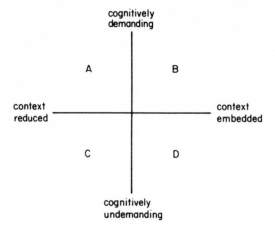

Figure 9.1   Cummins's conceptualization of language proficiency schematically represented

participants can refer to situational cues, they can give feed-back to guarantee under-standing of messages, and they can support language with all kinds of paralinguistic cues. In context-reduced communication, the other end of the continuum, parti-cipants have to rely primarily, or sometimes exclusively, on purely linguistic cues. In the classroom many activities are largely context-reduced.

The other dimension is that of cognitively demanding vs undemanding. Commu-nicative tasks are undemanding if they are largely automatized and require little active cognitive involvement. Many verbal activities in the classroom are cognitively demanding, because children do not master the task, and they have to organize their language production more or less consciously. Furthermore, many difficult concepts may occur in such tasks.

CALP can be situated in quadrant A of Figure 9.1. Examples of tasks requiring CALP are writing an essay, giving words with opposite meanings, and explaining a card game to somebody over the telephone. Quadrant D contains BICS. When a child tells a story on the basis of a drawing she has made, with the drawing present, BICS is at work. People talking about the weather rely on BICS. Cummins stresses that it is not his aim to suggest a precise model of language proficiency, but to present some distinctions relevant in relating linguistic skills to academic achievements of minority students. It is also important to note that the model presented in Figure 9.1 is perhaps more a model of tasks requiring certain forms of language proficiency than a model of language proficiency in itself.

In addition to the concepts discussed above Cummins proposed the *CUP-model* (Common Underlying Proficiency) as opposed to the *SUP-model* in explaining the linguistic effects of bilingual education. According to Cummins, the SUP-model, which claims that the underlying proficiencies of the two languages are separate, is inadequate. In the CUP-model, it is assumed that there is a common cognitive academic proficiency underlying both languages the bilingual speaks. Cummins (1984) argues that because of this non-language-specific, common underlying profi-ciency the literacy-related skills can be transferred from one language to the other. For example, reading lessons in Italian for bilingual Italian–English children also contribute to the development of their English reading skills, because they develop their common underlying proficiency.

Drawing on Cummins's views, we can give the following answers to the main question asked in this section. Bilingualism does not have detrimental effects on language skills, provided that first-language proficiency is adequately supported. Children from ethnic minority groups should receive instruction in their mother tongue in order to develop adequate cognitive language skills, before full weight is given to second-language acquisition in school. The skills developed in the mother tongue will also support the acquisition of academic and literacy-related skills in the second language. Then, and only then, will bilingualism be beneficial for these children. Children from majority groups, speaking a prestige language, will also profit from bilingualism if the second language is introduced at an early stage, because the first language, including the aspects relevant for the acquisition of literacy, is already developed outside school.

It must be emphasized that Cummins's hypotheses are indeed merely *hypotheses*, and have not yet found strong empirical support. They are very attractive, because they can explain many different phenomena. However, sometimes other explanations can be found as well, for instance with respect to the results of studies on bilingual education. It is a well known fact that social and psychological factors influence second-language development (cf. chapter 8). People will only acquire a second language successfully if their social-emotional state is not overly disturbed. Second-language learners have to feel more or less at ease, and if they experience social or cultural conflicts second-language acquisition will be impeded. This may be precisely the case in monolingual majority-language education for children from ethnic minority groups. Here bilingualism will not flourish because the social and psychological conditions affecting second-language acquisition are not favourable, while the first language is neglected.

Furthermore, we have to note that Cummins does not write about actual *linguistic* aspects of language proficiency. He does not provide an operationalization in linguistic variables of the concepts CALP and BICS, for instance he does not analyse the language spoken by people in a CALP-requiring task. 'Literacy-related skills' is merely a vague indication of the linguistic content of CALP. In fact Cummins's views apply to the relation between bilingualism and education, assuming that language proficiency is an important mediating variable without going deeper into the features of this variable.

Before turning to the cognitive consequences of bilingualism, where Cummins will also figure prominently, we will briefly discuss the concept of *semilingualism*, which frequently turns up in the descriptions of the linguistic effects of bilingualism. Somebody is semilingual when he or she speaks two languages but both at a lower level than monolingual native speakers.

The concept of semilingualism has often been misunderstood and misused. In the first place the notion should be worded as 'double semilingualism', because it refers to *two* languages: the semilingual child or adult knows two languages only partially, and if the skills could be added up, which is a rather impossible task, the total amount of linguistic knowledge would probably exceed that of a child speaking only one language. A second, more profound misunderstanding concerns the origins of semilingualism. Some authors have stated that the notion of semilingualism is part of a deficit theory, blaming the minority child for its low academic achievements (see, for instance, Edelsky *et al.*, 1983). As early as 1978, Skutnabb-Kangas made the case for the social origins of semilingualism. She argued that semilingualism should not be viewed as a characteristic of the minority children themselves, but as a reflection of the frustrating situation in which their home language is neglected in school while they are forced to learn the second language. Forms of subtractive bilingualism will be developed, resulting in relatively low levels of proficiency in both languages.

Another problem concerns the normativity of the concept. Why should the language skills of bilinguals be compared with those of monolinguals? Probably bilinguals use their languages in different domains or for different purposes, therefore comparisons with monolinguals do not seem justified. From a sociolinguistic perspective the two languages of the bilingual can be viewed as one linguistic repertoire which is probably adequate for all kinds of situations. The debates on this issue are of course similar to the discussions on the measurement of bilingualism.

Empirical support for the concept of semilingualism is largely derived from the assessment of language skills by means of language tests. From such tests it is concluded that semilingual children know less of each of their languages than monolingual children. Furthermore, analyses of spoken language have pointed out that bilingual children are not able to use all the morphological devices their monolingual age-mates use. They have a tendency to simplify both languages morphologically, for instance they only use the general rules and do not know the exceptions. Their vocabulary is also limited compared to children speaking only one language (cf. Stölting 1980 on the language of Serbo-Croatian children in West Germany). These data are in agreement with the perceptions of the people concerned. For instance, the parents of minority children often complain about the command of the home language, while many teachers argue that the skills in the majority language are insufficient.

Ideas on semilingualism are often phrased in terms of less or more proficient, as we have made clear above. However, because of this the nature of bilingual competence is neglected. The bilingual's verbal repertoire can also be viewed as *different* and not *deficient* when the monolingual quantitative norm is not taken into account. For instance, bilinguals have unique code-switching abilities which give them the opportunity to convey messages in a very subtle or sophisticated way (cf. chapter 10). Such abilities are not highly valued in schools, and it is evident that the concept of semilingualism, with its implications of socially motivated deficiency, was developed in relation to the educational problems of bilingual children from minority groups.

9.2 Cognitive effects

In a review on the literature on cognitive effects of bilingualism, Natalie Darcy concluded in 1953 that 'bilinguists suffer from a language handicap when measured by verbal tests of intelligence' (Darcy, 1953:50). Thirty years later, Rafael Diaz, again reviewing the literature, found 'a positive influence of bilingualism on children's cognitive and linguistic abilities' (Diaz, 1983:48). Darcy's conclusion was based on a number of studies in which large groups of monolingual and bilingual students were compared; for instance, Welsh–English bilinguals and English monolinguals by Saer (1923) and Jones and Stewart (1951). In the last study the bilingual subjects scored lower not only on verbal tests of intelligence, but also on non-verbal tests, a result contrary to the general trend in the research literature, namely that the detrimental effects on intelligence only surface in verbal tests.

Although a few of the 'older' studies pointed to positive intellectual consequences of bilingualism, an extensive study by Peal and Lambert (1962) heralded a major shift in the academic consensus about the relation between bilingualism and intelligence. According to Peal and Lambert, the negative findings of many of the 'older' studies can be explained from their methodological weaknesses. Important variables which could explain the test results were often not or insufficiently controlled for: socio-economic status, sex, degree of bilingualism, age, and the actual tests used. It will be evident, for example, that children who were tested via their second language, while not speaking that language well, performed poorly. Bilingual children from lower socio-economic classes scored lower on the tests than monolingual children from higher socio-economic classes, not necessarily because of their bilingualism.

In their own study, Peal and Lambert controlled for these variables. They compared the test performances of French–English bilingual and French monolingual 10-year-old school children in Montreal. Only 'true bilinguals' were included in the bilingual sample; i.e. the bilinguals were proficient in both their first and second language. Contrary to the results of the majority of the earlier studies, the bilingual subjects of Peal and Lambert performed significantly better than their monolingual peers on both nonverbal *and* verbal tests of intelligence. Unfortunately, this finding also had to be considered 'tentative', because of Peal and Lambert's selection procedure for bilingual subjects. Although the selection of 'true bilinguals' constituted a major methodological improvement, the way it was conducted might have introduced a bias in favour of the bilingual sample (cf. Macnamara, 1966). Children were only admitted to the bilingual sample if they scored above a certain level on the English Peabody Vocabulary Test. This test, however, is also frequently used to assess (verbal) intelligence in monolinguals. Furthermore, the French-Canadian children who had attained a high degree of bilingualism might have been more intelligent from the start. What Peal and Lambert saw as the consequence of bilingualism – higher intelligence – may have been the cause of it.

Since 1962, many studies have been conducted which corroborate Peal and Lambert's findings. For example, Hakuta and Diaz (1985) tried to determine the relation between degree of bilingualism and cognitive ability, and to assess the direction of causality between the linguistic and cognitive variables by following a group of Spanish–English speaking children through time. Their results indicated a significant positive relationship between degree of bilingualism and non-verbal cognitive skills as measured by the Raven's Progressive Matrices Test. (In this test the directions of the experimenter and the answers of the testee are non-verbal. The child has to complete partial geometrical patterns.) The longitudinal data support the view that the direction of causality is from bilingualism to cognition and not the other way around.

In various other studies more specific aspects of cognitive functioning of bilinguals were analysed. Ianco-Worrell (1972) investigated the *metalinguistic ability* of bilinguals on the basis of some observations by Leopold (1939–49) who analysed the simultaneous acquisition of English and German by his daughter Hildegard (see also section 8.3). Leopold noticed that Hildegard 'never clung to words, as monolingual children are often reported to do. She did not insist on the exact wording of fairy tales. She often reproduced even memorized materials with substitution of other words' (p. 187; quotation from the 1970 edition). Leopold attributes this attitude of detachment from words, or the lack of nominalism as it is sometimes called, to bilingualism. For Hildegard the link between the phonetic form and its meaning seemed to be looser than for monolingual age-mates.

Ianco-Worrell tried to find out whether this observation could be generalized to other bilingual children, in her case, the study of Afrikaans and English-speaking children, who had acquired both languages simultaneously, in South Africa. In one experiment she presented bilingual subjects and comparable groups of monolingual English and Afrikaans subjects orally with eight sets of monosyllabic words. Each set consisted of three words. One word was the key word, the second word was related to it phonetically, and the third word semantically. For instance, one set was made up of *cap*, *can* and *hat*. The subjects were asked which is more like *cap*: *can* or *hat*? Ianco-Worrell found that the bilingual children chose significantly more often along the semantic dimension. More than half of the young bilingual children (4–6 years old) consistently selected the semantically related word, while in the young groups of monolinguals only one English-speaking child (out of 25 subjects) did so. In the two monolingual samples and in the bilingual sample, the older children (7–9 years old) showed more semantic preference than the younger children (4–6 years old). Therefore, it could be concluded that the bilingual children were in a more advanced stage of metalinguistic development than their monolingual peers.

In a second experiment Ianco-Worrell tried to test whether there are any differences between bilingual and monolingual children with regard to their awareness of the arbitrary or conventional relation between an object and the name for that object. She borrowed a technique used by Vygotsky (1962) who asked his subjects about the relation between names and objects. Ianco-Worrell's test had three parts. In part 1 she asked the children for an explanation of six names or labels, for instance 'why is a chair called "chair"?' The two groups of children did not differ in the types of explanations offered. In the second part of the experiment, children were asked if names could be interchanged: 'Could you call a chair "table" and a table "chair"?' The bilingual subjects, more often than the monolinguals, replied that in principle this reversal was possible. Part 3 was a little bit more complicated. The experimenter proposed playing a game to the child and changing names for objects: 'Let us call a book "water".' Subsequently, she asked questions about the object, for instance: 'Can you drink this water?' and 'Can you read this water?' The bilinguals and the monolinguals did not perform differently in this part of the experiment.

In a study of Hebrew–English children Ben-Zeev (1977) replicated this last part of the experiment in a slightly different version. She also played a game with her subjects in which words were changed, for example, a toy aeroplane was named *turtle*. Then she asked questions like 'Can the turtle fly?'. In five of the seven test-items the task was made more difficult, because an obligatory selection rule of the language was violated. Ben-Zeev (1977:1012) gives the following example. 'For this game the way we say "I" is to say *macaroni*. So how do we say "I am warm?"' ' (Correct answer: Macaroni am warm). The bilinguals turned out to be significantly superior in this task, and Ben-Zeev concludes that bilinguals free themselves from the magical idea that there is a fixed relationship between a word and its referent at an earlier age than monolinguals. The bilinguals' success on the second, difficult part of the task suggests that bilinguals are better able to manipulate the syntactic rules of a language, probably because of their experience with two language systems.

Next to metalinguistic awareness, *cognitive flexibility* is another aspect of cognitive functioning frequently appearing in research on the effects of bilingualism. To evaluate results in this field, first a distinction must be made between divergent and convergent thinking. In a task assessing the level of convergent thinking, a subject must provide the one and only solution or answer on the basis of a number of pieces of information. In divergent thinking tasks subjects are required to generate a number of solutions without being channelled into the direction of one correct response. Divergent thinking is often equated with creative thinking. Many IQ tests require convergent thinking. Cummins and Gulutsan (1974) tested children's divergent thinking skills by presenting them with isolated words (for instance 'rake'), and asking them to give as many uses for the objects named as possible. Bilingual children outperformed their monolingual peers in this test. In her study mentioned above Ben-Zeev also included some tasks requiring cognitive flexibility or divergent thinking, and for those tasks that were directly related to language proficiency her bilingual subjects were cognitively more advanced.

Kessler and Quinn (1980) tried to investigate the cognitive consequences of bilingualism in a study on problem-solving abilities in science. English–Spanish bilingual and monolingual pupils (sixth class) followed an experimental educational programme consisting of 12 science inquiry film sessions and six discussion sessions. In each (short) film session a single physical science problem was presented, and the pupils (12-year-olds) were asked to produce as many hypotheses as possible explaining what they had seen in the film. In the discussion sessions the Hypothesis Quality Scale was used to show them how they could evaluate their hypotheses and improve them. After this instruction, three additional science problems were presented in films to elicit hypotheses that were scored for quality on the basis of the Hypothesis Quality Scale. Kessler and Quinn found that the bilinguals outperformed the monolinguals in the quality of the hypotheses generated.

The bilinguals' superiority in tasks requiring cognitive flexibility is probably due to the fact that they are confronted with two systems of linguistic rules. They will probably develop a more analytical view of language, and must therefore have a greater awareness of language than monolinguals. Hakuta and Diaz (1985) suggest that this results in a greater flexibility in the manipulation of non-verbal as well as verbal symbols. According to Peal and Lambert (1962) bilingual children may show cognitive advantages because they are better able to dissociate concepts from the words with which they are verbalized. This can make the mind free, i.e., it will foster 'intellectual emancipation' (Segalowitz, 1977:131) which will be closely related to cognitive flexibility. In this line of reasoning the results with regard to metalinguistic awareness and cognitive flexibility are accounted for by the same explanation.

Considering the evidence presented above, is it reasonable or justified to conclude that bilingualism will not impede cognitive development and that it will even affect certain aspects of cognitive functioning positively? Probably such a conclusion is too simplistic. As early as 1976 Cummins (1976) suggested that the results of the 'older, negative studies' can not be neglected completely, despite their methodological shortcomings. It was noted that the children participating in these studies could be characterized as subtractive bilinguals. In their community the mother tongue did not have social prestige and it was in danger of being replaced by a prestigious majority language. Contrary to this situation, the children involved in the more recent, positive studies were developing into additive bilinguals. Even the Spanish–English bilingual pupils in Kessler and Quinn's study whose Spanish language development was supported in a bilingual programme, and who were literate in both Spanish and English, could be characterized as additive bilinguals. In view of the differential effects of additive vs subtractive bilingualism, one can state that it is not bilingualism in itself which causes cognitive advantages or disadvantages, but certain social factors that influence the levels of proficiency the bilingual attains in both languages (cf. Lambert, 1977). These social factors include the social-economic position of the bilingual (and his or her community or group), the prestige of the two languages, and the educational situation. Bilingual proficiency is therefore not a causal variable, but only an intervening variable, mediating the effects of the causal variables which are social in nature, and which determine the bilingual learning situation.

Following Toukomaa and Skutnabb-Kangas (1977), Cummins (1979) has formulated the *threshold hypothesis* which claims that bilingual children must achieve threshold levels of bilingual proficiency to avoid detrimental effects on cognition *and* potentially to allow positive effects. In this hypothesis it is stated that bilinguals must attain these thresholds in both of their languages. Cummins proposes two threshold levels (see also Figure 9.2). Children below the lower threshold will show cognitive difficulties. These children are double semilinguals, which will restrict their cognitive learning experiences. Children above the higher threshold level can benefit cognitively from the fact that they are relatively proficient in the two languages. The thresholds can not be defined in absolute terms, since they vary according to the child's stage of cognitive development.

Together, the threshold hypothesis and the developmental interdependence hypothesis (see section 9.1 of this chapter) can explain the generally positive results of bilingual education programmes, as described in chapter 6. The developmental interdependence hypothesis accounts for the successful second-language acquisition by children instructed in their first language for a considerable part of the curriculum. The resulting relatively high levels of proficiency in the two languages foster certain aspects of cognitive development, as the threshold hypothesis predicts. Therefore,

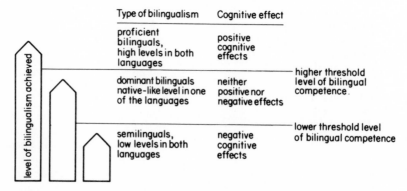

Figure 9.2 Schematic representation of the threshold hypothesis (adapted from Toukomaa and Skutnabb-Kangas, 1977)

the academic achievements of students from bilingual programmes will be higher than those of minority language students from monolingual schools.

9.3 Effects on personality development

It is said that speaking two languages is a negative factor in personality or identity development. Bilinguals are often expected to experience a conflict of values, identities and world views because these are probably strongly related to the two different languages. Therefore they will become cultural hybrids. Bilingualism, in this view, can cause emotional lability, and even alienation or anomie (cf. Diebold, 1968). These ideas are often based on anecdotal evidence provided by individual bilinguals. To illustrate this negative view of bilingualism, Weinreich (1953:119) cited the words of the Luxembourger Ries: 'The temperament of the Luxembourger is rather phlegmatic . . . We have none of the German sentimentalism (*Gemut*), and even less of French vivacity. . . . Our bilingual eclecticism prevents us from consolidating our conception of the world and from becoming strong personalities. . .'. This position was especially defended in the 1930s in Germany where Nazi ideology required the 'purity' of the nation, which implied purity of language and a strong relation between a people and a language. For instance, Müller (1934) writes that the Polish-German population of Upper Silesia suffered from some kind of mental inferiority as a result of their bilingualism.

Methodologically sounder studies, however, have shown that bilingualism may have detrimental effects on personality development, but only when social conditions are unfavourable. Again, bilingualism is not a causal, but only an intervening variable, mediating the influence of social factors. Diebold (1968) reviewed the literature on bilingual psychopathology, concluding that there is 'basically a crisis in social and personal identity engendered by antagonistic accumulative pressures on a bicultural community by a sociologically dominant monolingual society within which the bicultural community is stigmatized as socially inferior' (p. 239). This explanation seems apt for many groups of bilinguals with sociopsychological problems, such as migrant workers and their families in Western Europe. The adults frequently suffer from psychosomatic illnesses, but this is evidently not caused by their bilingualism, but by the social and cultural conflicts they experience as members of an often discriminated-against ethnic minority, whose language and cultural values are not appreciated. The same goes for children with social or emotional problems in school, often manifested in apathy, aggressive behaviour or isolation. When the minority's language and culture are included in the curriculum, as in bilingual/bicultural programmes, pupils often show fewer social or emotional problems. In a study of the social and emotional development of Turkish and Moroccan children in a transitional bilingual programme in the Netherlands, it was found that these children had fewer problems than a comparable group of children in monolingual Dutch schools (Appel, Everts and Teunissen, 1986). Dolson (1985) studied the effects of Spanish home language use on the scholastic performance of Hispanic students, comparing children whose families had maintained Spanish as the main home language ('additive bilingual environment' in Dolson's terms) and children from homes where a shift towards English had taken place ('subtractive bilingual environment'). On three out of four measures of psycho-social adjustment there were no differences between the two groups, while on one measure (having to repeat a certain year) the pupils in the subtractive, i.e. more monolingual, group performed less well than the additive bilingual pupils. In any case, additive bilingualism did not seem to have negative effects on the children's adjustment to school.

A shift from bilingualism to monolingualism does not prevent problems. Because of the assimilative forces of the majority community many members from ethnic minority groups adopt the cultural values of that community, try to learn and speak its language, while they are in the process of losing their mother tongue. At the same time, they are not really 'admitted' to the majority community, i.e. to the better jobs, houses and educational opportunities. They will often encounter discriminating and racist attitudes of the majority population who nevertheless require them to assimilate. It is not surprising that this may lead to psychological or emotional problems. In stable bilingual communities this type of problem does not have to occur because a kind of bilingual or bicultural identity has been established. All over the world, individuals use two or more languages in their daily verbal interactions, but this does not cause any psychological strain. Swedish–Finnish bilinguals in Finland do not experience special emotional problems because of having to cope with two languages. The same goes for other additive bilingual groups, such as English-speaking Canadians who have acquired French as a second language. Both their languages and their culture carry social prestige.

In subtractive bilingual groups different reactions to the strain of biculturalism are found. Child (1943) did a now classic study of the ethnic attitudes of second-generation Italians in the USA. His results showed three types of reactions: (a) an identification with American social and cultural values; (b) rejection of everything American and strong orientation towards the Italian heritage; and (c) a refusal to think in ethnic terms. Tosi (1984) investigated bilingualism and biculturalism of Italian immigrants in Great Britain. He points to the conflict between the first generation, which shows a highly conservative attitude, and the second generation, which feels the pressure of the wider bilingual, bicultural context. He also found Child's first two reactions, which he calls the 'apathic reaction' and the 'in-group reaction'. The term 'apathic' is chosen because this reaction 'develops when the individual feels unable to cope with the conflicting values of two opposing environments, and naturally slides towards the acceptance of one – the one from which the stronger pressure comes' (Tosi, 1984:116). In cases of in-group reaction the individual primarily identifies himself or herself with the Italian community. The third type of reaction Tosi distinguished, which is different from that of Child, is the 'rebel reaction'. Only a few young people displayed this reaction, refusing to choose between the old and the new culture, and trying to become really bilingual/bicultural.

Although the issue does not relate to personality development *per se*, but perhaps more to psychological functioning in general, here we also want to deal with the implications of the hypothesis that languages and ways of thinking are closely related. This hypothesis was tested by Susan Ervin-Tripp in a series of experiments with (a) first- and (b) second-generation Japanese women in the USA. They were compared with English and Japanese monolingual women. In two experiments she found support for a language–culture relation. In the Japanese part of a word-association task, both groups of Japanese–English bilingual women gave more associations typical of women in Japan, while the group of first-generation bilinguals also produced more typically American associations in the English part. As Ervin-Tripp (1967:84) concluded, '(the) over-all effect was that content shifted with language for both groups', for instance *tea* as an English stimulus word elicited words like *lemon* and *cookies* while in the Japanese part names of utensils of the tea ceremony were frequently given as associations. Ervin-Tripp also asked her subjects to complete a story. The bilinguals showed a preference for Japanese solutions to the social problems in the stories presented in Japanese. Analysing her data further, Ervin-Tripp found however that the women who gave typically American responses in both languages seemed to identify more with American cultural values, while the subjects who gave typically Japanese responses irrespective of the language being used were more oriented towards (traditional) Japanese culture.

The relation between language and culture does not seem to be as strong and fixed as is often assumed. It is not true that speaking a certain language inevitably leads to holding certain cultural values, as the famous Sapir–Whorf hypothesis would claim. According to this hypothesis the language an individual speaks determines his world view. Sapir and Whorf considered language to be the guide and the programme for the mental activities of the individual, and the interpretation of the surrounding world to be channelled via linguistic categories. If the world view of the members of a linguistic community constitutes their non-material culture, then this implies a strong relation between language and culture. However, the Sapir–Whorf hypothesis is much disputed, and it has never been properly and extensively supported empirically. In the field of bilingualism the question is even more vexed. What is the world view of a bilingual? By which of the two languages is it determined? Or has a bilingual two world views between which he has to switch depending on the language being used? Many questions can be generated, but it is difficult or even impossible to provide the answers (cf. Macnamara, 1970). It remains to be explained why many bilinguals and monolinguals feel or experience a strong relation between language and culture. This relation, which we discussed in chapter 2, is probably brought about by the fact that each language is associated with a community and its cultural values and social life. For instance, a Greek–English bilingual in Great Britain will associate Greek with the Greek community, Greek friends, ouzo, souvlaki, stuffed tomatoes, the Greek orthodox church, Greek newspapers, etc., while English is connected with aspects of public life where that language is commonly used. This does not mean that there are specific Greek and specific English concepts or that the bilingual views or interprets the world according to the language he/she speaks. The language–culture relation is rooted in the bilingual's social life, and it is not prominently reflected in cognition. Therefore, the social and emotional problems of certain bilinguals are not caused by their bilingualism as a cognitive phenomenon, but by the social context.

Further reading

Specialized books (or even readers with collections of articles) on the effects of bilingualism are not available, but much information can be found in the following books. P.A. Hornby (ed.), *Bilingualism; Psychological, social and educational implications* (1977), T. Skutnabb-Kangas, *Bilingualism or not* (1983), and J. Cummins, *Bilingualism and special education*, 1984. Cummins's book also contains information on the developmental interdependence and the threshold hypothesis discussed in this chapter.

L.G. Kelly (ed.), *Description and measurement of bilingualism* (1969) is a collection of many articles on language assessment in bilinguals. Skutnabb-Kangas's book (mentioned above) also includes an extensive discussion of this issue.

III Language use in the bilingual community

10 Code switching and code mixing

In many situations speakers make use of the grammar and lexicon of just one language when producing utterances, but this is not absolutely necessary. Thus we find utterances of the following type:

(1) You can it ZONDAG DOEN   English–Dutch (Crama and van
    You can do it on Sunday.   Gelderen, 1984

(2) Les femmes et le vin NE PONIMAYU   French–Russian (Timm, 1978)
    Women and wine I don't know much about.

(3) Lo puso UNDER ARREST   Spanish–English (Lance, 1975)
    He arrested him.

(4) Salesman ŞE OVED KAŞE can make a lot of money   Hebrew–English
    A salesman who works hard can make a lot of money.   (Doron, 1983)

This type of utterance, known as code mixing, has been studied in considerable detail since about 1970, from a *sociolinguistic* point of view: why do people switch between languages; from a *psycholinguistic* point of view: what aspects of their language capacity enable them to switch; and from a *linguistic* point of view: how do we know that they are really switching and have not simply introduced an element from another language into their linguistic system? Many outsiders see code mixing as a sign of linguistic decay, the unsystematic result of not knowing at least one of the languages involved very well. The opposite turns out to be the case, as we will show in this chapter.

Switching is not an isolated phenomenon, but a central part of bilingual discourse, as a number of studies have shown. An example is the following narrative, drawn from Valdés Fallis (1976):

(5) OYE (listen), when I was a freshman I had a term paper to do . . .
    . . .
    And all of a sudden, I started acting real CURIOSA (strange), you know. I started going like this. Y LUEGO DECÍA (and then I said), look at the smoke coming out of my fingers, like that. And then ME DIJO (he said to me), stop acting silly. Y LUEGO DECÍA YO, MIRA (and then I said, look) can't you see. Y LUEGO ESTE (and then this), I started seeing like little stars all over the place. Y VOLTEABA YO ASINA Y LE DECÍA (and I turned around and said to him) look at the . . . the . . . NO SÉ ERA COMO BRILLOSITO ASI (I don't know, it was like shiny like this) like stars.
    . . .

On the basis of material such as this narrative it is possible to distinguish three types of switches textually:

(a) Tag-switches involve an exclamation, a tag, or a parenthetical in another language than the rest of the sentence. An example is 'OYE, when . . .' at the beginning of the text. The tags etc. serve as an emblem of the bilingual character of an otherwise monolingual sentence. That is why Poplack (1980) has named this type of switching *emblematic* switching.

(b) *Intra-sentential* switches occur in the middle of a sentence, as in 'I started acting real CURIOSA.' This type of intimate switching is often called *code mixing*.

(c) *Inter-sentential* switches occur between sentences, as their name indicates.

As the above fragment shows, it is not always easy to distinguish between the different types: the use of 'Y LUEGO' in the text has some characteristics of tag-switching, but it involves the rest of the sentence in a more intimate way than a real tag. Sociological studies of code switching tend to generalize across the three kinds of switches, and in the following section, which deals with the sociolinguistic motivation for code switching, we will refer to code switching in general. In the next section, 10.2, which deals with grammatical constraints on code mixing, we return to the distinction between different kinds of switches.

10.1 Why do people switch between languages?

Why do people switch between languages in the course of a single conversation? This question has been discussed extensively in the sociolinguistic literature. We will organize our survey using the functional framework of Jakobson (1960) and Halliday *et al.* (1964) developed in chapter 3: quite obviously the same model that could potentially account for the choice of a given language could be used to explain the switching between languages. In presenting the reasons explored, we will have occasion to refer to a number of sources, including work by Gumperz and associates (Gumperz, 1976; Gumperz and Hernández-Chavez, 1975), Poplack (1980), and Scotton (1979).

Using the functional model suggested, switching can be said to have the following functions:

1 Switching can serve the **referential** function because it often involves lack of knowledge of one language or lack of facility in that language on a certain subject. Certain subjects may be more appropriately discussed in one language, and the introduction of such a subject can lead to a switch. In addition, a specific word from one of the languages involved may be semantically more appropriate for a given concept. Hence all topic-related switching may be thought of as serving the referential function of language. This type of switching is the one that bilingual speakers are most conscious of. When asked why they switch they tend to say that it is because they do not know the word for it in the other language, or because the language chosen is more fit for talking about a given subject.

One example of this is radio or television news broadcasts for immigrant groups. Usually the immigrant language is used, but at many points words from the majority language are introduced into the broadcast to refer to concepts specific to the society of the country of migration. The same pattern is found in discourse about technical subjects in many languages of the Third World. Scotton (1979) gives an example from a university student in Kenya, who switches between Kikuyu and English:

(6) Atiriri ANGLE niati HAS ina DEGREE EIGHTY; nayo THIS ONE ina mirongo itatu. Kuguori, IF THE TOTAL SUM OF A TRIANGLE ni ONE-EIGHTY ri IT MEANS THE REMAINING ANGLE ina ndigirii mirong mugwanya.

Even for people who do not know Kikuyu it is easy to guess what the student is talking about.

2 Switching often serves a **directive** function in that it involves the hearer directly. This being directed at the hearer can take many forms. One is to exclude certain persons present from a portion of the conversation. The opposite is to include a person more by using her or his language. A person may have joined the participants in an interaction. All participant-related switching can be thought of as serving the directive function of language use. Recall Giles's accommodation theory for language choice discussed in chapter 3; it is directly formulated along the lines of the directive function. Again, examples easily come to mind. Many parents try to speak a foreign language when they do not want their children to understand what is being said. If they do this too often, they find out that the children have learned the second language as well, or make up a language of their own to exclude their parents.

3 Poplack (1980) in particular has stressed the **expressive** function of code switching. Speakers emphasize a mixed identity through the use of two languages in the same discourse. An example is Spanish–English code switching in the Puerto Rican community. For fluent bilingual Puerto Ricans in New York, conversation full of code switching is a mode of speech by itself, and individual switches no longer have a discourse function. This function may not be present in all code switching communities, however – a point to which we return below.

4 Often switching serves to indicate a change in tone of the conversation, and hence a **phatic** function. This type has been called metaphorical switching by Gumperz and Hernández-Chavez (1975). Think of the stand-up comedian who tells the whole joke in a standard variety, but brings the punch line in a vernacular type of speech, e.g. an urban dialect. This type of switch has been documented extensively in a paper on switching between London Jamaican and London English by Sebba and Wootton (1984). They give a number of examples in which a stretch of basically Jamaican discourse is interrupted by an English 'meta-comment'. One of them is the following:

(7) m:an . . . Leonie 'ave party . . . WHEN . . . DON' REMEMBER WHEN IT WAS bot shi did tel aal o dem no fi (t) se notin . . . kaaz shi no waan tu moch Catford gyal di de . . . an Jackie av wan tu . . . neva se notin

Here the fact that the speaker has forgotten the date of the party is mentioned as a side-comment, but in the other language.

When Jamaican fragments are inserted into an English context, the main function seems to be that of highlighting the information conveyed, as in conversation (8):

(8) A: I mean it does take time ge??in' to n-..find the right person
    B: Let me tell you now, wiv every guy I've been out wiv, it's been a? -. . . . UOL IIP

> A MWONTS before I move wiv the nex' one
> A: next one, yeah!

The crucial point of this conversation is the amount of time it takes to get over a love affair; that it takes a whole heap of months, as we all know, is the essence here.

5 The **metalinguistic** function of code switching comes into play when it is used to comment directly or indirectly on the languages involved. One example of this function is when speakers switch between different codes to impress the other participants with a show of linguistic skills (Scotton, 1979). Many examples of this can be found in the public domain: performers, circus directors, market salespeople.

6 Bilingual language usage involving switched puns, jokes, etc. can be said to serve the **poetic** function of language. To pay homage to the twentieth-century poet who has perhaps been the most accomplished code switcher, here is a quote from Ezra Pound's Canto XIII:

(9)   Yu-chan to pay sycamores
              of this wood are lutes made
      Ringing stones from Seychoui river
      and grass that is called Tsing-mo' or μῶλυ
      Chun to the spirit Chang Ti, of heaven
      moving the sun and stars
                  que vos vers expriment vos intentions
                  et que la musique conforme

Pound works with complex internal rhymes across languages: Chinese gods, rivers, emperors and mountains are matched with elements from Homeric Greek and French, Italian, or Provençal verse. The result is at once an erudite evocation of all human civilizations and a panoply of sounds.

One thing to keep in mind is that it is by no means certain that code switching has the same functions within each community. While it can be described in linguistics terms fairly straightforwardly as the use of several languages in the same discourse, there may not be one sociolinguistic definition. Puerto Ricans in New York may code switch for very different reasons than the Flemish in Brussels. A sociolinguistic typology of code switching communities, focusing not only on who switches but also on why people switch, is one of the research priorities for the immediate future.

What now are the typical features of a fluent switcher? Poplack (1980) shows that only fully bilingual Puerto Ricans are capable of using both Spanish and English in one sentence. Only those speakers who have learned both languages at an early age will reach the level of proficiency necessary to be able to use two languages in one single sentence. This does not hold for all type of switching: often people will include a single word from another language because of having forgotten or not yet learnt that word in the base language of the sentence. In any case, the speakers who switch most are also those who are capable of switching in the middle of a sentence. McClure (1977) argues that children start switching only when they are eight years old, which suggests that considerable linguistic proficiency is called for. For the rest, code switching does not appear to be limited to certain age levels, even if in many immigrant communities it is particularly teenagers who mix (Pedrasa *et al.*, 1980).

10.2 Where in the sentence is code mixing possible?

One of the big problems that confronted the sociological literature on switching is that all the reasons given for switching may explain why switching occurs at all, but not why a particular switch-point is chosen. Gumperz and Hernández-Chavez, in a very important article, recognize this problem: 'It would be futile to predict the occurrence of either Spanish or English in the above utterances (instances of Spanish–English code switching such as the narrative given above) by attempting to isolate the social variables which correlate with the linguistic form. Topic, speaker, setting are common in each case. Yet the code changes sometimes in the middle of a sentence' (1975:155). This realization has caused a shift in the research on code switching, and particularly on intra-sentential code switching, called code mixing. Recognizing the general sociolinguistically determined nature of code mixing, a considerable part of recent research has focused on the syntactic properties of code mixing: where in the sentence do we find it, and when is it impossible? In other words, what are the constraints on code mixing? This research has undergone three stages: (1) an early stage in which grammatical constraints specific to particular constructions were focused on; (2) a stage which has produced the classical studies in which universal constraints on code mixing were explored, around 1980; (3) the present stage, which may be characterized by the search for new perspectives: what alternative mixing strategies are there and are constraints perhaps relative to a particular strategy?

Before we turn to these three strategies we should mention an important methodological problem in the empirical study of code mixing within sentences. How do we distinguish a case of mixing from the simple situation of word borrowing? Many foreign words are simply integrated into the language, such as French *maitre d'* (hotel) pronounced phonetically as [me:tR di:], used for head waiter in American English. Therefore we would not call a sentence such as:

(10) The maitre d' put us in a little dark corner of the restaurant

an example of code mixing. At the same time it is clear that in the example at the beginning of this chapter expressions such as *y luego*, 'and then', have not become a part of American English. But where do we draw the line? Using the distinction introduced by Ferdinand de Saussure, we could say that in abstract terms borrowing involves the integration of two languages at the level of *langue*, and code mixing integration at the level of *parole* (for borrowing, see chapter 14).

A second, in part theoretical, in part methodological, preliminary issue is whether we accept the notion of base or host language for a particular analysis of code mixing. There are several ways to think of the base language: *Psycholinguistically* it makes most sense to think of the base language as the dominant language of the bilingual speaker making the switch, since that language is the most important one in determining his verbal behaviour. *Sociolinguistically*, however, the notion of base language may be defined as the language in terms of which the discourse situation is defined, the unmarked linguistic code in a particular setting. *Grammatically*, the base language may be the one imposing a particular constraint for a particular case of switching if the notion makes any sense at all. We will see below that some researchers adopt the notion of base language, while others do not. In any case, the fact that there are three definitions means that in some situations, there may be several base languages possible, depending on the criterion used.

A third methodological problem which makes it difficult to evaluate the evidence for any particular proposed constraint, is whether we are looking for absolute constraints, admitting no counter-examples, as in generative grammar, or for quantitative constraints, suggesting statistical trends, as in the theory of variation developed by Labov (1972) and Sankoff (1978). The state of the research does not permit a choice at this moment, but it is clear that either choice has weighty methodological consequences.

(A) Particular grammatical constraints
Most of the early code mixing studies drew on Spanish–English data recorded from conversations of Mexican Americans and Puerto Ricans. Gumperz and Hernández-Chavez (1975) noted that switching was easily possible in some contexts, but not so much in others. Contexts allowing a switch include:

(11)   Between a head noun and a relative clause:
    . . . those friends are friends from Mexico QUE TIENEN CHAMAQUITOS (that have little children)
(12)   Between a subject and a predicate in a copular construction:
    An' my uncle Sam ES EL MÁS AGABACHADO (is the most Americanized)

Switches as in (13) are not allowed, however:

(13)   *. . . que HAVE chamaquitos

In a more systematic treatment Timm (1975) proposed the following restrictions:

(14)   Subject and object pronouns must be in the same language as the main verb:
    * YO (I) went
    * mira (look at) HIM
(15)   An auxiliary and a main verb, or a main verb and an infinitive must be in the same language:
    * they want A VENIR (to come)
    * ha (he has) SEEN

In these studies two methodologies are combined: the analysis of recorded conversations and grammaticality judgements. The stars in the above examples reflect judgements of bilinguals about possible switches, but that these judgements do not always correspond to actual switching behaviour is clear when we compare two observations by Lipski (1978) with findings of Pfaff (1979):

(16)   It is difficult to switch inside a prepositional phrase (PP):
    ?? in LA CASA (the house)
(17)   It is impossible to switch between the article and the noun:
    ?? I see the CASA (house)

Both observations contrast, however, with a large number of cases of precisely these switches found in the corpus analysed by Pfaff (1979). PP internal switching (of English nouns into Spanish PPs) occurs far more often than switching at PP boundaries. We also find more cases of a switch between the article and the noun than switches between article + noun combinations and the rest of the sentence. Clearly it is difficult if not impossible to rely on judgement data.

The studies of code switching carried out in the 1970s provide us with a large body of analysed data, with a number of inductive generalizations, and with insights into what type of constraints on code switching we may expect. Lacking is an overall theoretical perspective, and this is what the studies of the early 80s have tried to contribute.

(B) Universal constraints

The universal constraints proposed in the literature cluster around two fundamental grammatical and psycholinguistic concepts: linearity and dependency. We will discuss them in turn. *Linearity* constraints generally state that switching from one language to another in the middle of a sentence is only possible if the linear order of sentences in both languages is preserved. Although Lipski (1978) and Pfaff (1979) had already made a similar observation, we find the first explicit statement of this principle in Poplack (1980): 'Code-switches will tend to occur at points in discourse where juxtaposition of L1 and L2 elements does not violate a syntactic rule of either language, i.e. at points around which the surface structures of the two languages map onto each other.'

To see what Poplack meant, consider an example such as the following involving possible switches between Spanish and English:

(18) Eng I   told him   that   so   that   he   would bring it   fast

Sp (Yo)le dije   eso   pa' que   (el) la   trajera rápido

In (18) the vertical lines indicate places where the word order in both languages is equivalent, and hence, where a switch is possible. Where there are crossed lines, switching is impossible. Note in passing that the idea of base language plays no role in Poplack's theory.

Woolford (1983) gives a reformulation of Poplack's equivalence constraint in generative terms: when the phrase structure rules (that specify word order) of both languages are identical, switching is possible; otherwise, it is not. An example would be the relation between a verb and a full noun phrase in English and Spanish. In both languages we have a phrase structure rule as in (19):

(19) VP → V NP

This implies that in (20) it is possible to switch:

(20) Eng sees the house

Sp ve   la   casa

Joshi (1981) and Doron (1983) come up with the claim, on the basis of considerations from the mathematical theory of syntactic parsing, that the first word of a sentence or a constituent determines the host or base language, and properties of the host language determine whether switching is possible or not. For a case such as (20) this leads to the same predictions as the theory of Poplack and Woolford, but for adjective–noun order different predictions follow. For a large class of Spanish adjective–noun combinations, we have a phrase structure rule as in (21a), and for all English cases a rule as in (21b):

(21)   a. Sp   NP → Det N Adj
      b. Eng   NP → Det Adj N

Poplack's Equivalence Constraint predicts no Spanish/English adjective–noun switches, while the model of Joshi and Doron predict that the following are possible:

(22)   a. the BLANCA house
      b. la casa WHITE

In (22a) the English determiner imposes English syntax on the noun phrase, and in (22b) the Spanish determiner Spanish syntax. Predicted to be impossible, on the other hand, are the forms in (23), the mirror of (22):

(23)   a. * the house BLANCA
      b. * la WHITE casa

Sobin (1984), finally, comes up with the following constraint: when there are semantically relevant word-order contrasts within a given language, it is impossible to switch at that point. Again, the example of adjective–noun combination is pertinent, since in Spanish the pre-noun position of the adjective is semantically restricting, and the post-noun position modifying. This implies that (22b) and (23b), where the adjective is English, would be all right, and (22a) and (23a) out. Clearly the predictions of all these theories differ wildly; we will not go into the question here of which of these theories is right. Most probably none of them is in its present form, and the data, in part recorded, and in part panel judgement, are contradictory. What the theories share, however, is that the linear order of the elements determines what is an allowable switch or not.

A rather different approach is taken within models which stress dependency rather than linearity. The basic idea in this approach is that there cannot be a switch between two elements if they are lexically dependent on each other. A first implicit statement of this restriction comes from Schaffer (1978), but the most explicit formulation is given in work by DiSciullo, Muysken and Singh (1986). These authors develop a restriction in terms of *government*, a traditional grammatical notion which has received a formulation within the theory of Government and Binding of Chomsky. The restriction is that whenever constituent X governs Y, both constituents must be drawn from the same language. Typical cases of government would be case assignment, as in the Latin example (24), or subcategorization, as in (25):

(24)   ad urbem
      'to the city'
(25)   to wait for somebody

In (24) the Latin preposition *ad* takes an accusative complement (*-m*), and in (25) the verb *wait* subcategorizes for the preposition *for*.

    The goverment restriction on code mixing predicts that ungoverned elements, such as tags, exclamations, interjections, and most adverbs can easily be switched. This prediction is overwhelmingly supported by the available evidence. However, governed elements also are sometimes switched. How can this be reconciled with the government restriction? DiSciullo, Muysken and Singh (1986) claim that this is accomplished through a neutralizing element, such as a determiner. The theory predicts the following contrast in acceptability:

(26) a. veo los HORSES
      b.* veo THE HORSES
         I see the horses.

The switch in (26a) would be acceptable, since the Spanish determiner *los* would make the whole noun phrase Spanish, as far as the government restriction is concerned, and (26b) would be an impossible switch because the whole noun phrase, even though governed by a Spanish verb, would be English. Again, it is much too early to see if the predictions made by the government theory are factually correct, but the large number of switches between the determiner and the noun found, among others, by Pfaff (1979) suggest that something like the contrast between (26a) and (26b) may be relevant.

Proposals similar to the one by DiSciullo, Muysken and Singh (1986) have been put forward by Klavans (1983) and by Bentahila and Davies (1983). Klavans argues that it is the language of the inflected main verb or the auxiliary of a clause that determines the restrictions on code mixing in that particular clause, since those elements constitute in some sense the syntactic head of the clause and govern the rest. Bentahila and Davies, using Moroccan–French code mixing as an example, argue that the subcategorization properties of a word determine what elements, including elements of another language, may appear within the phrase syntactically headed by that word. The switches in (27) and (28) are ungrammatical, in their view, because the French determiners *cette* and *un* in (27) subcategorize for a simple noun without the Arabic article *l*, and the Arabic determiners in (28) subcategorize for a noun with an article. In neither case is there a violation of the word order of either language:

(27) * CETTE l xubza   'this the loaf'
      * UN l fqi   'one the teacher'
(28) * had PAIN   'this loaf'
      * wahed PROFESSEUR   'a teacher'

Again, something like the notion of government is at play: for Bentahila and Davies's proposal to work, they have to assume that the determiner and the rest of the noun phrase are in a government relation.

Work from an entirely different perspective, which in some sense combines the linearity and the dependency approaches, has been carried out among immigrant groups in Australia by Michael Clyne (1967; 1972). Clyne distinguished two types of switching: *externally* conditioned switching (due to external factors) and *internally* conditioned switching or *triggering*. Certain words will be used in bilingual discourse from another language, and these words will often trigger code switching in anticipation of the trigger word or following it. In the following example the form in italics is the trigger, and the words in capitals the switched items:

(29) . . . haben wir ON A *farm* gewohnt.
         There we have lived on a farm.

In (29) the switch is in anticipation of the trigger, but often it follows the trigger, as in (30):

(30) Das is' ein/handelt von einem alten *secondhand-dealer* AND HIS SON
      That is a/has to do with an old secondhand-dealer and his son.

Stretching it a bit, you could say that switching in anticipation of a trigger recalls the dependency approach, and switching following a trigger the linearity approach. The relation is a remote one, however. Note furthermore that Clyne's theory contains plausible elements, but that it makes no predictions to speak of. It does raise the question of how grammatical constraints on code mixing, if these exist, may have psycholinguistic correlates in the sentence production system of the bilingual speaker. This issue is far too complex to go into in detail here, and we know little about the psycholinguistic aspects of bilingualism (cf. chapter 7). It may just be useful to stress that the linear and the dependency approaches to code switching correspond to two aspects of the sentence planning process: linear planning (how am I going to put the words in a string) and content word planning (which main content words, and therefore governors, is my sentence going to contain).

(C) Relativized constraints: the search for neutrality
The third stage in the study of code switching, which started around the mid 1980s, is characterized by the search for relativized constraints, resulting from the interaction of universal principles and aspects particular to each code mixing situation. The need for relativized constraints becomes clear when code mixing involving more languages is studied and when different types of mixing are taken into account. On the empirical level we find the extension of code mixing studies to mixing involving non-Indo-European languages. On the theoretical level there is a widening of the scope of the concept of neutrality. So far we have seen two general kinds of neutrality, claimed to allow for intra-sentential mixing: linear neutrality and grammatical independence. Linear neutrality involves a parallel word order of the two languages around the switch point, and grammatical independence the absence of strong syntagmatic links across a switch point.

Other types of neutrality exist and are systematically being explored, however. One type involves closely related languages, where neutrality may be achieved by a word being phonetically identical or very similar in both languages. This idea we find already in Clyne's work, who terms these identical words *homophonous diamorphs*, and it is systematically explored in Crama and Van Gelderen (1984). They give examples such as the following Dutch–English switch:

(31) weet je *what* SHE IS DOING (do you know . . .)

Here the form in italics could equally well be Dutch *wat* pronounced with a somewhat English accent or the English *what*. This type of ambiguity can be seen as an additional type of neutrality.

Another form of neutrality can be achieved by morphological means: the introduction of a morpheme that serves to nativize a word. A very frequent pattern here is the introduction of a 'helping verb', often a form such as 'make' or 'do'. This is very common in the Indic languages, and here are some examples of Surinam Hindustani–Sranan/Dutch/English mixed verbs (from Kishna, 1979):

(32) ONTI kare   'to hunt'   Sranan
      BEERI kare   'to bury'

      TRAIN kare   'to train'   English

      BEWIJS kare   'to prove'   Dutch
      DISCRIMINEER kare 'to discriminate'

You might say that the elements in capitals in (32) are really borrowings (from Sranan, English and Dutch, respectively), but note that the process is completely productive and does not entail phonological or semantic integration into the host language. In fact there is a lexical structure of the type *(V kare)* available to insert alien elements into, in which *kare* 'do' serves as the helping verb.

It is not clear whether this type of example counts as a counter-example to the Free Morpheme Constraint formulated by Poplack (1980): no switch may take place between two morphemes which are morphologically bound to each other. Poplack illustrates this constraint with examples such as:

(33) * eat–IENDO
        'eating'

This switch would be ungrammatical because the verbal root is from English, and the gerund affix attached to it from Spanish. Now *-iendo* '-ing' is not a free morpheme, and hence there is a violation of the constraint. At the same time, she proposes to subsume lexicalized expressions under the constraint, and this would presumably include lexicalized expressions such as the ones in (32). One way out would be to say that the Free Morpheme Constraint holds for affixation, as in (33), but not for compounding, as in (32). This may not be a possible solution however, for examples such as the following. We also find helping verbs in switches involving Amerindian languages with a complex morphology. The following example is from Navaho-English mixing (Canfield, 1980); here the Navaho verb *anileek* 'make-2nd person' carries the inflection, and is added to the uninflected verb *show*:

(34) Nancy bich'i   SHOW anileek
      Nancy 3rd: to   show 2nd:make
      Show it to Nancy.

In examples such as the Surinam Hindustani and the Navaho cases, the helping verb can be thought of as forming a complex with the verb from the other language, and neutralizing it as it were. With nouns, we often have case suffixes functioning as morphological neutralizers. An example may be one drawn from the Hindi–English data in DiSciullo, Muysken and Singh (1986):

(35) BREAD ne   nas mar diya
            erg.   ruin   aux
      The bread ruined it.

Perhaps the ergative particle *ne* serves here to neutralize the offending English element *bread*, to which it is attached.

A strategy similar to the use of helping verbs as in Surinam Hindustani, (32), is by incorporating the alien element as a stem into a verbal compound. An example, again from Navaho (Canfield, 1980):

(36) na'iish   −CRASH la
     1st: pass out   crash emphatic
     I am about to pass out.

We return to this strategy in the following chapter, when discussing strategies of sociolinguistic 'neutrality'. A final pattern of neutralization is found in Japanese–English switching (Nishimura, 1984). Here the verb is included in both languages, to avoid the problem of the conflicting VO/OV order of Japanese and English (switches between which would pose a problem for the equivalence constraint).

  We have seen a number of ways in which neutrality may be achieved by auxiliary strategies that interact with the general constraints mentioned. These strategies depend on the characteristics of the particular language-pair involved, and perhaps also on the type of bilingual community.

Further reading

There is no book entirely devoted to code switching and code mixing available yet. The most important general articles have been mentioned in the text: Pfaff 'Grammatical constraints on code switching' (1979) and Poplack, 'Sometimes I'll start a sentence in English Y TERMINO EN ESPANOL' (1980). The introduction to bilingualism by Grosjean, *Life with two languages*, has an interesting chapter on code switching (1982).

11 Strategies of neutrality

When you call train information in Toronto, the automatic answering tape says HERE VIA RAIL/ICI VIA RAIL, underlining the company's wish to present itself as a truly national enterprise in a bilingual nation. In the same way the national government in Canada is careful to preserve neutrality, in its policies and publications, with respect to both the English-speaking and the French-speaking population. The way in which neutrality is achieved is by using both languages, but this language doubling is but one of the strategies that can be employed to be neutral. This chapter is devoted to a more systematic exploration of these strategies.

The term 'strategy of neutrality' was introduced into sociolinguistics by Scotton (1976), who described intertribal interaction in urban Africa. Below we return in more detail to her research. Here we will use 'neutrality' in a rather loose sense and perhaps ambiguously, to describe two types of neutrality:

– neutralization in *in-group* communication, which may be schematically represented as:

(1) A/B → X ← A/B.

In this type of neutralization, a 'neutral' communicative mode expresses a group's mixed ethnolinguistic identity.

– neutralization of the communicative mode in situations of *intergroup* communication in which two groups of speakers with clearly separate ethnolinguistic identities do not speak the same language. This type of neutralization may be schematically represented as:

(2) A → X ← B.

Here X refers to the strategy of neutrality, and A and B to the languages and identities of the speakers involved in the interaction. This second interpretation of neutrality is the one intended by Scotton (1976).

In this chapter we will describe the strategies in terms of these two types: neutralization of identity in section 11.1, and neutralization of communicative mode in 11.2, before attempting a more general perspective on neutrality in sociolinguistics, in section 11.3. We should say right away that the way 'neutrality' was used in chapter 10 on code switching was rather different. There we referred to the points of neutrality between the structures of the two languages involved in code switching, a form of grammatical neutrality. Here we are talking about the neutrality between the different languages and identities of speakers involved in bilingual interactions.

11.1 Neutralization of linguistic identity

Owing to changing circumstances in life, many people or groups of people do not have one linguistic identity, but two, or a mixture of two identities, which could perhaps be called a bilingual identity (cf. our chapter 2 on language and identity). Given the crucial function of language as a way of expressing identity, we may ask ourselves how speakers will express such a complex double or mixed identity in the way they speak, even when they are interacting with speakers with a similar background. In fact, there turns out to be a number of ways of doing this: code switching, relexification, mixed reduplication, maintaining an accent. We will deal with these in turn.

Code switching as a strategy of neutrality was dealt with *in extenso* in the last chapter, but we want to return to it here in relation to the analysis of language choice in chapter 3. In chapter 3 work by Fishman and Ferguson was discussed which implies that stable bilingualism is only possible in a situation of diglossia, i.e. when there are two languages with clearly separated functions (Ferguson, 1959; Fishman, 1965). Language choice was argued to be functionally determined, given the social meanings attached to different languages within a bilingual speech community. The phenomenon of frequent code switching in conversations, and particularly of intrasentential code mixing casts doubt upon the classical analysis in terms of functional differentiation. An article by Pedrasa *et al.* (1980), appropriately titled 'Rethinking Diglossia', explores this shift. Pedrasa *et al.* explore a much more concrete approach to bilingualism, taking into account the phenomenon of age grading: even if the younger generation of Puerto Ricans in New York seems to know less Spanish than their elders, they go back to Spanish more when they are adults. In addition, the fact that new Spanish-speaking Puerto Ricans arrive in New York continuously and that older speakers may go back to Puerto Rico (the phenomenon of 'cyclic' migration) causes the role of English and Spanish to be much more complex than the static models of functional separation suggest. Within the fluid division of Spanish and English existing in New York, there is ample space for strategies of neutrality, and this space is taken up in part by code switching and mixing.

Relexification is a process by which the vocabulary of a language is replaced by that of another language, while its grammatical structure (morphology, syntax, phonology) is maintained. It sometimes occurs when a minority group in a language-contact situation undergoes a shift in cultural or ethnic identity, for whatever reasons. The most extensively documented case of relexification is Media Lengua, as analysed by Muysken (1981). In this case, groups of Quechua speaking Indians living at the fringe of the truly Indian world have developed a kind of mixed language with an overwhelmingly (87 per cent) Spanish vocabulary, but a Quechua grammar. This mixed language is called *Media Lengua* (halfway language) or *Utilla Ingiru* (little Quechua). An example of a Media Lengua sentence, with the corresponding Quechua and Spanish sentences, is (3):

(3) ML miza despwesitu kaza – MU   i – NAKU – ndu – GA
    Q   MIZA k'ipa   wasi – mu   ri – naku – pi – ga
        Mass after   house to   go **pl**   **sub**   **top**
    Sp Yendo a la *casa despues* de la *Misa*
    ML ahi – BI buda da – NAKU – N
    Q   chi – bi BUDA ku – naku – n
        that **loc** feast give **pl**   **3**
    Sp *ahi da*n una *boda*.

      'When you go home after Mass, they then give a feast there.'
In this rather complicated example, Quechua elements in Media Lengua are in capitals (in the first line), elements of Spanish origin in Quechua are in capitals (in the second line), abbreviations for grammatical formatives are printed bold (in the third line with glosses), and Spanish elements in the fourth line that also occur in Media Lengua are italicized. **pl** is 'plural', **sub** is 'adverbial subordinator', **top** is 'topic marker', **loc** is 'locative marker', and **3** is 'third person marker'.

    Note that in Media Lengua all the *lexical roots* are Spanish, and most affixes (*-ndu*, derived from Spanish *-ndo*, being the exception) Quechua. *i-* is from the Spanish infinitive form *ir* 'to go', and *da-* from the Spanish verb *dar* 'give'. In addition, the word order is Quechua, with the verb at the end in both the main clause and the subordinate clause, with a noun/postposition complex (*miza despwesitu*), and a morphologically indicated subordinate clause preceding the main clause. This is the effect of relexification. It is important to realize that relexification is something very different from lexical borrowing (a process focused on in chapter 14). In ordinary Quechua there is extensive lexical borrowing, as is clear from the example in (3), where even the Quechua sentence contains two Spanish borrowings: *miza* 'Mass' and *buda* 'feast'. These borrowings are part, however, of the extensive cultural Hispanic influence that Indian society has undergone since the Conquest. Both words are associated with the cycle of saint's day celebrations, etc. brought in by Catholicism. In Media Lengua, however, it is also the core vocabulary that has been replaced, verbs such as 'go' and 'give'.

    Relexification has not been explored very much yet in the study of language contact, but particularly studies of creole languages suggest the possibility of extensive relexification. We return to this in chapter 15. The only thing that should be mentioned here is that the type of relexification we get in Media Lengua, involving Spanish roots and Quechua suffixes, may be different from relexification in creoles, where there are hardly any suffixes. The only way there to argue that relexification has occurred (replacement of vocabulary while maintaining the grammar), is by showing that specific syntactic constructions or phrases have been given a new lexical filling. An example might be the relexification of French *s'il vous plait* as English *if you please* or Dutch *als't u blieft*. In languages with little morphology, relexification is much less 'visible'.

    Mixed reduplication refers to the result of a process of hybridization found in Hindi (Singh, 1982). In Hindi it is possible to partially reduplicate nouns, giving the result an 'etcetera' meaning;

(4) roti   roti voti   namak   namak vamak
    'bread' 'bread etc.'   'salt'   'salt etc.'

A very similar process of reduplication, however, does not involve the phonological modification of the reduplicated second element, but rather its replacement by a synonymous form with a Perso-Arabic origin. The examples in (5) all illustrate this pattern:

(5) tan **badan**   dhan **daulat**
    body body   money money
    'body etc.'   money etc.

    vivah **sadi**
    marriage marriage
    'marriage etc.'

Here *tan, vivah* and *dhan* are of Hindi origin, and *badan, sadi,* and *daulat* (printed bold in (5)) of Perso-Arabic origin. Singh claims that the forms in (5) are modelled upon those in (4), maintaining the semantics of partial reduplication, but born in the time when a Persian dynasty ruled Northern India and there was a continuous opposition between Persian and Hindi, calling for some type of neutralization. The processes involved are lexical rather than syntactic: the forms in (4) and (5) are one-word forms. Singh stresses the fact that this strategy of neutrality depends on the structural possibilities of Hindi. We do not have *storm-tempest, even though English and French were in contact for a long period of time, after the invasion of Britain by William the Conqueror.

Maintaining an accent is a fourth way in which a bilingual group may maintain or create some kind of double identity (see also the discussion in chapter 2). We will discuss examples here from Polish and Italian immigrants in the USA, French Canadians in Montreal, and Surinamese immigrants in Amsterdam. Carlock (1979) and Carlock and Wölck (1983) have shown that particularly prosodic features are very important in identifying speakers of Polish and Italian extraction in heavily 'ethnic' industrial cities such as Buffalo. Polish speakers of American English tend to have two- and three-beat contours, Italian speakers one- and two-beat contours. In (6a) the way a Polish American would say an American sentence (with italics for the stressed vowels) is represented, and in (6b) the Italian American pronunciation:

(6) a. So I w*i*sh / they would f*i*nd / a c*u*re / for a c*o*ld.
    b. My / y*ou*ngest / d*au*ghter / *a*lways / seems to / have a / c*o*ld.

These features characterize the speech even of third-generation immigrants, but mostly that of those speakers who have remained in the traditional neighbourhoods of the group involved. (This may go so far that in fact the ethnic speech variety evolves into a neighbourbood variety.) The creation of an 'ethnolect' is a successful strategy of neutrality of an immigrant group. The immigrants have access to jobs and education because they have learned the majority language, but find a way to express their identity in a separate code through the accent with which they speak the majority language.

Research by Segalowitz and Gatbonton (1977) points to two other interesting aspects of the maintenance of accents: that it may be related to feelings about ethnic loyalty, and that it may involve very specific, in fact arbitrary linguistic variables. Segalowitz and Gatbonton did not study immigrants, but rather a group of French Canadians with different degrees of mastery of English. They looked at the pronunciation of *th* (θ) in *three* and *thick*, of *th* (δ) in *there* and *bother*, and of *h*. The results were that there was a very regular pattern in the correctness of pronunciation of all three variables across different linguistic environments (exactly as in the sociolinguistic studies of Labov and his associates; cf. Labov, 1972). The correctness of pronunciation of all three variables correlated positively with the speakers' overall mastery of English. However, only the correctness of pronunciation of (θ) (as in *three*) and (ð) (as in *there*) correlated negatively with the speakers' feelings of being Quebecois as opposed to Canadian, not the pronunciation of *h*, nor the overall degree of mastery of English. So the more Quebecois the speakers felt, the more they were likely to say *tree* and *dere*. From the point of view of ethnic identification, some features of bilingual speech may matter more than others; 'they may carry the symbolic load of signalling ethnic group affiliation more heavily than do other features' (1977:82). (See chapter 2 for a more extensive survey of the relation between language and identity.)

Research by Charry (1983) has focused on variation within the ethnolect. He interviewed immigrants from Surinam in Amsterdam, in Dutch, and looked at several phonological variables. The most striking effects show up in the pronunciation of Dutch *w*. In standard Dutch this is a labio-dental glide, but in the Surinamese ethnolect it is often realized as a bilabial glide (as in English). The informed lay opinion in the Netherlands is that the Surinamese pronunciation is the result of transfer from Sranan, the Surinam creole language, which indeed has a bilabial *w*, and that the Surinamese ethnolect is simply a case of incomplete second-language learning. Charry (1983) gives several arguments why this cannot be the case: (1) The bilabial pronunciation appears even with speakers who do not know Sranan. (2) It occurs more often with younger speakers (who tend to be less proficient in Sranan) than with older speakers. (3) The use of bilabial *w* is subject to stylistic variation: as could be expected, it is much more frequent in casual speech.

All these findings concur with the analysis of the Surinamese ethnolect, and in particular of bilabial *w*, as a strategy of neutrality along the lines of Buffalo Polish and Italian English analysed by Carlock and Wölck (1983) and Quebecois English studied by Segalowitz and Gatbonton (1977).

11.2 Neutralization of communicative mode in inter-group communication

We do not find neutralization only in in-group communication, however, but equally between groups with different language backgrounds. Generalizing grossly over different analytical levels, we can mention a number of these strategies here: foreigner talk, the choice of a third language, the creation of a new language, often a lingua franca, and doubling.

The term *foreigner talk* refers to the way in which native speakers adjust their speech when they are interacting with foreigners perceived as not speaking the language well. In chapter 3 we briefly sketched the theory of accommodation, which postulates that there are intricate processes of adjustment between speaker and hearer in interaction situations. The first part of chapter 12 is devoted to foreigner talk and its different characteristics. Now many aspects of foreigner talk should be seen as instances of simplification rather than of neutralization. But we do find the latter process at work as well. One finds it in a certain internationalization of the vocabulary (e.g. in the use of expressions derived from French) still within the limits of the language spoken, as well as in the use of foreign expressions (often picked up while on vacation in the Mediterranean, etc.), even when the foreigner addressed does not know the language involved. An example (translated from a sort of Dutch) from a store near the market:

(7) mañana cheese here
'Tomorrow there will be cheese again.'

Here the supposedly 'international' word *mañana*, taken from Spanish, is used with a Turkish speaker who may not have the slightest idea what it means. In the next chapter we will turn to foreigner talk in much more detail.

Particularly in post-colonial societies a very common strategy of neutrality is the use of a *third language*. This is the strategy that Scotton (1976) systematically explored in her work in African cities, and that led to the concept of a strategy of neutrality in the first place. Scotton studied the language choices made in the workplace in three African cities: Kampala (Uganda) and Nairobi (Kenya) in East Africa and Lagos (Nigeria) in West Africa. Since the cities have grown enormously in recent years because of the influx of tribesmen from the countryside, most work environments are multi-ethnic. Even though particular African tribal languages have a wide distribution in the cities (many non-Yoruba tribesmen know Yoruba in Lagos, for instance), in the workplace a non-tribal, 'neutral' language is used. In all three cities two neutral languages were available: English as the language accessible mostly to educated speakers, and a *lingua franca* accessible to everyone. In East Africa this lingua franca is Swahili, and in West Africa it is pidgin English. While using a neutral language was already a way to avoid the conflict between two different tribal identities, switching between the standard and the lingua franca provided an even higher degree of neutralization. Why a neutral language if people share several other languages as well, and if language-specific functions are associated with each (cf. chapter 3)? It is not because there are no rules for language choice, but rather because often the components of a rule give conflicting results and the speakers do not know which component should carry the greatest weight in a given situation.

Rather similar to the choice of a third language is the creation of a *new language* as a strategy of neutrality. This new language may be related to any of the languages involved in the interaction situation, but should not be identified with it. A rather successful example of such a new language is Bahasa Indonesia, the official language of the Indonesian republic. Bahasa is now widely used, in addition to the many local languages of the individual islands and ethnic groups, throughout the Indonesian archipelago. How did the Indonesian revolutionary government manage to impose Bahasa so successfully? Bahasa was developed from Malay (an Austronesian language), a lingua franca of the colonial and perhaps even pre-colonial period, which functioned as an auxiliary language at lower governmental levels during the Dutch period. It was promoted during the Japanese occupation of World War II and embraced by Sukarno during the struggle for independence as a symbol of national identity. The most important factor behind Bahasa as a fully-fledged lingua franca, however, Tanner (1967) claims, is the fact that it is not the language of any one prominent ethnic group. It is therefore a safe first choice in any conversation between two Indonesians. Even in Java, the most populated island, where Javanese is spoken, Bahasa has a function because through Bahasa it is possible to avoid the pitfalls of deciding which variety of Javanese: high (could be interpreted as overly formal) or low (may be seen as much too familiar) to use in talking to another Javanese speaker.

In many societies the dominant strategy of neutrality is the creation or adoption of a lingua franca, a partly or completely elaborated system that can be used for communication between different groups, and is easily learnable by new speakers. Sometimes the lingua franca is elaborated into a national language, as in Indonesia (see chapter 5 on language planning), and elsewhere it has a kind of unofficial recognition, as in many East African countries, and plays a complex role in the patterns of language choice.

Particularly in official discourse, or in other circumstances where code mixing is impossible, *doubling* is taken recourse to as the strategy of neutrality. An example from Canada was given at the beginning of this chapter. But we do not only find doubling in official prose (immigration forms, etc.). An interesting example is the entertainer in a Cuban nightclub in the Bautista years, as recorded by Cabrera Infante in the opening sentences of his Jazz novel *Tres tristes tigres* (1965):

Showtime. Señoras y señores. *Ladies and gentlemen.* Muy buenas noches, damas y caballeros, tengan todos ustedes. *Good-evening, ladies and gentlemen. Tropicana,* el cabaret MÁS fabuloso del mundo. *Tropicana, the most fabulous nightclub in the WORLD* presenta . . . *presents* . . . su NUEVO espectáculo . . . *its new show* . . . (and so on and so forth)

A type of strategy of neutrality which needs to be studied in much greater detail is a *multi-level generative system*, a system which consists of two very different grammars which produce identical or similar surface outputs. Such a system is Chinook Jargon, at least as Silverstein (1972) describes it. American traders and Chinook Indians created a jargon, which is a kind of common denominator of the structures of Chinook and English. Each language can function as the basis but all the 'marked' or language-particular structures are dropped so that speakers (given a small common vocabulary drawn from various sources) can understand each other. It remains to be seen whether the historical Chinook jargon is like the system described here, and whether other contact systems function in the same way. An example may be Michif, a French–Cree language spoken in some places in North Dakota (USA) and Manitoba (Canada) (Crawford, 1983).

11.3 An integrative perspective

One way of comparing strategies of neutrality is in terms of notions derived from information theory and anthropological linguistics. What is the *density* of points at which the neutrality of the code is established? How closely is the neutral code *linked* to both non-neutral codes? Density refers to the frequency within the speech signal. In our case, density is high when the neutrality is marked many times within two seconds of spoken speech, for instance. Linkage involves explicit representation of the outer form (vocabulary, morphology, sounds, perhaps surface word-order) of a language. Linkage is high when a code is present in the speech signal very frequently and explicitly. The ideal strategy of neutralization rates high on both density and linkage. High density makes it possible for even a very short message to be perceived as being in a neutral code. High linkage has several advantages: it may make the neutral code easier to learn, it may make switching between the neutral and the non-neutral code more meaningful, and it provides a way to relate the bilingual identity conveyed by the code to the separate identities associated with the non-neutral codes.

Before going on to evaluate the different strategies of neutrality, we should look at the relation between different components of the grammar and the notions of density and linkage. A rule of thumb could be perhaps that the more a component belongs to the outer form of the language, the larger its potential role in linkage. People are more aware of the way a language sounds than of the structure of the quantification system. When someone utters the French word *cheval* 'horse', anybody who knows French realizes French is somehow involved in the utterance. When someone says 'a horse black', however, it will not be immediately obvious to the hearer that the French word-order pattern of *un cheval noir* is involved here. Phrase structure rules have at best intermediate linkage. Intonation patterns have high linkage, in being instantly recognizable, but not all individual sounds do. Many occur in different languages, and therefore we may say that segmental phonology as a whole has only intermediate linkage.

For density, matters aren't so simple. Segmental phonology has the highest density, of course, given Saussure's definition of human language as a system with secondary articulation: sounds make up words, words make up sentences, etc. Intonation has lower density, since it has clauses, or at least, phonological phrases, as its domain. The vocabulary has intermediate density: every utterance consists of several words, but not all lexical items are equally frequent in speech. Phrase structure rules have varying amounts of density: some apply several times in most utterances, some are less frequent. Suppose that it is possible to generalize over several phrase structure rules through X-bar theory, establishing the basic word-order patterns of a language, then we could say that phrase structure has intermediate density. Schematically, these considerations yield the following picture:

Table 11.1 The evaluation of the different grammatical components in terms of the notions density and linkage

	Density	Linkage
vocabulary	intermediate	high
segmental phonology	very high	high
intonation	high	intermediate
phrase structure	intermediate	intermediate
semantics	intermediate	low
discourse	low	low

Given this very rough evaluation of the grammatical components in terms of the notions of density and linkage, how do the different strategies of neutrality, that make use of these different components in different ways, rate? Table 11.2 gives a first analysis:

Table 11.2 Rating the different strategies in terms of the concepts of density and linkage

	Density	Linkage
code switching		
intersentential	low	high
emblematic	intermediate	high
intra-sentential	high	high
relexification		
rich morphology	high	high
poor morphology	high	low
maintaining accent	high	low
foreigner talk	low	low
third language	high	low
new language	high	intermediate
Chinook system	high	high
doubling	low	high

Strategies which show high density and linkage are intrasentential code mixing, relexification in languages with rich morphological systems, and new languages which are related in some way (perhaps derivationally, as in the case of Chinook jargon) to the non-neutral languages involved. What they share is outer forms which are a mixture of various ingredients, and involving the non-neutral languages. What makes relexification a less frequent strategy than intrasentential code mixing? First, we do not know much about strategies of neutrality involving languages with a complex morphology. Second, code mixing and relexification both share high density and high linkage, whereas relexification requires the manipulation by the speaker of two systems within the lexicon; in code mixing this is within the syntax. Since the lexicon is the component which is largely stored in the brain, and the syntax the component which is largely creative, we can expect mixing processes in speech *production* to affect predominantly the syntax. Only in highly agglutinative languages such as Quechua, where speakers are constructing words productively in the same way that speakers of English construct sentences, can we expect mixing inside the word to occur.

It should be clear, however, that this comparison of strategies needs much more work; we hope that the notions of density and linkage give a grip, at least, on the complexity of the phenomena involved.

Further reading

Beyond the work by Scotton, 'Code-switching as a "safe choice" in choosing a lingua franca' (1979), 'Strategies of neutrality' (1976), and later articles by the same author, there is no systematic treatment of strategies of neutrality.

12 Strategies and problems in bilingual interaction

In bilingual communities the fact that different people speak different languages corresponds to a division in different communicative networks. Take for instance West Berlin. The (native German) Berliners will tend to speak to other Berliners, and the 300,000 Turks living there will tend to speak to other Turks. The social division allows the linguistic separation to continue, and is symbolically expressed by it. At the same time the linguistic separation helps to maintain the social division. Ignorance of German for Turks means being cut off from access to desirable jobs; ignorance of Turkish for Germans implies, among many other things, not knowing what goes on in the Turkish community.

The two language groups are not independent: they live in the same city, and form part of the same economy. This leads to frequent contacts, even if these contacts are often limited in range and depth. This chapter is dedicated to the nature of contacts such as these between Turks and Berliners. In many bilingual communities the two groups of speakers do not have equal status. In Berlin, of course, the Turks have fewer opportunities for social advancement, worse jobs with lower wages, a higher unemployment rate, and smaller and older houses than the native Berliners.

This inequality is reflected in the patterns of interaction: German rather than Turkish is used in interethnic contacts. Only a few Berliners (social workers, teachers, lawyers, researchers, an occasional shopkeeper perhaps) know some Turkish, the majority of Turks speak some German at least. The use of German, however, poses problems for both participants in the interaction:

a. The native speakers have to adapt their speech to make themselves understood to foreigners. In section 12.1 we will study in detail what forms of adaptation we find, centring the discussion around what is called 'foreigner talk' (Ferguson, 1975).
b. The non-native speakers face innumerable problems in making themselves understood to native speakers. Therefore we will discuss problems and misunderstandings in native/non-native interaction in section 12.2.

In section 12.3 we will attempt to integrate the perspective in terms of adaptive strategies (section 12.1), and the perspective of communicative problems (section 12.2).

Of course foreigner talk and inter-cultural misunderstandings are only two aspects of bilingual interaction. When the two groups have roughly equal status or when all interlocutors are to some extent bilingual, the situation changes drastically. In chapter 3 we discussed the factors influencing language choice in such cases, and in chapters 10 and 11 the complicated switching back and forth or attempts to find more neutral modes of speech when it is not obvious immediately that one speaker can impose his code on the interaction.

12.1 Adaptive strategies: foreigner talk

Speakers adjust their language when they are talking to people who do not speak it very well. This holds for mothers speaking to their young children and for people speaking to foreigners. Since the early 1970s the adjustment in the speech directed at foreigners has been studied systematically, leading to an increasingly detailed and complex picture of what actually goes on, much beyond the conglomeration of holiday anecdotes and memories coloured by fiction that characterizes the lay view of foreigner talk. Foreigner talk, it should be stressed once again, is the type of language used when to speaking *to* foreigners, not the language *of* foreigners (which we have termed 'interlanguage' in chapter 8). One way in which speakers adjust is by simplifying their language, perhaps imitating an impression that they have of how the foreigner speaks. A classical example of this we find in *Robinson Crusoe* (1719; ed. 1977, p. 156):

and said (Friday), 'yes, yes, we always fight the better'; that is, he meant always get the better in fight; and so we began the following discourse:
'You always fight the better'; said I, 'how came you to be taken prisoner then, Friday?'
Friday. My nation beat much, for all that.
Master. How beat? if your nation beat them, how came you to be taken?
Friday. They more many than my nation in the place where me was; they take
         one, two three, and me; my nation over-beat them in the yonder place,
         where me no was; there my nation take one, two, great thousand.
Master. But why did not your side recover you from the hands of your enemies
         then?
Friday. They run one, two, three and me, and make go in the canoe; my nation
         have no canoe that time.

Friday is portrayed as speaking some sort of broken English. The colonial tradition has produced a stereotyped foreigner talk throughout the Western world. Paradoxically, its literary reflection is the way in which foreigners (Indians, Africans, Arabs) are presented talking in dialogue rather than the speech directed at them by Europeans.

Ferguson (1975) reports on a study in which American students were asked how they would say certain things to foreigners with very little English. Typical features of their self-reported speech included:

(1) a. absence of articles   *man come*
    b. absence of the copula   *him no good*
    c. absence of overt plural marking   *build two house*
    d. absence of auxiliaries or overt tense marking   *me come last year*
    e. short sentences   (self explanatory)

f.   simplified negation   *him no mine friend*
g.   not polite second person form   (Spanish) *tu trabajar!*
                                                                   (you work!)

This conglomeration of features, which could still be expanded if we include related studies, leads to sentences such as:

(2) Two man come, burn down family cabin yesterday, two man no good.
(3) you come here, you cut down tree, then you make fire, is cold

The Dutch Workgroup on Foreign Workers' Language (1978) repeated the study of Ferguson's in Amsterdam, asking one group of students how they would say certain things to foreigners, and another group how they thought foreigners would say the same things. Interestingly enough, the results were identical. Intuitions about stereotypical foreigner talk are identical to stereotypes about interlanguage. The reader might well object that stereotyped intuitions are one thing, actual behaviour being quite something else.

Some researchers have gone so far as to suggest that there are in fact two entirely separate modes of adaptation: foreigner *talk* (a separate code with the features described above) and foreigner *register* (slight deviations from the normal code of speech) (e.g. Arthur *et al.*, 1980). In the foreigner register, speakers tend to avoid the type of blatantly ungrammatical, socially stigmatized forms mentioned above, however, modifying their speech only in subtle ways that become obvious under quantitative analysis. Modifications in this case go no further than slower and clearer speech, shorter sentences, avoidance of idioms, avoidance of complex or exceptional grammatical patterns, avoidance of rare vocabulary items, etc.

Do people *actually use blatantly ungrammatical foreigner talk* when speaking to non-native speakers?
It appears that they do, but only when special conditions hold:

(a) The speakers perceive their own status as (much) higher than that of the foreigners;
(b) The level of proficiency of the non-native speaker in the language of the interaction is low;
(c) The native speakers tend to have had frequent but limited interactions with foreigners before;
(d) The interaction is entirely spontaneous: most often centred around a specific task or problem in shops or factories.

These four conditions, all of them necessary but none of them sufficient by themselves, were discovered by Long (1981) on the basis of an extensive survey of the available literature on foreigner talk (by then some 40 articles). Of course, many native/non-native bilingual interactions do not conform to all four criteria given above, together leading to typical or even stereotypical interaction. Often speakers tend to see their status as relatively equal (e.g. two families of tourists on a camping site), the non-native speaker is in fact fairly fluent, etc. Still, participants in these cases modify their speech, but only to produce what was called foreigner register above, something quite distinct from foreigner talk. In this view, foreigner talk creates a distance between the interlocutors, involving a put-down of the foreigner, and foreigner register is an instance of accommodation (already discussed in chapter 3), leading to easier input for the learner and less difference between the native and non-native ways of speaking.

A number of studies has shown that often native speakers adapt their speech in subtle degrees, depending on the level of proficiency of the foreigner. In Amsterdam (Snow *et al.*, 1981) this was found to be the case with officials who had frequent dealings with foreigners (in housing and civil registration offices). An example (rather literally translated) of an interaction of this type is:

O: And when did she die? Do you know that as well?
F: Ye . . es, nine, six.
O: Nine, six.
F: Six.
O: Nineteen . . .
F: Seventy-six
O: Seventy-six. And where?
F: In Turke.
O: In Turkey? Istanbul? Do you have a paper of that?
F: Paper of?
O: Of dying. Of the passing-away act?
F: Paper, yes.
O: But not here. Not with you.
F: Yes, is home.
O: Home. O.K.

On the basis of the immediate context the official manages to make sense of what the foreigner is saying and at the same time he makes himself understood, repeating what the foreigner says and slightly elaborating on it.

At the same time the dialogue presented shows that foreigner 'talk' and 'register' cannot be separated: the official does both, and in fact many native/non-native interactions show both processes occurring, foreigner 'talk' being the more extreme continuation of foreigner 'register'. This is very clear as well in market interactions between Spanish-speaking 'mestizo' sales people and Quechua-speaking Indian customers in Ecuador. The market interaction is characterized by long bargaining sessions, joking, the going away of the customer, and by a number of specific forms of address. The most interesting one is *casera/casero/caserita/caserito*, derived from *casa* 'house', and used reciprocally by buyer and seller. In the foreigner register addressed to the Indian customers we find three classes of address forms:

(4) a. polite and usable with any adult customer
     casero) 'house-keeper'
     casera
     caserito) 'house-keeper' (affectionate diminutive)
     caserita
   b. familiar, endearing, slightly marked
     jovencito 'young man'
     negrita 'little black one'
     madrecita 'little mother'
   c. impolite or endearing, marked for Indians
     mamita 'little mother' (familiar form)

> *hijito* 'little son'
> *cholito* 'Indian peasant'
> *taytiku* 'little father' (Quechua)

Striking is the high number of diminutives in each category. In the address forms we see the curious mixture of the two dimensions of bilingual interactions: accommodation (the reference to the customer as a family member, the endearing use of the diminutive) and hierarchy (the use of expressions such as 'little son' and *cholito* 'peasant'). The same thing shows up with respect to pronominal address. In Spanish there is both a polite and a familiar second-person pronoun. Indians tend to be addressed with the familiar form, but this is subject to variation. In several interactions the use of the polite and familiar forms is manipulated as part of the bargaining process. Here a dialogue is represented between a market-seller and an Indian customer. *Usted* is the polite form used, and *vos* the familiar form:

(5)   Seller: . . . usted . . . usted . . .
      Buyer: refuses
      Seller: . . . vos . . . vos . . . vos . . .
      Buyer: indignant
      Seller: . . . usted . . . usted . . .

Sometimes *vos* and *usted* alternate within one single stretch of monologue. In the market interactions we also find the frequent repetitions, short sentences, avoidance of marked terminology and constructions that were mentioned earlier. What makes the dialogues different is that here the interaction patterns are ritualized, embedded in the weekly routines of buying and selling that are part of the economic reality of the Andes. The use of accommodative strategies such as typical foreigner-register features and the adoption of Quechua pragmatics are combined with distance-creating strategies such as special forms of address and impolite second person pronouns.

Two questions need to be asked before we conclude our discussion of foreigner talk: *Is foreigner talk imitative of the way non-native speakers use the language?* Again, the answer to this question is both yes and no. On the one hand, foreigner-talk speech, including the ungrammatical type first described by Ferguson (1975), has many features of the speech of beginning learners. Both will include phrases such as *him no come* (for 'he didn't come'), and the list of features in (1) corresponds fairly directly to a similar list for early interlanguage.

Also Snow *et al.* (1981) demonstrate that in the interactions between officials and immigrants there is a correlation between the type and frequency of the foreigner-talk features in the speech of the officials and of the deviant features in the speech of the immigrants. The imitative nature of foreigner talk and foreigner register (at this point there is no difference) stems from its cooperative accommodative aspects.

Hatch (1983) gives some examples of exchanges between Zoila, a Spanish speaker learning English, and her friend, Rina, an English native speaker. Rina clearly adopts Zoila's interlanguage forms in some instances:

Zoila: Do you think is ready?
Rina: I think is ready.

Zoila: Why she's very upset for me?
Rina: She is upset for you?
Zoila: Yeah, is.

On the other hand, Meisel (1980) has shown that the simplification in foreigner talk and the speech of foreign workers in West Germany is the result of similar strategies of simplification which, however, do not always lead to the same linguistic features. For example, whereas use of the full, uninflected verb is characteristic of foreigner talk, some of the second-language learners Meisel studied did not show this feature in their interlanguage, but rather another invariant form. Probably in foreigner talk speakers often make use of stereotypes that are not directly imitative of the non-native speaker. Compare the example given in chapter 11 of the Dutch shopkeeper who says *mañana* (Spanish for 'tomorrow' and interpreted by tourists in Spain to mean 'some other time') to a Hindustani customer, to indicate that some goods have not yet arrived. This is obviously not based on what the Hindustani has said. Nor is it likely to clarify much, of course.

If the foreigner register is adapted to the level of proficiency of the foreigner, *does it help the learner acquiring the second language?* This question is hard to answer because of the double nature of foreigner talk. German research by both Meisel (1977) and Dittmar (pers. comm.) suggests that foreigners, even those who are not fluent, find ungrammatical foreigner talk offensive. The implicit insult can negatively influence the acquisition process, leading to psychological and social distance (Schumann, 1978). Also it can be negative for the more advanced learner if the input remains reduced (and there have been cases of this documented).

On the other hand, and this has been stressed in the work of Long and associates, and much related research, the type of foreigner talk characterized by slow, careful, simple and unmarked input, full of repetitions, is ideal for beginning learners, as it is meant to be.

12.2 Problems and misunderstandings in native–non-native interaction

Meeting a foreigner (e.g. an Englishman), a Japanese might introduce himself, for instance, as 'I belong to Bank of Tokyo', and continue asking questions such as 'What is your job', 'How old are you?' and 'What is the name of your company?' (Loveday, 1982b). It is quite clear that the Japanese is following a rule of convention stating that identity and status of interlocutors has to be established prior to interaction. The native English speaker (like many members of Western societies) will introduce himself with his name, and might interpret the questions of the Japanese as threatening or offensive. Meanwhile, the Japanese could think that the English speaker does not dare to give information about his status; also when status is not established, the Japanese will have problems in continuing the conversation in a manner which seems appropriate to him, because he can not define the (status) relation between him and his interlocutor. This is one of the many misunderstandings that might come up in the interaction between speakers of different languages. In this case the problem seems to be a consequence of the fact that the Englishman and the Japanese employ different rules for introducing themselves in opening a conversation with a stranger. Although both speakers might feel uncomfortable, often the non-native speaker will be blamed for 'not talking appropriately'. This asymmetry defines many bilingual interaction situations.

In verbal encounters between a native speaker of a prestige language and a non-native speaker of that language, the native speaker will have a higher status, and he will expect the non-native speaker, consciously or unconsciously, not only to use that language but also to speak the way he does. Otherwise, the non-native speaker will be considered as strange, offensive, devious, etc., depending on the type of communicative collision or friction. Compare the following short dialogue between a Dutch stall-holder and a Moroccan man in an Amsterdam streetmarket:

(6) Moroccan: Ik moet een kilo uien ('I must have one kilo of onions')
    Dutch: Zoiets vragen we hier beleefd ('Such a thing we ask here politely').

These interaction problems are expressions of inter-ethnic or inter-cultural differences, and they might become sources of inter-ethnic conflicts. People tend to judge each other often on the basis of their communicative behaviour, and in cases like the example given above, majority-language speakers negatively stereotype the non-native speakers, because 'they do not know how to behave', 'they are hardly civilized', etc.

Interaction problems between native and non-native speakers can be distinguished with regard to their origin. A first cause for such a problem might be the *limited formal second-language proficiency of the non-native speaker*. The latter does not have sufficient grammatical, phonetic and or lexical second-language skills to express himself adequately when talking to a native speaker, or he does not understand the native speaker completely, which will certainly result in communicative difficulties. In such cases the native speaker will often make allowance for the relatively low second-language proficiency of the non-native speaker, and adjust his language, i.e. speak some kind of foreigner talk (see section 12.1).

The second type of interaction problem originates in a specific form of limited second-language proficiency: *the non-native speaker lacks the skills necessary for distinguishing and adequately using the different stylistic variants and registers of his second language*. Sociolinguistic research in many speech communities has shown that speakers select certain stylistic variants or registers appropriate to the speech situation, or in order to define the speech situation (cf. also the discussion on language choice in chapter 3). For example, in formal interactions like a job interview, the interlocutors will use formal stylistic variants – in any case the applicant will try – , while at a certain point one of the interviewers might switch over to informal variants, which will often be non-standard forms, to indicate that the 'interview part' is over, and that it is time or some small talk to finish up.

Often the non-native speakers' second-language competence will not include stylistic variants. The speakers are only proficient then in one style or in one variety. This implies that they might use an informal style when a more formal way of talking is required; native speakers may judge this as too personal or too intimate. Not only the native speaker, but also the non-native speaker will be annoyed or frustrated if stylistic skills are lacking. People who have learned a second language in the classroom will feel uncomfortable in an informal exchange (Segalowitz and Gatbonton, 1977).

Even if the various stylistic variants of the second language are part of the non-native speaker's verbal repertoire, he may not be proficient in using them appropriately. A famous example is the *tu/vous*-distinction, lacking in English. English–French bilinguals, with English as their first language, will undoubtedly know the two forms in French where English only has *you*, but they might not have the skills to use the appropriate form in a particular situation. Even when the bilingual speaks two languages that have both the T/V-distinction (for example Dutch and German), the bilingual might have problems in selecting the appropriate pronoun, because there might be an incomplete correspondence between the two languages with regard to the social distribution of the two forms. According to Brown and Gilman (1960), the factors 'power' and 'solidarity' determine the selection procedure, and in most Western societies the solidarity factor has become the dominant one, i.e. when the power relation between two persons is such that one is more powerful because of social or occupational status or age, but at the same time a positive solidarity relation can be established (for example, they work for the same company), there is a growing tendency to choose the T-pronoun, or 'informal' pronoun. This is also the case in the Netherlands. Dutch has *jij* (T) and *u* (V) for *you*, and in exchanges between interlocutors with unequal status – for instance, between university students and junior faculty – often *jij* is used by both interlocutors, because of the need to stress the solidarity relation. In Germany, however, more weight is given to the power relation, and a student who addresses a lecturer or professor with *du* (the T-pronoun) is acting very rudely or impolitely. A Dutch–German bilingual with Dutch as his first language will often have problems in selecting the socially correct pronoun, and will often be rude, probably, in the view of a German.

A third source of problems in native–non-native interaction lies in the fact that *the cultural presuppositions of the two interlocutors are not the same*. The meaning of utterances is not only determined by their semantic content (and syntactic structure), but also by presuppositions accompanying the utterance. Consider for example sentences (7) and (8).

(7) Let John go!
(8) Donald accused him of always taking the initiative in the group planning
     meetings.

(7) contains the presupposition (connected with 'let go') that the addressee holds John. Utterance (8) contains the presupposition (connected with 'accused') that it is wrong always to take the initiative in meetings. This last type is of interest here, termed *cultural presuppositions* because they are related to the cultural norms of a community. If in a certain speech community people are admired if they always take the initiative, utterance (8) will sound strange to members of this community. Consider also Lakoff's famous example 'John called Mary a virgin, and then she insulted him'. It will be very difficult to interpret for members of communities with traditional, restrictive norms for women's sexual behaviour. In bilingual communities not only are two languages in contact, but also two cultures or two partly different sets of cultural values, which enter into language use via cultural presuppositions. The non-native speaker of language A might not share the cultural values of native speakers of language A, and therefore, attach different cultural presuppositions – and thus,

different meanings – to utterances in A. For example, in many Western societies for women to know how to act independently, is often positively evaluated. However, in many other communities women are expected to be more or less subordinated to their husbands (of course, this attitude is also held by many members of Western communities, but here we are sketching a general image). Now imagine a verbal encounter between a Dutchman and a Moroccan immigrant worker in the Netherlands. They talk about a certain woman, and the Dutchman says:

(9) Ik bewonder haar onafhankelijkheid ('I admire her independence')

For the Moroccan this utterance can be strange or ambiguous, because of his cultural values regarding the social position of women: an independent woman is not to be admired. Cross-cultural misunderstanding might be the result.

Problems in native–non-native interaction might also be due to the fact that *interlocutors employ different sets of interaction rules*. The term 'interaction rule' is used here to refer to all kinds of rules in addition to rules of grammar, semantics and phonology (the formal linguistic rules) that specify which (sequence of) utterances and which type of non-verbal behaviour are considered appropriate in certain situations. Compare Hymes's concept of 'communicative competence' that contains this type of interaction rules as an extension of Chomsky's 'linguistic competence' (Hymes, 1972).

Philips (1972) gives a clear example of how cross-cultural differences in interaction rules can be a source of misunderstanding. She studied the verbal behaviour of American Indian children from the Warm Springs Indian Reservation in classrooms with a white teacher. She concluded that – compared with non-Indian children – Indian children are less interested in the development of a one-to-one interactional relation with their teacher; they take more interest in maintaining and developing relationships with their classmates, no matter what is going on in the classrooms. Philips observed that the Indian students were reluctant to participate verbally in educational settings where students must speak out individually in front of the other students. Also with the teacher in a small group, the Indian children much more frequently refused to say something than the non-Indian children did. To the teachers the children might often seem taciturn or withdrawn. On the basis of this behaviour, teachers can draw the wrong conclusions about the educational motivation or the cognitive level of the children.

Differences in the evaluation of speech and the function of speech are noted by many authors. Loveday (1982a, 1982b) writes about the differences between the Japanese and most Western speech communities. In Japan, the verbal expression of personal ideas and emotions is not positively valued as in the West. Loveday points to the potential misunderstandings in Japanese–English verbal encounters: if someone expresses his thoughts or feelings explicitly, the Japanese take this often as a sign that the speaker is neither profound nor sincere, but on the other hand, native speakers of English frequently regard the Japanese as 'distant', 'cool' and 'cautious'. Communicative problems can also arise when speakers are accustomed to different rules with regard to the organization of conversations, e.g. the expected length of verbal turns and the occurrence of interruptions. Barkowski *et al.* (1976) report on the language problems of Turkish immigrant workers in West Berlin in this perspective. These Turks are used to interactions with undisturbed long monologues containing many narratives. They have difficulties functioning in a German speech community where shorter exchanges are more common, and people interrupt each other sometimes frequently, especially in informal, personal interactions.

Until now, we have only given some examples of more general interaction rules referring to general discourse principles. However, there are also many cross- cultural differences in more specific interaction rules, i.e. rules with regard to the appropriate form of utterances or the expression of certain speech acts. Gumperz *et al.* (1982), for instance, analyse the characteristics of the English spoken by British citizens from India or Pakistan, and they contrast Indian English with standard Western English. One of their examples is utterance (10).

(10)   Building societies and the council have got no objection, doesn't mean that if a council house, council mortgage, you can still sell it.

They note that the most obvious interpretation (one cannot sell a council house) is not right. When analysed in the light of the preceding discourse, it becomes clear that the opposite is meant: one is free to sell a council house. According to Gumperz and his associates 'doesn't mean' bears no surface syntactic relation to the succeeding clause, but it serves to mark the entire utterance as a refutation of something expressed in the preceding part of the interaction. Indian English diverges from standard Western English in the use of a device like 'doesn't mean' in this example. Therefore, native speakers of Western English often judge Indian English as disconnected and hard to follow.

In his publications on inter-ethnic or cross-cultural communication, Gumperz often stresses the importance of paralinguistic aspects of language, like pitch and intonation. In Gumperz (1977) an example is given of newly hired Indian and Pakistani women in a staff cafeteria at London airport. The women exchanged only relatively few words with their superiors and the cargo handlers whom they served. But the intonation and manner in which the women pronounced these words were interpreted negatively, and the women were perceived as surly and uncooperative. For instance, a customer who had chosen meat at the counter needed to be asked whether he wanted gravy. The Indian and Pakistani women pronounced this word with a falling intonation (*Gravy*), while a British attendant would have asked *Gravy?* with rising intonation.

Many authors have noted that native–non-native interaction is often more or less disturbed because the non-native speaker does not follow the same rules for expressing certain speech acts as the native speaker does. Scarcella and Brunak (1981) give an example in which an Arabic non-native speaker of English says as a greeting 'Hello, welcome', which is rather odd for native speakers. Non-native speakers often have problems in applying the regular (i.e. native) strategies for politeness in their utterances. For instance, for formulating a request all languages have many options. Utterances (11a-e) are five of the potential ways of asking someone in English to give a book (and there are more utterances possible).

(11)   a.   Give me that book
      b.   Please, give me that book
      c.   Could you give that book?
      d.   Would you be so kind as to give me that book?
      e.   I need that book.

The appropriateness of each of these utterances depends mainly on the social relation between the speaker and addressee, and non-native speakers often have difficulties in selecting the appropriate utterance in a given situation. Scarcella and Brunak (1981), for example, found that Arabic non-native speakers of English used many more requests in the imperative mood than native speakers did, and not only to the 'subordinates' in a role-playing experiment, but also to the 'superiors'. The utterances of the non-native speakers might not only seem odd to the native speaker, but also impolite.

In fact, this discussion of the expression of speech acts must be related to the earlier discussion of stylistic differences. With regard to both issues, cross-cultural interaction problems might occur, because (a) the non-native speaker's competence does not contain all the formal options of the target language; or (b) the non-native speaker does not use the same rules as the native speaker for selecting the appropriate option. In the last case, a linguistic minority group might have developed a set of rules that differs from the 'majority interaction rules' and marks a social or ethnic variety of the language considered (see also, section 2.1 on ethnic varieties). This seems to be the case in Gumperz's description of Indian English.

Conventions for non-verbal behaviour we will consider to be a separate type of interaction rules. Speech communities can, for instance, differ substantially with regard to the amount of gesturing that is judged 'normal': in Northern Europe, Italians are famous for their 'exaggerated gesturing'. According to Loveday (1982a), in contrast with many other communities, the Japanese try to avoid eye contact with interlocutors in face-to-face interaction: 'Unlike the Latin or Middle Eastern or certain North European patterns, the Japanese consider being repeatedly looked at or intensively focused on with the eyes as unpleasant or even rude. Intent gazing at the person one is talking to does not signal respect' (p. 95).

Body distance between interlocutors is an important variable in interaction. It is often observed that people from Arabic countries are used to much smaller distances in personal face-to-face interaction than people from Western speech communities. It is easy to imagine the frustration or irritation both participants may experience in Arab–Western language contact: in an extreme case, the one does a step forward, and the other a step backward, etc. These cross-cultural misunderstandings can be a source of further conflicts, since the non-verbal behaviour (like the verbal behaviour) is *always* socially interpreted. In the example above, the Arab might think that the Westerner is reluctant to talk to him or does not want to talk informally, while the Westerner might suppose that the Arab wants to talk too intimately.

Non-native speakers in bilingual communities often are second-language learners in intermediate acquisition stages. An interesting question is whether there is *a relation between formal and functional competence*. Or to put it otherwise: do non-native speakers with a relatively low formal second-language proficiency differ more from native speakers with regard to the use of interaction rules than non-native speakers with a higher second-language proficiency? This question was included in a study by Fonck (1984) on pragmatic differences between English learners of Dutch and the Dutch of native speakers. She found that the non-natives had a preference for more polite, or more indirect utterances expressing the speech act 'to complain' than the Dutch natives. Within the group of non-natives there was a tendency for those with less grammatical second-language skills to diverge most from the Dutch native speakers.

The data of Scarcella and Brunak (1981) also point to a relation between formal and functional proficiency. In their comparison between American native speakers of English and Arabic non-native speakers of English, they found that in a role-playing situation both groups used small-talk in opening a conversation with a 'friend'. However, when the native speakers talked with a 'superior', they only used short openings such as attention-getters. The non-native speakers, and among these especially the students with limited English proficiency, also used extended openings, i.e. small talk, towards a 'superior'.

A further issue with regard to interactional differences between native and non-native speakers is, *whether the interaction rules employed by the non-natives are transferred from their first or source language* (for the concept of 'transfer', see chapter 8). Loveday (1982b) stresses the occurrence of what he calls 'cross-cultural communicative interference'. He gives many examples to show the influence of Japanese interaction rules on the communicative behaviour of Japanese speakers of English. For instance, Loveday argues that in the Japanese speech community the collective is given more importance than the individual, so the Japanese rarely express disagreement in conversation. This behaviour is transferred to language contact situations; therefore, the verbal participation of Japanese in English conversations seems dull and unsatisfactory for native speakers of English: they tend to judge the Japanese as polite, but withdrawn or insincere, as was already remarked above.

Gumperz *et al.* (1982) discuss the thematic structure in discourse, and contrasts between British and Indian English in signalling the connections the speaker intends to convey between the utterances. One of their examples is the use of conjunctions. In Indian languages, conjunctions never receive stress and they are more often optional than in English. This implies that the occurrence of an optional conjunction carries signalling value. Gumperz *et al.* give the following part of a dialogue in which the Indian speaker A marks a shift of focus by the unstressed use of *and* without any further prosodic cues.

B: So so what was the outcome Mr. A?
A: Outcome was and that they had recommended that he has class discipline problem/language problem/so much problem/and but his lesson was well prepared/ and he had told us he needs more help . . .

Gumperz *et al.* note that A uses a listing prosodic pattern, but that 'he does nothing to signal the distinction between the list of criticisms in the first three clauses and the contrasting commendation in the last. This last clause is marked off only by being conjoined with "and" ' (p. 46). It is clear that interactional transfer from the native language into the second language occurs. But research data are still rather scarce and anecdotal. Furthermore, in many cases non-native speakers do *not* transfer interaction rules from their first language: the Arab speakers of English in the above-cited example from the study of Scarcella and Brunak (1981) do not use more requests in the imperative mood because they apply an Arab interaction rule, but because of their limited skills in English. Therefore, it is difficult to judge the extent and the importance of this type of transfer, and the way it influences native–non-native interaction.

Language is embedded in society, and interaction rules as well. They relate to the social structure and cultural values of that society. In the beginning of this section an example was given of the differences between Japanese and people from Western societies in introducing themselves when starting a conversation with a stranger. The Japanese apply an interaction rule specifying that in such an introduction interlocutors have to establish their status. According to Loveday (1982a) this rule must be connected with the vertical structure of Japanese society whose members are bound in tightly organized groups.

When interaction rules express certain cultural values, these values clash where interaction rules clash. This means that the social consequences of native–non-native interaction problems must not be neglected: the result may be further social and cultural stigmatizing of linguistic minorities.

12.3 An integrative perspective

If we want to relate the foreigner-talk strategy discussed in section 12.1 to the communication problems dealt with in the preceding section, it is necessary to look at the concept of 'conversation' in more detail. In general a conversation can be seen as a 'joint venture' of the people participating in it. The content and form of the conversation is not given beforehand (except in certain institutionalized interactions), but the interlocutors make it, construct it while they are talking. Therefore, interlocutors have to cooperate, otherwise interaction can not be successful, i.e. meanings and intentions will not be understood. It must be stressed that 'cooperation' does not imply that participants in an interaction help each other or agree with each other continually. 'Cooperation' refers to the fact that interlocutors are generally applying the same rules for expressing and interpreting speech acts.

Interlocutors may not have equal power, and this will be expressed in the interaction. The most powerful participant has the chance to direct the conversation, to reduce the turn-taking possibilities of other participants, etc.

In native–non-native interaction problems often occur because the interlocutors do not have the same set of rules at their disposal for expressing and interpreting speech acts. In many cases, the interlocutor with the most power can determine what language is used, imposing his native language on the other speaker. The latter will have considerable difficulty, however. Therefore, the interaction can only be successful when the native speaker gives much credit to the cooperation principle: he must make extra efforts to understand the non-native speaker, and to make himself understood. He must often adjust his speech, and use a kind of foreigner talk which gives the non-native speaker extra chances to grasp the meaning. This is exemplified in the following dialogue, taken from a study by Josine Lalleman (1986). She made recordings of the verbal interactions between Turkish and Dutch children at play. In general, the Turkish children had a lower Dutch proficiency than the Dutch children (a difference which was even more striking in their test results). But most of the time that did not lead to interactional problems. However, now and then such a problem occurred, for instance in the following dialogue.

Soraya (Dutch)	Moet je ook pleister? ('Do you need band-aids?')
Özlem (Turkish)	Wat? ('What?')
Soraya:	Moet je ook pleistertjes? ('Do you need little band-aids?')

Özlem:	Watte? ('Wot?')
Soraya:	Moet je ook beetje van dees? (Do you need any of these?')
Özlem:	Nee ('No').

Özlem clearly does not know the word 'pleister', and Soraya probably tries to help her by using the diminutive ('pleistertjes'), which is very common in Dutch, especially among and towards young children. If Özlem still fails to understand, Soraya solves the interaction problem by using a demonstrative pronoun and pointing to the band-aids, i.e. she is very cooperative in her behaviour.

But interlocutors may also fail to cooperate, or they may (implicitly) refer to the power-relation. In native–non-native interaction, the native speaker will generally be more powerful. He can express this power by not cooperating, not trying to resolve interaction problems, or indeed by increasing the interactional gap between him and the non-native speaker. There are two means for increasing this gap: (a) by not adapting his speech; (b) by adapting it too much or wrongly, and using the particular type of offensive, ungrammatical foreigner talk that will further frustrate inter-ethnic communication in the bilingual community.

Further reading

The starting point for anybody interested in foreigner talk is the work of Ferguson (1971; 1975; Ferguson and DeBose, 1977), who has related it to simplified registers in general, pidgins, and the process of linguistic simplification. Michael Long (1981; 1982) has stressed the relation between foreigner talk and second-language learning, and has written several 'state of the art' reports. For German the most interesting article is Meisel (1975; 1977), and for French we have Valdman (1977a). Volume 28 of the *International Journal of the Sociology of Language*, edited by Michael Clyne (1981), is dedicated to foreigner talk, presenting both sociological and psychological perspectives.

Loveday (1982a) deals with interaction problems between native and non-native speakers from the perspective of second-language acquisition. Sanches and Blount (1975) is a reader with articles on culture-specific interaction rules. Discourse processes and problems in inter-ethnic interaction are dicussed in Gumperz (1982a and 1982b). Extra and Mittner (1984) contains a section with papers on (mis)understandings in conversations between native speakers and second-language learners. Articles on this issue are collected in two special issues of journals: *International Journal of the Sociology of Language*, Vol. 27 (1981) and *Applied Linguistics*, Vol. 5, No. 3 (1984).

IV Linguistic consequences

13 Language contact and language change

Can one language influence another one structurally? Or, put differently, can languages borrow from each other? This issue has been hotly debated, both in historical linguistics and in language contact studies, and no consensus has been reached. One of the reasons for this is that there are widely divergent views on what language is really like. At opposite ends we find the 'system' view and the 'bag of tricks' view. The system view holds that languages, or more specifically grammars, are tightly organized wholes, of which all elements are related by complex syntagmatic and paradigmatic relationships. A prominent advocate of the system view was Ferdinand de Saussure, the founder of structuralism, who claimed that language was a system 'ou tout se tient' (where everything hangs together). The bag of tricks view holds that languages are primarily complex tools for referring to the world and for communication, and that these tools easily adapt to new communicative and referential needs. A prominent proponent of the bag of tricks view was Hugo Schuchardt, the creolist referred to in chapter 1. Schuchardt (1914) went as far as proposing language chemistry for handling creole data: the 'formula' for two creole languages spoken in Surinam was CEP_1D for Sranan and CEP_5D for Saramaccan (C = Creole, E = English, P = Portuguese, D = Dutch), and the different numerical subscript for P indicates the different amount of Portuguese present in both creoles.

On purpose we have cited two scholars from the early twentieth century as holding these rather opposite points of view. In modern linguistics the distinction is not as clear, as we will see below. One would tend to associate Chomsky and the generative tradition with the system view, and Hymes and other functionalists with the bag of tricks view. The notion of system itself, however, has undergone important changes. The holistic systems of early structuralism have been replaced by modularized systems in modern grammatical theory. These systems contain a number of independent components: the lexicon, the phonological component, etc. The implication of this conception of the grammar for borrowing is that borrowing a word does not imply necessarily that the sounds of which the word are composed are borrowed in the same way. Of course words are phonologically adapted in the process of borrowing. What this means is that words are borrowed in a fairly abstract shape, which is then mapped onto the sound patterns of the language.

One of the reasons why so little agreement has been reached with respect to the question of what can be borrowed in language is that the focus has been on the elements borrowed, and not as much on the processes of borrowing, i.e. the type of contact situation. We claim that this makes all the difference in the world, and therefore we discuss different scenarios for linguistic borrowing in section 13.1. Section 13.2 focuses on the type of evidence needed to argue for borrowing with the example of one grammatical structure, relative clauses, which has been the subject of language-contact studies in four continents, and continues to cause controversy. In section 13.3 we take the perspective of historical linguistics: how does grammatical change due to language contact compare with other kinds of grammatical change?

One thing should be mentioned before going on: lexical borrowing is something that all researchers acknowledge. How could they otherwise, since lexical borrowing is as old as the oldest cuneiform tablets and rock inscriptions, and older yet. It will be discussed in the next chapter, by itself. Here we limit ourselves to grammatical borrowing – the incorporation of foreign rules into a language. The alternative term, linguistic influence, has a disadvantage: it suggests that it is the donor language that determines what is borrowed or not, and neglects the creative and adaptive aspects of the process that we will return to below. It would be easy to make up a new scientific term, but we will refrain from doing this given that the field is already riddled with confusing terminology.

13.1 Five scenarios

There are at least five ways in which grammatical borrowing could potentially take place:

(1)   through convergence
      through cultural influence and lexical borrowing
      through second-language learning
      through relexification
      through imitation of prestige patterns

We will discuss these one by one, presenting them in terms of a hypothetical scenario:

(a) Gradual convergence due to prolonged coexistence
In a situation in which several languages have been spoken in the same area and mostly by the same people for a long time they may start converging. This convergence is most apparent on the phonetic level: the sound systems of the languages may grow to be more and more similar, without clear influence in one direction. One example from Ecuador may illustrate this. Here the dialect variation in the pronunciation of palatal *l* is parallel in both Spanish and Quechua:

(2)		Spanish	Quechua
	North Eduador	[kaže]	[aži]
	South Ecuador	[kal̄e]	[al̄i]
		'street'	'good'

Both in Quechua and in Spanish the 'Northern' pronunciation is an innovation; hence it is not easy to argue for influence is one direction. Note also that the consequences for the linguistic systems involved are rather limited: the fricativization of palatal *l̄* is a late phonological rule, without consequences for the rest of the sound systems.

Roman Jakobson has described a number of cases of phonological convergence, in terms of the notion 'phonological *Sprachbund*' (1931), a notion derived from work of Trubetzkoj. In several cases, for instance, unrelated languages spoken in the same area have developed a tone system. Chinese and Tibetan are one example, and another example is formed by the languages of the Baltic sea: Swedish, Norwegian (excluding the Northwestern dialects), most dialects of Danish, some dialects of North German, North Cashubic, Estonian, Lettish, Lithuanian.

The situation is a little different in the Balkans and in Northern India, regions for which extensive convergence of complete grammatical systems has been claimed. We will discuss these in turn. The Balkan peninsula is the home of a number of languages, from four Indo-European and one non-Indo-European language families:

(3) *Indo-European*
Slavic: Bulgarian, Macedonian, South East Serbian dialects
Romance: Romanian
Greek
Albanian
Non-Indo-European
Turkish

Disregarding Turkish, which may well have contributed to the linguistic levelling (homogenization, cf. Birnbaum, 1966) of the Balkan area but cannot be seen as part of the *Sprachbund* itself, the other languages share several remarkable features. One is that several (but with the exception of Greek) have developed post-nominal articles:

(4) | Albanian | qiel**li** | lul**ja** |
|---|---|---|
| Bulgarian | nebe**to** | cwet**jat** |
| Romanian | cer**ul** | floar**ea** |
| (Greek | **o** ouranos | **to** louloudhi) |
| | 'the sky' | 'the flower' |

This grammatical feature does not exist in earlier stages of these languages nor in related languages. There is no explanation, of course, for why Greek does not share this feature, under the convergence hypothesis.

Another example is the replacement of the infinitive by a subjunctive construction. Instead of something like 'je veux partir' (I want to leave) speakers of Balkan languages will say something like 'je veux **que** je parte (subjunctive)' (I want **that** I leave):

(5) | Albanian | due | **te** shkue |
|---|---|---|
| Bulgarian | iskam | **da** otida |
| Romanian | veau | **sa** plec |
| Greek | thelo | **na** pao |
| | 'I want that I leave'. | |

The verb after the complementizer is in the present tense and corresponds in person and number to the main verb. Hence it is completely redundant information and this corresponds with the idea that this construction emerged in a language contact situation (Civian, 1965). It is less plausible that all these languages had developed post-nominal articles for that same reason.

It is also difficult to discover why this type of convergence takes place. In the Ecuadorian case of phonetic convergence, cited above, you might think of the convergence as being due to the mere proximity of the two languages, but for syntactic convergence it can not be so simple. It could be that a large population speaking two languages will tend to start using the same structures in both languages. Another possibility is that two converging languages are influenced, independently of each other, by yet a third language spoken in the region (see below under (d)). Finally, one might think that people living in one region may start developing common linguistic norms, norms which are then imposed on the languages of the region.

In studies of linguistic convergence on the Indian subcontinent the term 'areal feature' has been coined (as opposed to 'genetic feature', for features due to linguistic ancestors). Languages spoken in a *Sprachbund* area then have both genetic and areal features. Below, we return to one such feature when discussing Konkani.

Care should be taken, of course, when determining what the areal features are not to include features that are so common that their areal distribution could be due to chance. To give but one example, in many Ecuadorian dialects of Quechua initial consonants of suffixes are voiced after a nasal and a vowel, giving the following distribution:

(6) ñan – **da**   road (acc.)
     papa – **da**   potato (acc.)
     krus – **ta**   cross (acc.)

It would be silly to argue that this voicing is due to the fact that there are voiced as well as voiceless consonants in Spanish. The process is much too natural and expected to need an explanation in terms of borrowing.

(b) Cultural influence and lexical borrowing

A very important scenario for borrowing is through cultural influence. The most important effect of this type of influence is lexical borrowing, to which we turn in the next chapter, devoted to the borrowing of words. Therefore we will not pursue this here.

(c) Drastic relexification

In chapter 11 we explored the notion of relexification: the replacement of the vocabulary of one language with that of another language, while maintaining the original grammar. We should briefly mention here that sometimes it is not quite possible to maintain the original grammar in the process of relexification, particularly if function words from the new language are introduced as well. In Media Lengua, the language resulting from the relexification of Quechua with Spanish vocabulary, some changes have occurred due to this. An example is first-person reflexive. In Quechua reflexive is generally marked with a suffix **-ku** on the verb, as in (7):

(7) riku – ku– ni
     see   **refl** 1
     'I see myself.'

Since Media Lengua has formed a non-subject first-person pronoun **ami** 'me' (from Spanish *a mí* '(to) me'), it is possible to form first person reflexives in Media Lengua without the suffix **-ku-**, by simply adding **-lla-di** 'self' to the object pronoun:

(8) ami – 11a –(da)– di bi – ni
     me   self   acc   see 1
     'I see myself.'

(Here **acc** = accusative case, **1** = first-person agreement).

We will return to the syntactic consequences of relexification in chapter 15.

(d) Language acquisition and substrate

In order to explain how daughter languages came to diverge widely from the mother language some scholars have appealed to *substrate* influence. When a language is brought into another region than that of its original use, and when speakers of other languages in that region adopt it as their second language, because of its cultural and political prestige, then the original language of these speakers may influence the new language in various ways. Schematically:

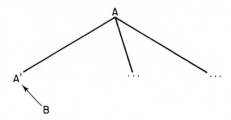

Figure 13.1

Thus Romance scholars have sometimes argued that French is derived from Vulgar Latin not only through a series of linguistic changes internal to the system, but also because of Celtic influence on Vulgar Latin in the late Roman era. This type of influence would explain a number of the differences between French, Spanish (Basque substrate), Portuguese (Celtic substrate?), Romanian (Thracian substrate), etc.

Presumably this type of substrate influence would occur because the Celts learned Vulgar Latin as a second language, but only imperfectly, and introduced many elements from their own language into it. The process requires three steps:

(a) One or more features of language **B** (cf. the schema above) are transferred into the **B/A** *interlanguage*, i.e. the result of the attempts by speakers of **B** to learn **A** (cf. chapter 8 on second-language learning);

(b) These features remain in the interlanguage, even when speakers of **B** learn **A** rather well.

(c) The features, originally characteristic of **B**, are adopted by native speakers of **A** in successive generations, sometimes as a stylistic variant of the original corresponding feature of **A**, sometimes as the only variant.

For this reason, arguing for a substrate feature in a particular system involves three steps as well:

(a) first showing that there is *variation* (diachronic, stylistic, sociolinguistic);

(b) then showing that one of the variants is characteristic of the *acquisition* process;

(c) and finally showing that it could have resulted from *borrowing*: it is present in fact in the other language system as well.

(e) Imitation of prestige language patterns

In addition to the four scenarios discussed so far, we find cases in which sentence patterns or complex expressions of a prestige language are imitated. This scenario is by necessity limited to fairly superficial phenomena. Only aspects of the grammar that are easily perceived can be imitated, of course. The case of Turkish discussed in 13.2 below may be illustrative of this type of development. We can also think of all kinds of Latin turns of phrase that appeared in the European vernaculars when the latter developed as literary languages in the Renaissance.

13.2 Is there syntactic borrowing? The case of relative clauses

We will now turn to a number of specific cases, to see how relevant the scenarios presented above may be. For the sake of clarity and ease of comparison, all cases will involve relative clauses.

(a) India: influence from Kannada on Konkani?

An apparently very clear case of syntactic influence involves some dialects of Konkani, an Indo-European language related to Marathi spoken in central India. Some centuries ago a group of Konkani speakers moved into an area where Kannada, a Dravidian language, is spoken, and they were forced by circumstances to become bilingual: Konkani inside the home, Kannada outside. That their bilingualism was maintained and shows no sign of disappearing is perhaps due to the rigid ethnic, religious and caste divisions that cut through Indian society: the Konkani speakers were Brahmins and kept themselves separate socially. Nadkarni (1975) claims, however, that the structure of the Konkani dialects involved was directly affected, becoming very much like the structure of Kannada. The original Konkani relative clause, formed with a relative particle as in (9a), was gradually replaced by a Kannada-type relative clause, formed with a question word and a yes/no interrogation element as in (9b):

(9) a. jo   mhāntāro   pepar vāccat āssa, to   dāktaru āssa
        REL old-man   paper reading is   that doctor is
    b. **khanco** mhāntāro pepar vāccat āssa-**ki**, to dāktaru āssa
        which   Y/N
        'The old man that is reading the newspaper is the doctor.'

This replacement can only be explained through the postulation of Kannada influence; it is not motivated structurally. In fact, the change implied a decrease in the expressive potential of Konkani, Nadkarni claims, because in the Kannada-type structure extraposition becomes impossible. At the same time extraposition is a very useful device for structuring the information, particularly in languages with prenominal relative clauses like Kannada and Konkani. (10) gives the relevant contrast:

(10) to   dāktaru āssa   jo/***khanco** mhāntāro pepar vāccat āssa- ***ki**
       that doctor is   REL/ which   old-man   paper reading is   Y/N

On the whole the case presented by Nadkarni is very strong and hard to explain otherwise. People who claim that syntactic borrowing is impossible can try to argue two things: (a) What we have in (9) is not the replacement of one type of relative clause by another one, but rather the loss of the possibility to relativize, and its replacement by a question-like structure, which functions somewhat like a relative clause. (b) What we have is not Konkani grammar undergoing some change, but the replacement of a Konkani grammar rule by a rule of Kannada grammar, while maintaining Konkani vocabulary. This may be called resyntactization (as opposed to relexification), and is a strategy of anti-neutrality (see chapter 11). Centuries of coexistence and massive bilingualism have led to the convergence of the grammars of the Indian languages, but the existing social divisions called for pluriformity. Therefore the languages remained as separate as possible on the lexical level. An extreme case of this is the distinction of Hindi and Urdu, which holds for none of the grammar and only a small part of the lexicon, but is very real for Hindus and Muslims in India and Pakistan.

(b) Turkish: influence from Persian

An intriguing case of syntactic borrowing involves the introduction of Persian relative clauses into Turkish. Turkish has undergone extensive lexical influence, from Arabic and Persian successively, and at the Ottoman court a very complex and flexible form of Turkish was spoken, full of Arabic and Persian expressions and phrases. One element introduced was the Persian particle *ki*, somewhat like English 'that', which created the possibility of having Indo-European-like relative clauses such as (11b) in addition to original Turkish patterns such as (11a):

(11) a. kapıyı kapamıyan   bir çocuk
         door   not-shutting a child
    b. bir çocuk ki   kapıyı kapamaz
        a child   REL door   not-shuts
        'A child who does not shut the door'

In (11a) the relative clause is formed with a participial form of the verb, and in (11b) with the particle *ki* and a fully inflected verb. Furthermore, the original type of relative clause precedes the head noun, and the 'Persian' type follows the head noun.

Again, this seems to be a clear example of syntactic borrowing, in this case through cultural influence and lexical borrowing: the introduction into Turkish of the element *ki* opened the way, not only for new types of relative clauses, but also of complement clauses, just as with English 'that'. Again, however, there are two ways to argue that there is no borrowing: first, Lewis (1972) (who gives the two examples in (11) as well) notes that there is an old Turkish interrogative element *kim*, which through its phonetic similarity may have paved the way for the extension in syntactic use of *ki*. Second, there is some doubt that constructions of type (11b) ever really became part of Turkish. Lewis suggests that foreigners should not use this construction since it 'is regarded as alien and is increasingly rare in modern Turkish'. The use of *ki* may be a peculiar type of code-mixing (see chapter 10), triggering a non-Turkish syntactic pattern in speech production, without this pattern really entering the grammar.

(c) Spanish influence on Nahuatl in Mexico

The two cases described show how complex the study of syntactic borrowing is. Another complication is introduced in work by Karttunen (1976) on relative clauses in the Amerindian language Nahuatl, spoken in Mexico by the Aztecs before the Spanish Conquest and since then by various Indian peasant groups. In one variety of modern Nahuatl we find several ways of forming relative clauses. (12) corresponds to the original Nahuatl construction, in which the relative clause is embedded without a particle or pronoun:

(12)   inon tlacatl ica   oni-hua Cuauhnahuac cualli tlahtohua
      that person him-with I-went Cuernavaca   well-able speaks

      Mexica-tlahtolli
      Mexican speech
      'That person I went to Cuernavaca with speaks Nahuatl well.'

In (13), a construction of more recent date, a question word (here *tlen* 'which') is put at the beginning of the relative clause:

(13)   onicnexti in tonin   **tlen**   otimopolhui ye yalhua
      I-it-found the money which you-lost   yesterday
      'I found the money which you lost yesterday.'

It cannot be excluded that the innovation in (13) is due to Spanish influence. In Spanish many relative clauses are formed with a question word. That the influence must be indirect is also clear, however: in the specific case of (13) Spanish would have the conjunction *que* rather than a question word:

(14)   Yo encontré la plata **que** tu perdiste ayer.
      'I found the money that you lost yesterday.'

Furthermore, sometimes Nahuatl speakers introduce a deictic element rather than a question word into the initial position of the relative clause, and this innovation cannot be due to Spanish. Karttunen (1976) concludes, with respect to (12) and (13), that under the influence of Spanish something has been *added* to Nahuatl, but that nothing in Nahuatl has changed. (12) remains a perfectly productive construction.

(d) English influence on Quebec French?
To turn now to a language more familiar perhaps to many readers, it is often said that Quebec French is gradually changing under the influence of English. A striking example according to many newspaper editorialists is a type of preposition stranding: (15a) is used in popular Quebec French instead of (15b), and the source for the innovation would appear to be the English equivalent paraphrase in (16):

(15)   a.   la fille **que** je sors **avec**
      b.   la fille **avec qui** je sors
(16)   the girl **that** I go out **with**

Bouchard (1982) has argued persuasively against English influence, however. First of all, we find similar constructions already in the French of the fourteenth century. Second, several modern popular dialects in France, far away from English influence, also show the phenomenon of stranding. Third, related phenomena appear in other Romance languages, which suggests that it is a possibility inherent in the Romance language family itself. In addition, stranding in English is possible with almost all prepositions, and in French it is limited to phonologically strong prepositions. Hence the contrast between English (17) and impossible Quebec French (18):

(17) the guy I talked to
(18) * le gars que j'ai parlé **à**

Bouchard goes on to show that the construction in (15a) should not be treated by itself, but is part of a complex set of phenomena which can be analysed in a unified way as a simple distinction between Standard French and popular Quebec French.

(e) Spanish influence on Bolivian Quechua

Many scholars have assumed without question that Bolivian Quechua relative clauses such as the one in (19), replacing the original structure as in (20), are the result of borrowing from Spanish (Schwartz, 1971):

(19) riqsi – ni warmi – ta (pi – **chus** chay – pi hamu – ša – n)
      know 1 woman **acc** who **dub** that **loc** come **prog** 3)
      'I know the woman who is coming there.'

(20) (Chay – pi hamu –ša – q) warmi – ta riqsi ÷ ni
      that **loc** come **prog ag** woman **acc** know 1
      'I know the woman coming there.'

(In these examples **1** = first person, **acc** = accusative case, **dub** = dubitative marker, **loc** = locative, **prog** = progressive, **3** = third person)

    In (19) the relative clause is introduced by a question word, *pi* 'who', follows the antecedent noun *warmi* 'woman', and has a tensed verb. In (20) the relative clause precedes the antecedent noun, is marked with the agentive suffix *-q*, and has no tense and person marking. In both ways (19) is more like Spanish than (20), and the dialect of (20) has borrowed a great many words from Spanish. The case for borrowing would seem very strong then.

    Lefebvre (1984) argues, however, that there is no reason to assume borrowing here. Already in the oldest Quechua texts available to us, dating from the middle of the sixteenth century and almost certain not to show Spanish influence (the Spanish Conquest took place in 1532), we find a correlative structure as in (21):

(21) **ima** – hina kawsa – **nki**, chay – hina wañu –**nki**
      what like live 2 that like die 2
      'The way you live, that way you will die.'

The first clause modifies an element in the second clause, and the two clauses are coordinated. Like (19), the modifying clause is introduced by a question word and has person marking. What makes (19) different from (21) is that in (19) the modifying clause can be *embedded*. This possibility is due, according to Lefebvre, to the fact that in (19) there is a particle *-chus* attached to the question word, and that particle has come to function as the marker of a conjunction in Cochabamba Quechua, as a result of developments entirely independent of Spanish. The only thing not explained through developments internal to Quechua is the fact that in (19) the relative clause *follows* the antecedent. Perhaps here the general shift to SVO word order (which *is* perhaps related to Spanish influence at the same time as being motivated internally) may have stimulated the shift to antecedent noun–relative clause order, or direct Spanish influence may be involved.

(f) Summary

From cases such as the ones presented, and they are representative of the literature on the subject, it is hard to reach an unambiguous conclusion. Perhaps the fairest thing to say is that they do not support the 'bag of tricks' view, but that syntactic borrowing may take place as an internally motivated evolution (perhaps only superficially) going in the direction of the forms of another language. All the cases involving relative clauses where something like syntactic borrowing, however superficial, seems to have occurred (Turkish, Nahuatl and Quechua) would be cases of the fifth scenario, imitation of a prestige language pattern. A task for further research would be to develop a more general perspective on what kinds of grammatical elements or structures can be borrowed through what scenario.

13.3 Grammatical borrowing and linguistic change

The phenomenon of grammatical borrowing is first of all a special kind of linguistic change: there is one phase in which a particular feature does not occur, and a later phase in which it does occur. The only thing that makes grammatical borrowing different from other types of change is that the cause stipulated for it is the presence of the borrowed feature in another grammatical system in the linguistic environment. Not just the presence of another grammatical system, for there could be types of linguistic change due to language contact (in the wider sense) which are not cases of grammatical borrowing: one such case would be language loss and language death where there is reduction or simplification of a linguistic system without necessarily the adoption of features of the dominant language. This process was sketched in chapter 4.

When we place grammatical borrowing in the general context of a theory of linguistic change, a good way of organizing this is Weinreich, Herzog and Labov's discussion of the five problems that a theory of language change faces (1968):

(22) – the constraints problem
   – the transition problem
   – the embedding problem
   – the actuation problem
   – the evaluation problem

Different aspects of these problems have in fact been dealt with in various chapters throughout this book.

The *constraints* problem concerns the way in which linguistic structure restricts the type of change that is possible within a given language. This issue was addressed in the introduction to this chapter in terms of the 'systems' view and the 'bag of tricks' view. From our discussion of relative clauses it transpired that most changes are motivated internally, but that they may be in the direction of another language.

The *transition* problem concerns the intermediate steps in the process of change. With respect to grammatical borrowing, the most immediate problem related to transition has to do with the degree of integration of a foreign item or structure into a language. From the Turkish example with *ki* it is clear that there may be a 'borrowed syntax' present in the grammar, with a clearly separate status, and subject to rejection by purist grammarians. This 'borrowed separate syntax' is perhaps related to the phenomenon of code mixing, discussed in chapter 10.

The *embedding* problem concerns the way in which changes are embedded both within the overall linguistic structure, and within the speech community. What are the repercussions of a particular change? The linguistic aspects of the embedding problem, for grammatical borrowing, can best be considered together with the constraints problem: the overall linguistic system in fact imposes the constraints. The social aspects of the embedding problem have to do with the way a particular grammatical influence winds its way through the speech of the different social groups that constitute a speech community. Clearly a more articulated set of scenarios would be necessary to deal with this aspect of the embedding problem.

The *actuation* problem relates to the issue of how a particular linguistic change, which starts out with individual speakers, is generalized within the speech community. As such the actuation problem reflects a general issue in the social sciences: the *agglomeration* problem, to which we referred in chapter 1. How can we translate descriptions of individual behaviour into the language needed to describe group behaviour?

Finally, there is the *evaluation* problem, which involves the way that speakers react to the different languages or linguistic varieties in their community. We have dealt with this problem at considerable length in chapter 2 on language and identity. An interesting example for us here is the case of relativization in Quebec: it is the perception of preposition stranding ('la fille que je sors *avec*') as due to English which makes it a stigmatized construction, while the construction has an independent motivation within varieties of French grammar.

One thing that becomes clear from this more sociolinguistic way of looking at language change is that the question posed at the beginning of this chapter: can languages borrow rules of grammar?, may not receive a straightforward answer. Perhaps a crucial determining factor is the type and degree of language contact. Even if we conclude that in standard situations of linguistic change such as most of the cases surveyed in section 13.2, grammatical borrowing remains a rather superficial phenomenon, we will see in chapter 15 on pidgins and creoles that in cases of drastic restructuring of linguistic systems, as with creoles, grammatical borrowing may be by no means exceptional.

Further reading

Two good books on linguistic change are Lightfoot's *Principles of diachronic syntax* (1979, advanced) and Aitchison's *Language change: progress or decay* (1981, introductory). For those who can read French there is a special issue 'Grammaires en contact' of the *Revue Québécoise de Linguistique* (1983).

14   Lexical borrowing

It is hard to imagine a language that has not borrowed words from some other language, just as there is no culture that has developed entirely from scratch. At the same time it is amazing how this simple fact of linguistic life is hard to accept for the speakers of the language involved. English-speaking people tend to scoff at the purist policies of some sectors of the French government, aimed at blocking the wave of foreign, mostly English, words entering into French usage. Nonetheless, linguistic purism is extremely widespread and enjoys popular support in most countries. Since vocabulary, as we noted in chapter 11, is perhaps the most visible part of a language, lexical borrowing is perceived as affecting the language in its very being.

This chapter is devoted to the complex phenomenon of lexical borrowing. We begin by presenting a typology of borrowing phenomena. Then, in section 14.2, we look at social and cultural determinants of borrowing: why does one language take words from another one? A third issue is the grammatical conditions under which borrowing can take place. We conclude with some further issues about the relation between borrowing and other phenomena, in section 14.4.

14.1 Typology

In the simplest case, a word is borrowed as a whole: both sound and meaning. If this was the only possibility, not much would need to be said. Many other possibilities of lexical borrowing occur, however, forcing us to develop a more systematic approach. The most complex typology of borrowing is due to Haugen (1950), who has managed to systematize a hitherto rather confusing terminology. The primary distinction introduced is the one between *importation* and *substitution*. Importation involves bringing a pattern into the language, substitution involves replacing something from another language with a native pattern. When a Spanish speaker says:

(1) Dáme un **wheesky** 'Give me a whisky'

He has *imported* the English morpheme 'whisky' into Spanish, but inside that morpheme *substituted* the Spanish sound *-ee* for English *-i*. Using this distinction and applying it to the various levels of analysis of structuralist linguistics, Haugen comes up with the following types of borrowings:

(i) *Loanwords*: morphemic importation without substitution. This is the most common kind, such as the use of the word *chic* in English. Within the category of loanwords, we may then distinguish cases where there has been substitution at the phonemic level (phonologically adapted loans) from those where this has not been the case.

(ii) *Loan blends*: morphemic substitution as well as importation. This class includes 'hybrids' such as Dutch *soft-ware* **huis** from *soft-ware* **house**.

(iii) *Loan shifts*: morphemic importation without substitution. Here only a meaning, simple or composite, is imported, but the forms representing that meaning are native. A well-known example of a loan shift is German *Wolkenkratzer*, French *gratte-ciel*, and Spanish *rasca-cielos*, all based on English *sky-scraper*. But when the meaning is simple we can also find cases of a loan shift. This is also sometimes called a loan translation. In Dutch the verb *controleren* means mostly 'to check', but in recent years it also acquired the English meaning of *control*, 'to have power over'.

From an anthropological perspective, a different basic distinction in lexical borrowing is made by Albó (1970), who distinguished between *substitution* and *addition* of vocabulary. There is substitution if the borrowed item is used for a concept which already exists in the culture, and addition if it is a new concept. If we rephrase Albó's distinction in Haugen's terms, we can say that Albó's substitution is morphemic importation with semantic substitution, and Albó's addition morphemic importation with semantic importation. One distinction very relevant at this point is that between borrowing of *core* and of *non-core* vocabulary. Core vocabulary refers to items basic to a human society such as 'fire', 'hands', 'two', 'daughter'. Non-core items are elements of the very specific material and non-material culture and organization of a group: 'lawnmower', 'dictionary', 'psychiatry'.

A fundamental problem of course for any typology of lexical borrowings is how we distinguish between words that are taken from another language in discourse only accidentally, in which case we speak of *lexical interference* or *nonce borrowings*, and words that become fully integrated into the receptor language. This distinction we take up again in section 14.4.

14.2 Social and cultural determinants

Even though words can be borrowed quite freely in many contact situations, it is clear they don't travel like specks of cosmic dust, by themselves, pushed by unknown forces. Rather, we can generally determine why particular groups of words are borrowed, in other words, what the social and cultural determinants of borrowing are.

We will illustrate the social and cultural determinants of borrowing by looking at a number of different situations in which extensive borrowing has taken place, in different parts of the world. Weinreich (1953) gives a number of reasons why words may be borrowed (cf. also Taber, 1979):

(1) Through cultural influence;
(2) Rare native words are lost and replaced by foreign words;
(3) Two native words sound so much alike that replacing one by a foreign word resolves potential ambiguities;

(4) There is a constant need for synonyms of affective words that have lost their expressive force;
(5) Through borrowing, new semantic distinctions may become possible;
(6) A word may be taken from a low-status language and used pejoratively;
(7) A word may be introduced almost unconsciously, through intensive bilingualism.

Note that reasons (1), (2), (3) and (5) have to do with the referential function of language, and reasons (4) and (6) with the expressive and directive functions. We leave it to the reader to think of yet other reasons for borrowing.

(a) Loanwords in English

After the Anglo Saxon groups had settled here in the fifth century, England underwent two major invasions: by the Norse Vikings and Danes in the eighth, ninth and eleventh centuries, and by French-speaking Viking settlers from Normandy in the eleventh century. These invasions, and the migrations and cultural changes in their wake, transformed and enriched the English vocabulary, if not the language as a whole (Serjeantson, 1968). A parallel influence, from Latin, arrived through the conversion of the country to Christianity, starting in the sixth century. Some Latin was probably assimilated earlier by the raiders and traders along the 'Saxon Shore' of south-east England. Many loanwords are still recognizable as such for people who know French and/or Latin, but what to think of Old English words such as :

(2) **čēap** 'goods, price, market' CHEAP, from Latin *caupo* 'innkeeper, wineseller, tradesman'
   pund 'pound, pint' POUND, from Latin *pondo* 'measure of weight'
   čese, čiēse 'cheese', CHEESE, from Latin *caseus* 'cheese'

Most non-specialists would not recognize these words as 'foreign' in any way, as Serjeantson notes in the preface to her detailed study.

The coexistence of Norse settlers with the Anglo Saxon inhabitants, and the relatedness of Norse and Old English have led to considerable lexical influence, over a period much beyond the original invasions, and affecting different regions in different degrees. Early loans include *husbonda* 'householder, husband' and *wrang* 'wrong'; later we find *skirt* from Norse, which came in addition to 'shirt'.

The greatest number of loans came from French, however. Curiously enough, borrowing from French was limited during the early period of intense contacts between the Normans and the Anglo Saxons. There are a few borrowings, such as *prūd, prūt* 'proud', via French from Vulgar Latin *prōd-is*. In the eleventh and twelfth centuries French itself was used as the language of government and the courts. Only later, when Middle English replaced French as the language of the higher spheres of life, did English have to bear the full burden of referring to a culture that had arisen partly outside of its domain. At that time, words such as *capun* 'capon', *cuntesse* 'countess', and *bēst* 'beast' were introduced. This time is the beginning of the period of the massive introduction of 'learned' vocabulary, a vocabulary that has its own affixation rules and often also morphophonological rules associated with it. In certain respects the English lexicon consists of two parts: 'native' and 'learned'. Some people have claimed that an affix such as *-hood* attaches only to native words:

(3) brother-**hood**

father-**hood**
*chief-**hood**
*prince-**hood**

That this is certainly not the case etymologically is shown by formations with -*hood* on the basis of 'non-native' words, as in *nation-**hood*** and *priest-**hood***.

On the other hand, the affix -***ity*** attaches only to non-native words (exceptions being *nice-**ity*** and *odd-**ity***):

(4) absurd-**ity**
pur-**ity**
*good-**ity**
*red-**ity**

Again, that it is not a purely etymological criterion that counts is demonstrated by examples such as *proud-ity*, which should be grammatical since it is an early Norman loan (as we said above), but is not. In many languages we have this phenomenon of a lexicon with several compartments, that correspond roughly but not completely to differently etymological origins.

There is considerable disagreement between scholars to what extent lexical borrowing was responsible for syntactic borrowing. English underwent enormous changes between Old English and Middle English, for instance in its word order, and came to resemble French more, but whether this change is due to syntactic borrowing remains to be seen.

(b) Comanche in the South Western United States

The way in which the Comanches modified their language when confronted with the white man's colonial expansion is illustrative of many similar Amerindian experiences. Comanche linguistic acculturation has been described in detail by Casagrande (1954/5). After fighting and trading with the French and Spanish in the Spanish Southwest (now part of the United States) throughout the eighteenth century, they were confronted with American settlers soon after the Louisiana Purchase in 1803. The American expansion westward proved too strong for them, and by the middle of the nineteenth century they had lost their tribal autonomy and had become farmers. In analysing the way the Comanches have adapted their language to the changing circumstances Casagrande distinguishes between *primary accommodation*, the use of resources within the language itself, from *secondary accommodation*, the use of resources from other languages. Accommodation is a continuous process, and it takes many forms. Examples of primary accommodation include:

(i) Shifts in meaning of existing words, e.g. the word *tihi.ya*, which originally meant 'deer', came to mean 'horse', and a new word for 'deer' was coined: ʔarikaʔ.

(ii) Newly coined words, e.g.:

(5) na   – taʔ   – ʔai – ki – ʔ
reflexive   with the feet   go   causative   nominalizer
Thing to make oneself go with the feet.
nataʔaikiʔ 'bicycle'

(iii) Descriptive circumlocutory expressions, which function as fixed phrases, to designate less familiar foreign items and which may be made up on the spot.

(6)   ?ohapIti?a –   taka –   sikikamatI
    orange's   brother tastes-sour
    'lemon'

In Casagrande's view, secondary accommodation, borrowing in our terms, takes over when language contact becomes more intense or when the native language is under pressure, purist tendencies being overridden. There are a number of loans both from Spanish and from English in Comanche, many of which are quite old and are not recognized as foreign words by speakers of Comanche. These include:

(7)   po?ro?   'pig, bacon'   Sp. *puerco*
    pihú.ra   'beans, peas'   Sp. *frijoles*
    tehnsé.?   'ten cents'
    ?i.cin ?ecin '(Indian) agent'

In addition to these loans, there are cases of loan translation, only from English, which suggests that this process occurred later in the history of Comanche acculturation. Note that it requires more extensive bilingual knowledge. Examples are:

(8)   pïhïkavïrí.?sari.?   'sheep dog'
    sheep   dog
    ta?ahpi   'Our Father'
    our father

Borrowed here are the meanings of the components of the English compound, and the meaning of the whole.

Casagrande stresses the fact that borrowing in Comanche is a sign of the decline of Comanche itself; this conclusion may be due in part to the Whorfian perspective taken by Casagrande: language is seen as a direct reflection of culture. His pessimism with respect to borrowing may be justified in part for Comanche. A big difference between Comanche and the case of English cited earlier lies of course in the different social position of the two languages; another big difference may be that borrowing is a much easier and less disturbing process when the languages in contact are typologically similar, as was the case with Old English, Norse and French.

(c) Portuguese elements in Japanese

The Portuguese gained entry into Japan in 1542 or 1543, and traded intensively till the complete isolation of Japan started in 1639. Portuguese became in fact a lingua franca, also used by the Japanese when dealing with Dutch, Spanish and English merchants, and has had an influence far beyond the trade with the Portuguese themselves. Since the sixteenth century, there have been over 1000 Portuguese words in use in Japan, half of which refer to Christian religious vocabulary (Kim, 1976):

(9)

	Portuguese	**gloss**
zenchiyo	gentío	a heathen
terouja	teología	theology
resureisan	ressureição	resurrection
karujinaresu	cardinales	cardinal

It is clear from these examples that the Portuguese words have been adapted phonologically: consonant clusters have been broken up, both *l* and *r* are pronounced as *r*, vowels have been adapted, etc. Most borrowings referring to religious terminology have disappeared or have been replaced by Japanese equivalents. What has survived in the modern language is mostly words referring to material culture:

(10) | birodo | velludo | velvet |
pan	pão	bread
jiban/juban	gibão	doublet (garment)
furasuko	frasco	flask

Most or all borrowings into Japanese refer to materials or concepts added to Japanese culture. Hence we find almost exclusively nouns borrowed. When the Portuguese had left, the meaning of some of the terms evolved. The word *juban/jiban* referred originally to a Western type of wear, and now to a Japanese garment. The European style garment is called *shatsu* (derived from English 'shirt'), which is an example of the enormous influence from English since World War II.

(d) English in Costa Rica

It is remarkable how many English elements have entered into Costa Rican Spanish. English influence starts with the influx of Jamaicans in 1871, when the Atlantic–Pacific railway was constructed (Zuñiga Tristan, 1976). Jamaicans kept coming in when the United Fruit Company started exploiting the banana plantations. In a Spanish book with grammatical exercises from 1888 we find the following English expressions:

(11)   clown, high life, meeting
God save the King, God save the Queen
Happy New Year
reporter, self-government
that is the question
time is money

English influence intensified as the Costa Rican economy was integrated more and more into the American sphere of influence; most businesses operated bilingually. An additional source of English influence came from American retired people, gold diggers and adventurers who moved to Costa Rica. The net result is the use of hundreds of English words that are well integrated phonologically. Some examples:

(12) | chinchibí | 'ginger beer' |
espich	'speech'
ensuicharse	'to switch oneself on, to get organized'
odishit	'audit sheet'

At the same time, there is no morphological and syntactic influence to speak of, a minor exception being the use of English genitive *-s* in names of bars, e.g. *Fito's bar*. It is remarkable also to see the degree of morphological adaptation of English loans: in *ensuicharse* an English noun has been turned into a verb and has received a prefix.

(e) French loanwords in Sango

A final example concerns French loanwords in Sango, the lingua franca of the Central African Republic. The language is based on a tribal language, also called Sango, belonging to the Niger–Congo language family. The tribal language underwent geographical expansion, was pidginized as a result (losing most of its morphology and a large part of its lexicon), and later came to serve as a contact language for the French colonizers. Now it is used widely as a second language by speakers of many tribes. Sango has a lot of borrowings from French, particularly in non-core vocabulary (Taber, 1979). These borrowings are motivated in part by the fact that the original vocabulary of the lingua franca Sango was impoverished and that the language lacked morphological resources for 'primary accommodation' (unlike Comanche): French was needed as a source of lexical expansion. The interesting thing, however, is that there are a number of pairs of French–Sango synonyms that function as doublets in the language, including:

(13)
samba	bière	'beer'	NOUNS
mbétí	lettre	'letter'	
ndo	place	'place'	
buba	foutu, ruiner	'ruin'	VERBS
hǫ́	passer	'pass'	
nzoní	bien	'well'	ADJUNCTIVES
kóé	tout	'all'	

Many of these synonyms belong to the core vocabulary. When then did Sango borrow French words in these cases? Through a careful quantitative analysis of different kinds of texts Taber discovered that the French equivalents have an expressive function: they serve as a marker of security, in Taber's interpretation, for young people without very fixed tribal identities.

(f) Summary

We see that borrowing takes place in many different social and cultural contexts: invasions (as in England), conquest and domination by a majority culture (as in Comanche), limited culture contact (Japan), limited immigration and economic dependence (Costa Rica), coexistence in a colonial setting (Sango). In each case the extent, the type and the sociolinguistic effect of borrowing have been different.

14.3 Grammatical constraints

The words of a language are separate elements, of course, but at the same time they are part of a system: the lexicon is itself partly structured and also the context in which the words occur in the sentence imposes structural constraints on borrowing. These constraints manifest themselves in the fact that some categories can be borrowed more easily than others, or at least are borrowed more frequently than others. This was observed as early as the nineteenth century by the Sanskritist William Dwight Whitney (1881), who arrived at the following hierarchy:

(14) Nouns – other parts of speech – suffixes – inflection – sounds

This hierachy was elaborated on by Haugen (1950), using data from Norwegian immigrants in the United States, to include:

(15) Nouns – verbs – adjectives – adverbs – prepositions – interjections – . . .

Nouns are borrowed more easily than verbs, verbs more easily than adjectives, etc.

Independently of Haugen, Singh (1981) came to a comparable hierarchy on the basis of English borrowings in Hindi:

(16)   Nouns – adjectives – verbs – prepositions

On the basis of data from Spanish borrowings in Quechua, Muysken (1981) concluded tentatively that there may be something like the following hierarchy:

(17)   nouns – adjectives – verbs – prepositions – coordinating conjunctions – quantifiers – determiners – free pronouns – clitic pronouns – subordinating conjunctions

The data included, among other things, the following numbers of Spanish words in a given corpus of recorded speech (types, not tokens):

(18)
nouns	221	prepositions	5
verbs	70	interjections	5
adjectives	33	negation	2
sentence adverbs	15	manner adverbs	1
quantifiers	7	greetings	1
conjunctions	6		

Now what do we do with data of this kind? Obviously they cannot be directly used to establish a hierarchy of the type in (14) to (17), since there may be differing amounts of elements of each category available for borrowing. Spanish has many more nouns than verbs, and the fact that three times as many nouns as verbs were borrowed could be interpreted, if we take the *percentage* of elements of a category borrowed, as: verbs are *easier* to borrow than nouns. This conclusion is not very attractive either, since there is a consensus that nouns can be borrowed more easily. If we look at quantifiers, of which seven are borrowed, we could conclude that these elements can be borrowed easiest of all since almost all Spanish quantifiers were borrowed, and so on.

The data in (18) give a distorted picture for yet another reason: *types* are counted, not *tokens*. This makes a big difference, since one word may be used many times. In the Sango corpus studied by Taber 508 French loans accounted for 51 per cent of the types, but for only 7 per cent of the tokens: they are used relatively infrequently. A token analysis of the elements in (18) shows that Spanish nouns are much more frequent than (18) suggests, and elements such as prepositions, adverbs, and quantifiers, much less frequent.

For all these reasons it is not possible to establish hierarchies of borrowing simply by counting elements in a corpus or, worse yet, a dictionary (as we suspect many researchers have done). It is better to think of them as hypotheses that can help us understand the process of lexical borrowing rather than as clear empirical results. What could be the basis for these hypotheses, or, alternatively: how can we explain hierarchies of borrowing, like the ones given above? The most important explanation of course lies in the reasons for borrowing, of which the most important one is to extend the referential function of a language, as was noted in the previous section. Since reference is established primarily through nouns, these are the elements borrowed most easily. More generally, content words (adjectives, nouns, verbs) will be borrowed more easily than function words (articles, pronouns, conjunctions) since the former have a clear link to cultural content and the latter do not.

In some cases, borrowing extends beyond cultural content words, however, and there may well be other constraints on borrowing. It is clear from a number of cases that words which play a peripheral role in sentence grammar: interjections, some types of adverbs, discourse markers, and even sentence coordination markers, are borrowed relatively easily. Note that this is the same class of elements that participates in 'emblematic switching' (see chapter 10), the type of phenomenon halfway between inter-sentential and intra-sentential code switching. What this suggests is that switching and borrowing may to some extent be subject to the same type of constraints: both are difficult when the coherence of the language is disturbed. This coherence may take two forms: *paradigmatic* coherence and *syntagmatic* coherence.

Paradigmatic coherence is due to the tightness of organization of a given subcategory: the pronoun system is tightly organized, and it is difficult to imagine English borrowing a new pronoun to create a second person dual in addition to second person singular and plural. For this reason determiners, pronouns, demonstratives, and other paradigmatically organized words are rarely borrowed. Syntagmatic coherence has to do with the organization of the sentence: a verb is more crucial to that organization than a noun, and perhaps therefore it is harder to borrow verbs than nouns. This line of thinking needs to be explored in more detail, however.

14.4 Borrowing and integration: can we distinguish borrowing from code mixing?

In chapter 10 we discussed code mixing as the use of two languages in one sentence. This is something else, conceptually, than the introduction of foreign vocabulary items into a lexicon. In practice, however, it may not be so simple to distinguish between them. The classical view is that code mixing and borrowing can easily be kept apart: with code mixing the non-native items are not adapted morphologically and phonologically, with borrowing they are. This view is problematic for at least two reasons: first, there may be different degrees of phonological adaptation for borrowed items, second it is not evident that all non-adapted items are clearly cases of code mixing.

A case of phonological adaptation was cited already when we discussed Comanche. This language has regular correspondence rules for the treatment of foreign items: English *b* is realized as *p*, English *l* as *r*. Hence we get *barely* pronounced as *pa.re*? On the other hand, we have cases of non-adaptation such as English *computer* being realized as [kompyuteR] in Dutch, the sequence [pyu] being non-native to Dutch.

Spanish verbs in Quechua can be used to illustrate complete morphological adaptation. The old Spanish verb *parlar* 'to speak' shows up with complete Quechua verbal morphology in expressions such as :

(19) parla – na – ku – n – ku
      speak **rec re   3 plur**
      They speak with each other.
      (here **rec** = reciprocal, **re** = reflexive, **3** = third person, and **plur** = plural)

All Spanish verbs borrowed into Quechua pattern this way, but with nouns we see that sometimes morphological integration is not complete in that affixes, particularly plural and diminutive, are borrowed as well, and may even appear on Quechua nouns in Bolivian Quechua:

(20) a. polisiya – s – kuna
      police **plur** **plur**
      Policemen.

  a.′ runa – s – kuna
      man **plur** **plur**
      Men.

  b. kaball – itu
      horse   **dim**
      Little horse.

  b.′ rumi – tu
      stone   **dim**
      Little stone.

      (Here **plur** = plural, **dim** = diminutive)

In (20a) and (20b) Spanish nouns are borrowed with a Spanish plural (**-s**) and diminutive (**-itu**) suffix respectively, and in (20a′) and (20b′) we see that these suffixes have been incorporated into Quechua morphology to such an extent that they show up on Quechua nouns as well. The incorporation involves adaptation as well: the Spanish plural affix is used conjoinedly with the Quechua plural affix **-kuna**, and the diminutive affix has undergone a complex morphological adaptation to fit into the Quechua pattern.

Casagrande (1954/5) cites a number of linguists working on Amerindian languages in support of the idea that the integration of borrowed elements is a very gradual process, which may take generations, and that the degree of integration is generally indicative of the time of borrowing. A similar result was obtained in work by Poplack and Sankoff among Puerto Ricans in New York City (1984). Using very sophisticated statistical techniques to analyse elicited lexical reponses of both adult and child informants, they found that the integration of English items into Puerto Rican Spanish takes place only gradually, along four parameters: frequency of use, displacement of native language synonyms, grammatical integration and acceptability by the speaker.

All the relevant evidence points to the fact, then, that it is not possible to distinguish individual cases of code-mixing from not-yet-integrated borrowings on the basis of simple diagnostic criteria. The distinction has a theoretical basis in the difference between use of two systems (mixing) and adoption into a system (borrowing): further work on the implications of this difference will need to yield new operational criteria.

14.5 Lexical borrowing and language death

We saw above that sometimes massive borrowing has taken place without serious implications for the language involved (e.g. English) and that in other cases borrowing was a sign of language attrition and death (Comanche). In chapter 4 we saw that language death involves heavy lexical borrowing. We can easily explain, of course, the different fate of the two languages with reference to the difference in social cirumstances in medieval England and in the American South West, but the question is whether it is visible in the languages involved as well. For this we need to look at the structure of the language which has borrowed heavily. An example of a stretch of

Quechua text with several Spanish borrowings, at the same time indicative of language attrition phenomena, is the following fragment from the life story of a construction worker in Ecuador:

(21) chi – bi – ga ña   **once años** ri – rka – ni kitu – mun
     that LO TO already   eleven years go PA 1 Quito to

     ña **dos sucres gana** – sha ashta chi – bi – ga – ri   **casi**
     alr. two sucres earn   SUB more that LO TO EMPH almost

     casi dos sucres – ka **gana** – sha **cada** p'uncha **dos sucres**
     almost two sucres TO earn   SUB each day   two sucres

     gana – sha ña   kitu – bi ña – mi, ña **seis** hapi – sha ashta
     earn   SUB alr. Quito LO alr. AF alr. six grab SUB more

     contento – ri   na
     happy   EMPH alr.

Then there already eleven years old I went to Quito, earning already two sucres, more, there earning almost almost two sucres earning every day two sucres, in Quito already, already taking in six even happier.

What makes this fragment show signs of attrition is not the amount of Spanish borrowing; much more fluent speakers also use many Spanish words. Rather it is the lack of variation in the Quechua syntax: one main clause followed by a number of adverbial clauses marked with -*sha*, and in the Quechua morphology: only a few suffixes are used, and the frequent use *ña* almost as a hesitation marker, which betray that the story is told by somebody who does not know a great deal of Quechua any more. Heavy lexical borrowing often goes together with low esteem for the receptive language involved, and low esteem, as we have shown in chapter 4, is often related to processes of language loss and death.

Further reading

The literature on lexical borrowing combines an immense number of very interesting case studies (of which only a few could be summarized here) with the absence of general works. Haugen's work (1950, 1953, 1956, 1973) is perhaps the most general starting point. A convenient volume of collected articles of Haugen's is *The Ecology of Language* (1972). In addition, journals such as the *International Journal of American Linguistics* and *Anthropological Linguistics* have published a large number of articles on borrowing.

15 Pidgins and creoles

Not only can one language take over elements from another one, but an entirely new language can emerge in situations of language contact. In the field of pidgin and creole studies the main question is how, exactly, a new language can come into existence, and how the particular grammatical properties of the newly formed languages, pidgins and creoles, are related to the way in which they have emerged. A pidgin language is generally defined as a strongly reduced linguistic system that is used for incidental contacts between speakers of different languages, and that is the native language of nobody (DeCamp, 1971). A creole language is a language that emerged when the pidgin had acquired native speakers.

The following parable, drawn from Bickerton (1975), can perhaps clarify the subject matter of creole studies: A natural disaster destroys a family's home. They have to give it up, but they can re-use a part of the debris to build up a new house. The resulting structure is something quite different from their original dwelling, and, due to the lack of material, also something rather different perhaps from what they had in mind. The children of the family grow up in it and for them it is the only house that they know. Years later some bigwig comes along, who remarks that the house is not at all the way it should be and produces the construction plans that should have been used for the rebuilding of the house. A possible remodelling, however, has to take place while the family remains in the house. When the important visitor is gone again a quarrel breaks out concerning the question of whether, and if so, how the remodelling must be carried out. Finally everybody does something different. Whole rooms remain in their original state, others undergo drastic divisions.

This is the end of the parable. When you put 'language' for 'house', something like the following picture emerges (partially based on work by Mühlhäusler, 1974):

(a) The disaster that can lead to the emergence of a jargon (a very primitive contact system) and subsequently of a more stable pidgin generally involves the migration of a socially dominated group. This can be in the context of slavery or of contract labour in a colonial setting. Often trade carried out on an unequal footing is involved. A group of people is forced by circumstances to develop a new communication system, to be used with foreigners who speak a different language.

Even though various languages are involved at the moment in which a jargon or pidgin emerges, the vocabulary of a pidgin generally derives from one language: the language that is socially or politically dominant in the original contact situation. Because most pidgins have resulted from the European (and later more generally

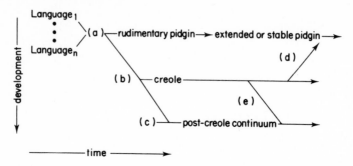

Figure 15.1   Schematic representation of the development of pidgins and creoles

Western) colonial expansion, starting in the fifteenth century, the vocabulary of most pidgins and creoles is derived from a European language (Portuguese, English, Spanish, French, Dutch). Later we will return in more detail to the question of how pidgins have emerged.

(b) When, after the original social disruption that led to the pidgin, a new society comes into existence, for instance on the Caribbean plantations in the colonial era or in the islands in the Pacific in this century, then children from newly formed marriages may grow up with only the pidgin as their linguistic model, and the pidgin may expand into a full natural language that becomes their native language. In this way a number of creole languages have emerged, which are distinguishable from non-creole languages by having emerged out of a pidgin. The figure above leaves open the possibility that the creole derives from a rudimentary pidgin, from a stable pidgin, or even from a structurally expanded pidgin. Below we return to these three options. In some cases, the pidgin never becomes a creole, but simply continues to evolve in the direction of the original target, and the result may be a slightly deviant version of the target, the upper end of a post-pidgin continuum.

Three things can happen to a creole language once it has come into existence. In the first place the language can remain as it is, without undergoing further major changes. In the second place the creole can lose its status as a native language and only continue as a lingua franca, used as a means of communication between different language groups (repidginization) (d). The latter has happened in some African communities, in Senegal and Guinea-Bissau, where the original colonial situation leading to the emergence of the creole has disappeared. Finally, a creole can develop further in the direction of the socially dominant language, so that a post-creole continuum emerges (e).

In this chapter we will first give a brief survey of some of the most important pidgin and creole languages and their geographical distribution, then, in section 15.2, sketch the development of creole studies and outline the theories that have been proposed to account for the genesis of pidgin and creole languages. Section 15.3 is devoted to the social position of creole languages and their speakers.

15.1 A survey of pidgin and creole languages

Most pidgins still in existence are spoken in Africa and in the Pacific Ocean. A few are

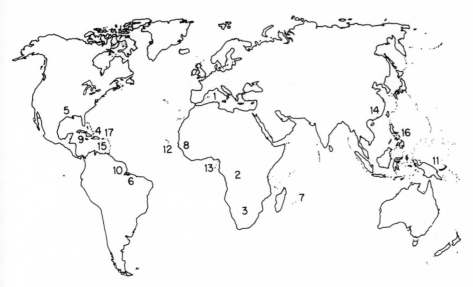

Map 15.1 The geographical distribution of some pidgin and creole languages

indicated on Map 15.1. In Africa pidgins primarily serve for communications between members of different tribes. Fanakalo, for instance, is used by workers in the mines in South Africa when they speak with a co-worker from another tribal background and sometimes with white or Indian South Africans.

Creole languages we find predominantly in the Caribbean, in West Africa, in the Indian Ocean, and in the Far East. The most well-known of the creoles are spoken, of course, by the descendants of the black slaves who were brought to the Caribbean to work in the sugar plantations. We will only mention a few pidgins and creoles here, organized by the origin of their vocabulary, and numbered corresponding to their location on the map. Furthermore, we will give examples for some pidgins and creoles to illustrate their grammatical properties.

Pidgins:
1. *Lingua Franca* (a pidgin with predominantly Romance vocabulary once spoken in the Mediterranean, but extinct since about 1900). An example of a Lingua Franca sentence would be:

(1) mi star contento mirar per ti
     me be happy   see   for you
     'I am glad to see you.'

This pidgin has several remarkable features: (a) the personal pronouns *mi* and *ti* are derived from the object pronouns of the Romance languages; (b) there is no person or tense marking, and the verb *star* is derived from the infinitive; (c) the object is indicated with *per*.

2 *Lingala* (spoken in Zaire)
3 *Fanakalo* (spoken in South Africa, but generally looked down upon). An example of this pidgin, related to Zulu, is:

(2) nikạ mina lo manzi
     Give me water.

Creoles with a vocabulary derived mainly from French:

4 *Haitian Creole* (spoken by five million Haitians living both on the island and in exile in France, the United States, and Canada.)

   Haitian has a syntax rather different from that of French, as can be seen when comparing (3) and (4):

(3) mwe pa **te** gegne yu gros fõ **sifi** pu m **te** reponsable
     I not **ant** have a big fund suffice for I **ant** responsible
     'I don't have money enough to be responsible.'

     (**ant** = anterior tense)

(4) Je n'ai pas assez d'argent pour être responsable.
     (same as (3))

Example (3) illustrates two important properties of many creoles: the verb is not inflected, like in pidgins such as Lingua Franca, but there is a tense marker: anterior tense *te*. In addition, there is a secondary verb, called 'serial verb', *sifi*, in the main clause, marking the degree of the action of the main verb.

5 *Louisiana French Creole*
6 *Cayenne or French Guyana Creole*
7 *Seychelles Creole.* On the Seychelles Islands, as well as on Mauritius, and Reunion a number of French creoles are spoken that in some way resemble the French creoles of the Caribbean, but in other ways are different.

Creoles with a vocabulary derived mainly from English:

8 *Krio* (spoken in Sierra Leone)
9 *Jamaican*
10 *Sranan* (the most important creole language spoken in Surinam). The following Sranan sentence, taken from Sebba (1984) illustrates the extensive use made of serial verbs in that language:

(5) a **fringi** a tiki   **trowe**   **naki** Kofi
     he fling the stick throw away hit Kofi
     He threw the stick at Kofi and it hit him.

11 *Tok Pisin* (a language spoken in New Guinea which is at the same time a pidgin with many speakers in the rural interior and a creole with mostly young native speakers in the urban areas). Again, its basic vocabulary is from English, but it has developed structures which are not like those of English, and only resemble those of the Caribbean creoles in some respects:

(6) mipela ol we i save kaikai saksak   em i putim long mipela tasol
     we **plur** that **pm** know eat sago   he **pm** put to us only
     'We who are used to eating sago, they gave it to us only.'

This example illustrates several important features: the use of *we* 'where' as a relative clause marker is found in the Caribbean as well. Plural is marked somewhat variably, with a separate particle *ol* 'all'; several Caribbean creoles also have plural particles.

Notice the verb of Portuguese origin *save* 'know', a remnant perhaps of a Portuguese nautical and trading language, used in Asia and the Pacific. Finally, there is reduplication in *kaikai* 'eat' and *saksak* 'sago', characteristic of many pidgins. (The particle *i* in (6) marks the predicate phrase, starting with the verb.)

Creoles with a vocabulary derived mainly from Portuguese:
12 *Cape Verdean Portuguese Creole*
13 *Sao Tomense Creole.* On the islands in the Gulf of Guinea we find creole languages which resemble those of the Caribbean. These islands played an important role in the slave trade. The following example illustrates the serial verb *da* 'give', used for benefactives and datives:

(7) komplá sapé **da** mu
     buy   hat give me
     'Buy a hat for me.'

14 *Macao Portuguese Creole* (now the most important centre of Portuguese creole in the Far East, of what was once a long chain of trading centres)

Creoles with a vocabulary derived mainly from Spanish:
15 *Papiamentu* (a creole with a mixed Portuguese and Spanish origin spoken on Aruba, Bonaire and Curaçao). A final feature of many creole languages that we would like to illustrate is the 'doubling' of the verb at the beginning of the sentence to emphasize the action:

(8) ta **traha** e homber-nan ta **traha**
     foc work the man **plur asp** work
     'The men are really working.'

The first particle *ta* is a focus marker, the second a tense/aspect marker. Note also the use of a plural particle, *nan*, which is identical to the third person plural pronoun, a feature of many creole languages.

16 *Philippine Spanish Creole*

Creoles with a vocabulary derived mainly from Dutch:
17 *Negerhollands* (now practically extinct, but once flourishing on the US Virgin Islands)
18 *Afrikaans* (it is a controversial question whether the language spoken by the descendants of the Boers is a creole; for many local whites the notion that Afrikaans has a 'mixed' origin is repugnant).

The examples that we have given of different creoles give a general idea of what the grammar of these languages is like. The following features are either shared by all of them or quite general:

(a) fairly rigid subject–verb–object word order;
(b) invariable pronouns;
(c) no inflectional morphology and little derivational morphology;
(d) preverbal particles marking negation, tense, mood and aspect;
(e) the use of serial verbs to modify the meaning of the main verb or to mark extra arguments;

(f) fronting and doubling of the verb to mark emphasis;

(g) the use of a conjunction meaning 'for' to mark purposive and infinitive clauses;

(h) the use of the third-person plural pronoun to mark plural of the noun phrase;

(i) the use of focus particles at the beginning of the sentence to mark a constituent focused on.

15.2 Creole studies

Creole studies originated as a systematic domain of studies over a century ago, with Schuchardt's (1842–1927) important series of articles, that started as an attempt to account for a more complex set of developments in the history of the Romance languages than was possible in the Neogrammarian preoccupation with the regularity of sound change. Hesseling's (1880–1941) work originally started out explaining the developments in Greek, from the early dialects through *koine* Greek in the Roman Empire to Byzantine and modern Greek. Both scholars found it necessary to allow for more complex types of linguistic change: mixture, simplification, reanalysis, and the complexity of their analyses characterizes modern creole studies as well.

Until 1965 the field remained rather marginal. Creole languages were studied by a few enthusiastic historical linguists, fieldworkers with an adventurous bent, and folklorists ahead of their time. Now the study of creole languages has moved to the centre of linguistic research, a research programme with universalist theoretical ambitions, half-way between theoretical linguistics and sociolinguistics. Reasons for this development are manifold, but include political and cultural emancipation of certain parts of the Caribbean (most notably Jamaica), the interest in Afro-American culture, particularly in the US, and a partial reorientation of linguistic research.

An important group of creole researchers wants to focus on the dynamic and variable aspects of language (Sankoff, 1980; Bickerton, 1975, 1981). While linguists working inside the paradigm of generative grammar tend to abstract away from variation and change, focusing on the universal and invariable aspects of linguistic competence, creolists have tended to put variation and change at the centre of attention: only by studying the changes that languages undergo and the ways in which these changes are manifested in the speech community can we find out about the phenomenon of language. Pidgin and creole languages form a natural field of study for these researchers, exactly because they present so much internal variation and because they tend to change so rapidly.

The main research effort in creole studies has been to find a principled explanation for the genesis of the languages involved. There is an implicit assumption that the creole languages share some property that calls for an explanatory theory. What property this is depends on the theory concerned. Any of three properties are assumed to play a role:

(1) Creole languages are assumed to be more *alike* than other languages. As we saw, creoles share many structural features, and many researchers believe that these resemblances can neither be simply due to the similarity between the languages of Western Europe nor accidental.

(2) Creole languages are assumed to be more *simple* than other languages. There is a wide-spread belief that creole languages are not just morphologically, but also syntactically and phonologically simpler than other languages.

(3) Creole languages are assumed to have more *mixed* grammars than other languages. Many people have drawn parallels between language and biology, when thinking of creoles. It is assumed that creole languages, in the same way as many of their speakers, have 'mixed' African, European, and in some cases Amerindian ancestry. The languages are thought to be simply European vocabulary coupled with African syntax and semantics.

These assumptions, even though none of them has been conclusively shown to be correct until this day, play a role in the various theories of creole genesis around in the field. In fact, these theories have been developed in part to explain the assumed similarity, simplicity and mixedness of the creole languages. Table 15.1 presents these theories in relation to the three underlying assumptions:

Table 15.1 Theories accounting for special properties of the creole languages

	Alike	Simple	Mixed
Semantic transparency (Seuren, 1983; Seuren and Wekker, 1986)	x	x	
Imperfect second language Learning (Valdman, 1981; Andersen, ed., 1983)	(x)	x	
Baby talk (Naro, 1978)	(x)	x	
Afro-Genesis (Alleyne, 1980)	x		x
Portuguese monogenesis (Whinnom, 1971)	x	(x)	
Bio-programme (Bickerton, 1981)	x	x	
Atlantic mono-source (Hancock, 1986)	x		
Common social context (Sankoff, 1980)	x	(x)	

We will briefly sketch the eight theories listed in Table 15.1.

The *semantic transparency* theory is not a full-blown genesis theory, but simply claims that the structure of creole languages directly reflects universal semantic structures. That they are alike, in this view, is due to the fact that the semantic structures are universal. They are simple because the semantic structures involved are fairly directly mapped onto surface structures, without a very complex transformational derivation. An example of this may be the fact that creole languages have separate tense/mood/aspect particles, which reflect separate logical operators, rather than incorporating tense, etc. into the inflection of the verb.

In the *imperfect second-language learning* theory creoles are the crystallization of some stage in the developmental sequence (cf. chapter 8). The speakers of the proto-creole simply did not have sufficient access to the model, and had to make up an approximative system. In this view the fact that creoles are simple is due to the simplification inherent in the second-language learning process. Thus we find in the intermediate stages of the acquisition of several European languages (e.g. English and German) a phase in which there is an invariant negative element in preverbal position:

(9) a. he **no** eat   'He doesn't/won't eat'
     b. ich **nix** arbeite   'I don't/didn't work'
         (compare standard German: ich arbeite nicht)

This same feature was mentioned before as characteristic of many creoles.

For some adherents of the imperfect second-language learning theory the creole languages are also similar, and this similarity is due to universal properties of the learning process.

The *baby-talk* theory is similar to the imperfect second-language learning theory in postulating that creoles are frozen (i.e. fossilized) stages in the second-language learning sequence. The difference lies in the fact that in the baby-talk theory the responsibility for the simplification is shifted from the learners to the speakers of European languages, who provide a simplified model (cf. our discussion of foreigner talk in chapter 12). The similarity between creoles would be due, in this view, to universal properties of the simplified input. The type of evidence adherents of the baby-talk hypothesis are looking for thus includes simplifications made by native speakers, not by learners, in pidgins. An example may be, as noted by Schuchardt (1909), the use of infinitives in Lingua Franca. Many people have pointed to the use of reduplicated forms in the creoles as evidence for the baby-talk hypothesis, but reduplication turns out to be a very general process in the creoles, while in baby-talk it has only very specific functions.

The *Afro-genesis* model really deals only with the creole languages spoken in the Atlantic region: West Africa and the Caribbean, and postulates that these languages have emerged through the gradual transformation of the West African languages spoken by the slaves under influence of the European colonial languages. The similarity of the languages involved is due, in this model, to the fact that they share the same African language features, mixed together with features of European languages. One thing shared by the Caribbean creoles and the languages of West Africa is the serial verb construction that we encountered in examples (3), (5) and (7) above. The Afro-genesis model would claim, in this particular case, that the African serial verbs have been relexified with European vocabulary, keeping their original meaning. Thus an African serial verb 'surpass' was relexified with the English adverb *more*, to yield Sranan *moro*, in examples such as (10a):

(10) a. Harold bigi **moro** mi
          Harold big surpass me
          'Harold is bigger than me.'
      b. angri **moro**   mi
          hunger overpower me
          'I am hungry.'

The form *moro* can also occur as a verb by itself, as in (10b). The main problem with the Afro-genesis model in its strict version is the large number of structural differences between West African languages and creoles. What must be claimed to save the hypothesis is that in the process of relexification syntactic and semantic properties of European lexical items were introduced as well, for instance that *more* is an adverb in English. Thus we also have a construction more like English in Sranan, equivalent to (10a):

(10) c. Harold bigi **moro liki** mi
      Harold big more than me
      'Harold is bigger than me.'

The *Portuguese mono-genesis* model has undergone several modifications. Crucial to all of these is the existence of a trade language with a predominantly Portuguese lexicon, used in the fifteenth through seventeenth centuries by traders, slave raiders and merchants from different countries throughout the then emerging Third World. The mono-genesis theory holds that the slaves learned this language in the slave camps, trading forts and slave ships of their early captivity, and then took this language, really no more than a jargon, with them to the plantations. The different creole languages as we know them are based on this jargon, but have replaced the Portuguese words by words from other European languages. The supposed similarity of the creole languages is due of course to the underlying Portuguese jargon, and their simplicity to the simplicity of this jargon.

The *bio-programme* theory claims that creoles are inventions of the children growing up on the newly formed plantations. Around them they only heard pidgins spoken, without enough structure to function as natural languages, and they used their own innate linguistic capacities to transform the pidgin input from their parents into a fully-fledged language. Creole languages are similar because the innate linguistic capacity applied is universal, and they are simple because they reflect the most basic language structures. One feature shared by all creoles that would derive from the innate capacity is the system of pre-verbal tense/mood/aspect particles. Not only do they seem limited in the creole languages to a particular set of meanings, but they also seem to occur in a particular order, illustrated in (11) and (12), taken from the now almost extinct language Negerhollands:

(11) yu **sa ka:** dra: di a yu han   MOOD ASPECT
     you **md asp** carry this in your hand
     'You shall have carried this in your hand'

(12) aster am **ha ka:** sit ne:r   TENSE ASPECT
     after he **tns asp** sit down
     'After he had sat down . . .'

The system of tense/mood/aspect particles, its interpretation, and its ordering would directly reflect universal aspects of the human language capacity.

The *Atlantic mono-source* hypothesis limits itself to the English-based creole languages of the Atlantic, and is based on the idea that there was an English jargon or pidgin spoken along the coast of West Africa that later formed the primary source for a wide range of English-based creoles. Clearly, common features of these creoles are then assumed to be due to this early pidgin.

The *common social context* theory, finally, adopts a strictly functional perspective: the slave plantations imposed similar communicative requirements on the slaves, newly arrived and without a common language, in many cases. The common communicative requirements led to the formation of a series of fairly similar makeshift communicative systems, which then stabilized and became creoles. To give an example of what this may imply, consider the following Tok Pisin relative clause, from an article by Sankoff and Brown (Sankoff, 1980):

(13) boi **ia** (i   gat fiftin yias **ia**) em i   tokim ologeta
     boy   **pm** have fifteen years   he **pm** tell   all

liklik boi ol   i   kam
little boy **plur pm come**
'This boy, who was fifteen years old, he told all the little boys to come.'
(**pm** = predicate marker, **plur** = plural)

Sankoff and Brown show that the marker *ia* 'here' has developed out of a conversational focus marker into a grammatical element setting a relative clause apart from the matrix clause.

15.3 The social position of the creole languages

The previous section may give one the impression that creole studies is only a very academic discipline, preoccupied with the abstract properties of the human mind or with who spoke what to whom where in the seventeenth century. There is a whole other side to the field as well, however, involved with the creole speaking communities in the post-colonial world. This is not the place to go into the literary developments in the creole languages, which have been remarkable, but in several ways the issues raised in earlier chapters of this book are of relevance to creoles as well. We will discuss a few here.

(a) The relation creole–standard in the Caribbean
We mentioned in the introduction to this chapter that sometimes the creole language continues to evolve in the direction of the European colonial language to which it is related, so that decreolization occurs and a post-creole continuum arises. This last development can occur when (a) in a given area the original dominant European language that has supplied the vocabulary for the creole continues to be spoken, (b) there is a certain amount of social hierarchy and mobility within the creole-speaking community itself. Under these two conditions some speakers of the creole adopt different features from the colonial language, so that a series of linguistic varieties emerges intermediate between the creole and the colonial language. These varieties can not be clearly kept apart, and speakers often are capable of producing and understanding a sizeable portion of varieties from the continuum. As Figure 15.1 indicates, the post-creole continuum may be formed in various stages in the development of the creole: both right at the beginning, e.g. when the slave plantation had creole-speaking overseers and other intermediate ranks, or much later, after the abolition of slavery. For individual cases, it remains a controversial matter when exactly decreolization set in, and why there seems to be a post-creole continuum in some communities but not in others. Thus, the Jamaican sociolinguistic situation has often been described in terms of a continuum (DeCamp, 1971) and this seems to be the case in many English-speaking areas. For French creoles, several scholars have argued that there is no continuum, but rather a sharp division between the creole *patois* and regional standard French (cf. Lefebvre, 1975, who argues this for Martinique). The same division exists in those societies where the creole spoken and the standard or

colonial language are in no way related: the Dutch Antilles (Papiamentu and Dutch), Surinam (Sranan and Dutch), and St Lucia (French Creole and English).

(b) Creoles in education
When there is a continuum there is a great deal of variation in creole speech, and this causes considerable problems for the school. First, when the decision is made that creole languages will serve as a medium of instruction (see chapter 6 on bilingual education), difficult decisions will have to made about the *type* of creole used. Will one choose a very 'deep' creole, which links the children to their heritage, or a more 'adapted' creole, that may be closer to what the children actually hear spoken around them? Second, when the decision is made not to use the creole in school, perhaps because it is close enough to the standard, there is often the problem of finding out how much the children know of the standard. The fact that they speak a creole which may resemble the standard only superficially in some cases makes this a very complicated issue. Third, in almost all cases the creole has very low prestige, and is not even recognized as a separate language with a positive identity associated with it. Creole speakers use 'bush talk', a 'dialect', a *'patois'*. Pejorative names for creole languages, such as Taki-Taki for Sranan, abound. The implication of this is that it is very difficult to involve creole languages in language planning and in educational programmes. It is not impossible, however, as the example of Aruba, Bonaire and Curaçao shows, where Papiamentu is rapidly acquiring a more important position in the educational system and is being standardized.

(c) Pidgins and creoles in the industrial West
So far the discussion has had a Third World flavour: plantations, tropical islands, trade routes, and Map 15.1 did nothing to correct this impression. Still, there are pidgins and creoles spokes in the industrial West as well. First, speakers of creoles have participated in the migration from the Third World to the industrial centres: New York, Toronto, London, Amsterdam, and Paris are full of creole speakers, and are confronted with the same educational problems as the Caribbean itself. Second, pidgins may be emerging in the urban centres of the West itself, according to some scholars. Schumann (1978) has labelled the incomplete learning of English by Central American migrants in the United States (see chapter 8) 'pidginization' and various German scholars have analysed the varieties of German spoken by socially isolated migrant workers in German cities such as Berlin as pidgins (Klein and Dittmar, 1979). An example of the 'pidginized' German discovered is:

(14) oytə fil koleega kuədsawaitə, nich arwaitə, pasia.
     Heute viel Kolega kurzarbeit nicht arbeiten pasieren.
     Now many colleagues short-terms jobs, not work, walk around.

(Cited from Heidelberger Forschungsprojekt 'Pidgin Deutsch' 1975; spelling slightly adapted.)

Is this a pidgin? The utterance is put together as a string rather than as a true structural whole, there is little or no inflection, the vocabulary used is quite limited.

Not enough is known about the sociolinguistic aspects of these varieties, and the word pidgin is not well enough defined, to make this a meaningful issue. It is clear in any case that many of the features of the speech of migrant workers recall those of the 'tropical' pidgins, and that the fact that they can be studied now makes them of particular importance to pidgin and creole studies. Most importantly, of course, the fact that something like pidgins emerge at all is indicative of the deep social divisions within the industrial West.

In some sense this chapter on pidgins and creoles provides a fitting conclusion to this book, which has tried to explore how different groups of speakers react, in different settings, to the confrontation with other languages. Creoles emerged out of one of the most inhumane and in many cases cruellest institutions in history: plantation slavery. It is a sign of human energy and of the human capacity for language and communication that in these circumstances languages emerged and flourished.

Further reading

The primary source for documentation about the different pidgins and creoles is still Reinecke's monumental bibliography (1975). There are a number of introductions to pidgins and creoles on the market, including Hall (1966), Todd (1974), Mühlhäusler (1986), and in French Valdman *Le creole: structure, statut, origine* (1979), in addition to a large number of collections of articles of which Hymes (1971) *Pidginization and creolization of languages*, Valdman's *Pidgin and Creole Linguistics* (1977b), and Valdman and Highfield (1981) *Theoretical issues in pidgin and creole linguistics* are the most general in scope. There are a few important books by single authors: Bickerton's *Roots of Language* (1981) contains a highly readable exposition of the bioprogramme hypothesis, Alleyne's *Comparative Afro-American* (1981) documents the Afro-genesis hypothesis with a wealth of detail, and Sankoff's *The Social Life of Language* (1980) has documented the view that the structure of creole languages is finely attuned to their functional requirements with a number of insightful articles.

References

Aitchison, J. 1981: *Language change: progress or decay*. London.

Alatis, J.E. (ed.) 1980: *Georgetown University Round Table on Languages and Linguistics* (Current issues in bilingual education), Washington, DC.

Albert, M.L. and Obler, L.K. 1978: *The bilingual brain; Neuropsychological aspects of bilingualism*. New York.

Albó, X. 1970: *Social Constraints on Cochabamba Quechua*, Dissertation Series no. 19, Latin American Studies Program, Cornell University, Ithaca, New York.

Alisjahbana, S.T. 1974: Language policy, language engineering and literacy in Indonesia and Malaysia. In Fishman 1974, 391–416.

Alleyne, M.C. 1980: *Comparative Afro-American*. Ann Arbor, Mich.

Andersen, R. (ed.) 1983: *Piginization and creolization as second language acquisition*. Rowley, Mass.

—— 1984: *Second languages; A cross-linguistic perspective*. Rowley, Mass.

Anderson, A.B. 1979: The survival of ethnolinguistic minorities: Canadian and comparative research. In Giles and Saint-Jacques 1979, 67–85.

Appel, R. 1983: Buitenlanders en taalbehoud. *Tijdschrift voor Taal- en Tekstwetenschap* 3, 152–66.

—— 1984: *Immigrant children learning Dutch; sociolinguistic and psycholinguistic aspects of second language acquisition*. Dordrecht.

—— 1987: The language education of immigrant workers' children in the Netherlands. In Cummins and Skutnabb-Kangas 1987 (forthcoming).

Appel, R., Everts, H. and Teunissen, J. 1986: Het Leidse onderwijsexperiment. *Moer*, 141–48.

Apte, M.L. 1976: Multilingualism in India and its sociopolitical implications: An overview. In O'Barr and O'Barr 1976, 141–64.

—— 1979: Region, religion and language: Parameters of identity in the process of acculturation. In McCormack and Wurm 1979, 367–75.

Arthur, B. *et al.* 1980: The register of impersonal discourse to foreigners: Verbal adjustments to foreign accent. In Larsen-Freeman, D. (ed.), *Discourse analysis in second language research*. (Rowley, Mass.), 111–24.

Baetens Beardsmore, H. 1982: *Bilingualism: Basic principles*. Clevedon.

Barkowski, H. *et al.* 1976: Sprachhandlungstheorie und Deutsch für ausländische Arbeiter. *Linguistiche Berichte* 45, 42–55.

Bender, M.L. *et al.* 1976: *Language in Ethiopia*. London.

Bentahila, A. 1983: *Language attitudes among Arabic-French bilinguals in Morocco*. Clevedon.

Bentahila, A. and Davies, E.E. 1983: The syntax of Arabic-French code-switching. *Lingua* 59, 301–30.

188 References

Ben-Zeev, S. 1977: The influence of bilingualism on cognitive development and cognitive strategy. *Child Development* 48, 1009–18.
Bickerton, D. 1975: *Dynamics of a creole system*. Cambridge.
— 1981: *Roots of language*. Ann Arbor, Mich.
Birnbaum, H. 1966: On typology, affinity and Balkan linguistics. *Zbornik za filologiju i linguistiku* IX, Novi Sad.
Blom, J.-P. and Gumperz, J.J. 1972: Social meaning in linguistic structure: code-switching in Norway. In Gumperz J.J. and Hymes D. (eds), *Directions in sociolinguistics* (New York), 407–34.
Bloomfield, L. 1933: *Language*. New York.
Bouchard, D. 1982: Les constructions relatives en français vernaculaire et en français standard: étude d'un paramètre. In Lefebvre, C. (ed.), *La syntaxe comparée du français standard et populaire: approches formelle et fonctionelle* (Quebec: Office de la langue française), 103–34.
Brown, R. and Gilman, A. 1960: The pronouns of power and solidarity. In Sebeok, T.A. (ed.), *Style in language* (Cambridge, Mass.), 253–76.
Burling, R. 1959: Language development of a Garo and English speaking child. *Word* 15, 45–68.
Cairns, H.S. and Cairns, C.E. 1976: *Psycholinguistics: A cognitive view of language*. New York.
Canfield, K. 1980: A note on Navajo-English code-mixing. *Anthropological Linguistics* 22, 218–20.
Carlock, E. 1979: Prosodic analysis of two varieties of Buffalo English. *The fifth LACUS forum*, 377–82.
Carlock, E. and Wölck, W. 1981: A method for isolating diagnostic linguistic variables: The Buffalo ethnolects experiment. In Sankoff, D. and Cedergren, H. (eds), *Variation Omnibus* (Edmonton), 17–24.
Carranza, M. and Ryan, E.B. 1975: Evaluative reactions of bilingual Anglo and Mexican American adolescents toward speakers of English and Spanish. *International Journal for the Sociology of Language* 6, (= *Linguistics* 166), 83–104.
Carrow, Sister M.A. 1957: Linguistic functioning of bilingual and monolingual children. *Journal of Speech and Hearing Disorders* 22, 371–80.
Casagrande, J.B. 1954/55: Comanche linguistic acculturation. *International Journal of American Linguistics* 20, 140–57, 217–37; 21, 8–25.
Chan, M-C. *et al.* 1983: Input/output switch in bilingual code switching. *Journal of Psycholinguistic Research* 12, 407–16.
Charry, E. 1983: Een sociolinguistische verkenning van Surinaams-Nederlands. In Charry, E. *et al.* (eds) *De talen van Suriname* (Muiderberg), 138–61.
Child, I.L. 1943: *Italian or American? The second generation in conflict*. New Haven.
Christian, C.C. Jr 1976: Social and psychological implications of bilingual literacy. In Simoës 1976, 17–40.
Civian, T.W. 1965: *Imja suscestvitel'noje v balkanskich jazykach*. Moscow.
Clark, H.H. and Clark, E.V. 1977, *Psychology and language; An introduction to psycholinguistics*. New York.
Clyne, M. 1967: *Transference and triggering*. The Hague.
— 1972: *Perspectives on language contact; Based on a study of German in Australia*. Melbourne.
— 1982: *Multilingual Australia*. Melbourne.
Cobarrubias, J. and Fishman, J.A. (eds), 1983 *Progress in language planning*. Berlin.
Cohen, A.D. 1975: *A sociolinguistic approach to bilingual education; Experiments in the American South-West*. Rowley, Mass.
— 1976: The case for partial or total immersion education. In Simoës 1976, 65–89.
Cohen, M. 1956: *Pour une sociologie du langage*. Paris.
Cooper, R.L. (ed.) 1982: *Language spread; Studies in diffusion and social change*. Bloomington.
Crama, R. and Van Gelderen, H. 1984: Structural constraints on code-mixing. University of Amsterdam, Institute for General Linguistics.

Crawford, J. 1983: Speaking Michif in four Métis communities. *Canadian Journal of Native Studies* 3.1, 47–55.

Cummins, J. 1976: The influence of bilingualism on cognitive growth: A synthesis of research findings and explanatory hypotheses. *Working Papers on Bilingualism* 9, 1–43.

—— 1978: Educational implications of mother tongue maintenance in minority-language groups. *The Canadian Modern Language Review* 34, 395–416.

—— 1979: Linguistic interdependence and the educational development of bilingual children. *Review of Educational Research* 49, 222–51.

—— 1980: The construct of language proficiency in bilingual education. In Alatis 1980, 81–103.

—— 1984: *Bilingualism and special education.* Clevedon.

Cummins, J. and Gulutsan, M. 1974: Some effects of bilingualism on cognitive functioning. Ms. University of Alberta, Edmonton.

Cummins, J. and Skutnabb-Kangas, T. (eds) 1987: *Education of linguistic minority children.* (Tentative title; forthcoming). Clevedon.

Cziko, G.A. and Troike, R.C. 1984: Contexts of bilingual education: International perspectives and issues. *AILA Review-Revue de l'AILA* 1, 7–33.

Dalbor, J.B. 1959: The English phonemes /š/ and /č/: A hearing and pronunciation problem for speakers of Spanish learning English. *Language Learning* 9, 67–73.

Darcy, N.T. 1953: A review of the literature on the effects of bilingualism upon the measurement of intelligence. *Journal of Genetic Psychology* 82, 21–57.

Davis, F.B. 1967: *Philippine language-teaching experiments.* Quezon City.

Day, R.R. 1982: Children's attitudes toward language. In Ryan and Giles 1982, 116–31.

DeCamp, D. 1971: Introduction: The study of pidgin and creole languages. In Hymes 1971, 13–39.

Defoe, D. 1719: *Robinson Crusoe.* London: Everyman's Library, 1977 edn.

De Houwer, A. 1983: Some aspects of the simultaneous acquisition of Dutch and English by a three year old child. *Nottingham Linguistic Circular* 12, 106–29.

Del Rosario, G. 1968: A modernization-standardization plan for the Austronesian-derived national languages of Southeast Asia. *Asian studies* 6, 1–18.

Diaz, R.M. 1983: Thought and two languages: The impact of bilingualism on cognitive development. *Review of Research in Education* 10, 23–54.

Diebold, A.R. Jr 1968: The consequences of early bilingualism in cognitive development and personality formation. In Norbeck, E. *et al.* (eds.), *The study of personality; An interdisciplinary appraisal* (New York), 218–45.

Diem, W. 1974: *Hochsprache und Dialect im Arabischen.* Wiesbaden.

Di Sciullo, A-M., Muysken, P. and Singh, R. 1986: Government and code-mixing. *Journal of Linguistics* 22, 1–24.

Dittmar, N. 1981: 'Regen bisschen Pause geht' - more on the puzzle of interference. Unpublished manuscript, Freie Universität Berlin.

Dolson, D.P. 1985: The effects of Spanish home language use on the scholastic performance of Hispanic pupils. *Journal of Multilingual and Multicultural Development* 6, 135–55.

Dorian, N.C. 1978: The fate of morphological complexity in language death: evidence from East Sutherland Gaelic. *Language* 54, 590–609.

Doron, E. 1983: On a formal model of code-switching. *Texas Linguistic Forum*, 22, 35–59.

Dressler, W. and Wodak-Leodolter, R. 1977: Language preservation and language death in Brittany. *Linguistics* 191, 33–44.

Dulay, H.C. and Burt, M.K. 1974a: Errors and strategies in child second language acquisition. *TESOL Quarterly* 8, 129–36.

—— 1974b: Natural sequences in child second language acquisition. *Language Learning* 24, 37–53.

Dulay, H., Burt, M and Krashen, S. 1982, *Language Two*, New York and Oxford.

Duškova, L. 1969: On sources of errors in foreign language learning. *International Review of Applied Linguistics* 7, 11–33.

Eastman, C.M. 1983: *Language planning; An introduction*. Novato, Cal.

Edelsky, C. *et al.* 1983: Semilingualism and language deficit. *Applied Linguistics* 4, 1–22.

Edwards, J. 1981: The context of bilingual education. *Journal of Multilingual and Multicultural Development* 2, 25–44.

Edwards, J.R. 1982: Language attitudes and their implications among English speakers. In Ryan and Giles 1982, 20–33.

Ehri, L.C. and Ryan, E.B. 1980: Performance of bilinguals in a picture-word interference task. *Journal of Psycholinguistic Research* 9, 285–302.

Ellis, H.C. 1965: *The transfer of learning*. New York.

Ellis, R. 1985, *Understanding second language acquisition*, Oxford.

Ervin-Tripp, S.M. 1967: An Issei learns English. *Journal of Social Issues* 23, 2, 78–90.

Ervin, S. and Osgood, C.E. 1954: Second language learning and bilingualism. Supplement to the *Journal of Abnormal and Social Psychology* 49, 139–46.

Extra, G. and Mittner, M. (eds) 1984: *Studies in second language acquisition by adult immigrants*. Tilburg: Tilburg University.

Faerch, C. and Kasper, G. 1983: Plans and strategies in foreign language communication. In Faerch, C. and Kasper, G. (eds), *Strategies in interlanguage communication* (London and New York), 20–60.

Fasold, R. 1984: *The sociolinguistics of society*. Oxford.

Feinstein, M.H. 1980: Ethnicity and topicalization in New York City English. *International Journal for the Sociology of Language* 26, 15–24.

Fellman, J. 1974: The role of Eliezer Ben Yehuda in the revival of the Hebrew language: An assessment. In Fishman 1974, 427–55.

Ferguson, C.A. 1959: Diglossia. *Word* 15, 325–40.

— 1968: Language development. In Fishman *et al.* 1968b, 27–36.

— 1971: Absence of copula and the notion of simplicity: A study of normal speech, baby talk and pidgins. In Hymes 1971, 141–50.

— 1975: Towards a characterization of English Foreigner Talk. *Anthropological Linguistics* 17, 1–14.

Ferguson, C.A. and DeBose, C. E. 1977: Simplified registers, broken language, and pidginization. In Valdman 1977b, 99–125.

Fishman, J.A. 1965: Who speaks what language to whom and when? *Linguistics* 2, 67–88.

— (ed.) 1968: *Readings in the sociology of language*. The Hague.

— 1972: Domains and the relationship btween micro- and macro-sociolinguistics. In Gumperz, J.J. and Hymes, D. (eds), 1972, 435–53.

— (ed.) 1974: *Advances in language planning*. The Hague.

— 1977: Language and ethnicity. In Giles 1977, 15–57.

— (ed.) 1978: *Advances in the study of societal multilingualism*. The Hague.

Fishman, J.A. *et al.* 1966: *Language loyalty in the United States*. The Hague.

Fishman, J.A. *et al.* 1968a: *Bilingualism in the Barrio*. New York.

— (eds) 1968b: *Language problems of developing nations*. New York.

Flores, N. de la Zerda and Hopper, R. 1975: 'Mexican-Americans' evaluations of spoken Spanish and English. *Speech Monographs* 42, 9–98.

Fonck, A. 1984: Klagen en aanbieden in het Nederlands: Pragmatische problemen voor de Engelsman? University of Amsterdam.

Gaarder, B.A. 1979: Language maintenance or language shift. In Mackey, W.F. and Andersson, T. (eds), *Bilingualism in early childhood* (Rowley, Mass.), 409–34.

Gal, S. 1979: *Language shift: Social determinants of linguistic change in bilingual Austria*. New York.

Gardner, R.C. 1979: Social psychological aspects of second language acquistion. In Giles, H. and St Clair, R. (eds), *Language and social psychology* (Oxford), 193–220.

Gardner, R.C. *et al.* 1976: Second-language learning: A social-psychological perspective. *The Canadian Modern Language Review* 32, 198–213.

Gardner, R.C. and Lambert, W.E. 1972: *Attitudes and motivation in second-language learning*. Rowley, Mass.

Giles, H. 1973: Accent moblity: a model and some data. *Anthropological Linguistics* 15, 87–105.

—— (ed.) 1977: *Language, ethnicity and intergroup relations*. London.

Giles, H. *et al*. 1973: Towards a theory of interpersonal accommodation through language: Some Canadian data. *Language in Society* 2, 177–92.

Giles, H. *et al*. 1977: Towards a theory of language in ethnic group relations. In Giles 1977, 307–49.

—— 1979: Prestige speech styles: The imposed norm and inherent value hypothesis. In McCormack and Wurm 1979, 589–96.

Giles, H. and Saint-Jacques, B. 1979: *Language and ethnic relations*. Oxford.

Glazer, N. 1978: The process and problems of language maintenance. In Lourie, M.A. and Conklin, N.T. (eds), *A pluralistic nation: The language issue in the United States* (Rowley, Mass.), 32–43.

Glazer, N. and Moynihan, D.P. 1975: Introduction. In Glazer, N. and Moynihan, D.P. (eds), *Ethnicity; Theory and Experience* (Cambridge, Mass.), 1–26.

Grosjean, F. 1982: *Life with two languages*. Cambridge, Mass. and London.

Guboglo, M. 1979: Linguistic contacts and elements of ethnic identification. In McCormack and Wurm 1979, 359–65.

Guitarte, G.L. and Quintero, R.T. 1974: Linguistic correctness and the role of the Academies in Latin America. In Fishman 1974, 315–68.

Gumperz, J.J. 1976: The Sociolinguistic Significance of Conversational Code-switching. Working Papers of the Language Behavior Research Laboratory No. 46, University of California, Berkeley.

—— 1977: Sociocultural knowledge in conversational inference. In Saville-Troike, M. (ed.), *Twenty-eighth Annual Round Table Monograph Series on Language and Linguistics* (Washington, DC), 191–211.

—— 1982a: *Discourse strategies*. Cambridge.

—— (ed.) 1982b: *Language and social identity*. Cambridge.

Gumperz, J.J. *et al*. 1982: Thematic structure and progression in discourse. In Gumperz 1982b, 22–56.

Gumperz, J.J. and Hernández-Chavez, E. 1971: Bilingualism, bidialectism and classroom interaction. In Gumperz, J.J. *Language in social groups* (Stanford), 311–39.

—— 1975: Cognitive aspects of bilingual communication. In Hernández-Chavez E. *et al*. (eds), *El lenguaje de los Chicanos* (Arlington), 54–64.

Gumperz, J.J. and Hymes, D. (eds) 1972: *Directions in sociolinguistics*. New York.

Hakuta, K. 1976: A case study of a Japanese child learning English as a second language. *Language Learning* 26, 321–51.

Hakuta, K. and Diaz, R.M. 1985: The relationship between degree of bilingualism and cognitive ability: A critical discussion and some new longitudinal data. In Nelson, K.E. (ed.), *Children's Language* Vol. 5. (Hillsdale, NJ), 319–44.

Hall, R.A. Jr 1966: *Pidgin and creole languages*. Ithaca.

Halliday, M. *et al*. 1964: *The linguistic sciences and language teaching*. London.

Hancock, I.F. 1986: The domestic hypothesis, diffusion, and componentiality. In Muysken P. and Smith N. (eds), *Substrata versus universals in creole genesis* (Amsterdam), 71–102.

Hartford, B. *et al*. (eds) 1982: *Issues in international bilingual education*. New York and London.

Hatch, E. 1977: An historical overview of second language acquisition research. In Henning C. A. (ed.), *Proceedings of the Los Angeles second language research forum*. (Los Angeles), 1–14.

Hatch, E. 1983: *Psycholinguistics; A second language perspective*. Rowley, Mass.

Haugen, E. 1950: The analysis of linguistic borrowing. *Language* 26, 210–32.

— 1953: *The Norwegian language in America: A study in bilingual behavior*, 2 vols. Philadelphia.

— 1956: *Bilingualism in the Americas: A bibliography and research guide*. Alabama.

— 1966a: *Language conflict and language planning: The case of modern Norwegian*. Cambridge, Mass.

— 1966b: Linguistics and language planning. In Bright, W. (ed.), *Sociolinguistics* (The Hague), 50–71.

— 1971: Instrumentalism in language planning. In Rubin and Jernudd 1971, 281–92.

— 1972: *The ecology of language*. Stanford.

— 1973: Bilingualism, language contact and immigrant languages in the United States: A research report 1956–70. In Sebeok, T.A. (ed.), *Current Trends in Linguistics* Vol. 10, (The Hague and Paris), 505–91.

Haugen, E. *et al.* (eds) 1981: *Minority languages today*. Edinburgh.

Heller, M. 1984: Ethnic relations and language use in Montreal. In Wolfson, N. and Manes, J. (eds), *Language of inequality* (New York).

Hesseling, D.C. 1899: *Het Afrikaansch; Bijdrage tot de geschiedenis der Nederlandsche taal in Zuid-Afrika*. Leiden.

— 1905: *Het Negerhollands der Deense Antillen; Bijdrage tot de geschiedenis der Nederlandse taal in Amerika*. Leiden.

Hewitt, R. 1982: White adolescent creole users and the politics of friendship. *Journal of Multilingual and Multicultural Development* 3, 217–32.

Hill, J. and Hill, K. 1977: Language death and relexification in Tlaxcalan Nahuatl. *Linguistics* 191, 55–68.

Hornby, P.A. (ed.) 1977: *Bilingualism: Psychological, social and educational implications*. New York.

Hymes, D.H. (ed.) 1971: *Pidginization and creolization of languages*. Cambridge.

— 1972: On communicative competence. In Pride and Holmes 1972, 269–93.

Ianco-Worrell, A. 1972: Bilingualism and cognitive development. *Child Development* 43, 1390–400.

Jakobson, R. 1931: Über die phonologischen Sprachbünde. In *Travaux du Cercle Linguistique de Prague* IV (reprinted in *Selected Writings* 1962 (The Hague), 137–43).

— 1960: Linguistics and poetics. In Sebeok, T. (ed.), *Style in Language* (Cambridge, Mass.) 350–77.

Jaroviskij, A. 1979: On the lexical competence of bilingual children of kindergarten age groups. *International Journal of Psycholinguistics* 6, 3, 43–57.

Jones, B.L. 1981: Welsh: Linguistic conservation and shifting bilingualism. In Haugen *et al.* 1981, 40–51.

Jones, W.R. and Stewart, W.A. 1951: Bilingualism and verbal intelligence. *British Journal of Psychology* 4, 3–8.

Joshi, A. 1981: Some problems in processing sentences with intrasentential code switching. Unpublished manuscript, University of Texas Parsing Workshop.

Karttunen, F. 1976: Uto-Aztecan and Spanish-type dependent clauses in Nahuatl. In Steever, S. *et al.* (eds), *Papers from the parasession on diachronic syntax* (Chicago), 150–58.

Kelly, L.G. (ed.) 1969: *Description and measurement of bilingualism: An international seminar*. Toronto.

Kessler, C. and Quinn, M.E. 1980: Positive effects of bilingualism on science problem-solving abilities. In Alatis 1980, 295–308.

Kiers, T. 1982: Taalvaardigheid en taalbehoefte van Marokkaanse jongeren in Nederlands. MA thesis, Institute for General Linguistics, University of Amsterdam.

Kim, T.W. 1976: *The Portuguese element in Japanese*. Coimbra.

Klavans, J.L. 1983: The syntax of code-switching: Spanish and English. (Unpublished manuscript).

Klein, W. and Dittmar, N. 1979: *Developing grammars; The acquisition of German syntax by foreign workers*. Berlin.

Kloss, H. 1966: German-American language maintenance efforts. In Fishman 1966, 206–52.

Kolers, P. 1963: Interlingual word associations. *Journal of Verbal Learning and Verbal Behavior* 2, 291–300.

— 1966: Reading and talking bilingually. *American Journal of Psychology* 79, 357–76.

Krashen, S.D. 1973: Lateralization, language learning, and the critical period: Some new evidence. *Language Learning* 23, 63–74.

Krashen, S.D. *et al.* 1979: Age, rate and eventual attainment in second language acquisition. *TESOL Quarterly* 13, 573–82.

Kremnitz, G. 1981: *Das Okzitanische, Sprachgeschichte and Soziologie.* Tübingen.

Labov, W. 1972: *Sociolinguistic patterns.* Philadelphia.

Lado, R. 1957: *Linguistics across cultures.* Ann Arbor, Mich.

Lalleman, J.A. 1986: *Dutch language proficiency of Turkish children born in the Netherlands.* Dordrecht.

Lambert, W.E. 1967: A social psychology of bilingualism. *Journal of Social Issues* 23, 2, 91–109.

— 1977: The effects of bilingualism on the individual: Cognitive and sociocultural consequences. In Hornby 1977, 15–27.

— 1978: Some cognitive and sociocultural consequences of being bilingual. In Alatis, J.E. (ed.), *Georgetown University Round Table on Languages and Linguistics* (Washington, DC), 214–29.

Lambert, W.E. *et al.* 1958: The influence of language acquisition context on bilingualism. *Journal of Abnormal and Social Psychology* 56, 239–44.

Lambert, W.E. *et al.* 1960: Evaluative reactions to spoken language. *Journal of Abnormal and Social Psychology* 67, 617–27.

Lambert, W.E., Anisfeld, M. and Yeni-Komshin, G. 1965: Evaluational reactions of Jewish and Arab adolescents to dialect and language variations. *Journal of Personality and Social Psychology* 2, 84–90.

Lambert, W.E., Havelka, J. and Gardner, R. 1959: Linguistic manifestations of bilingualism. *American Journal of Psychology* 72, 77–82.

Lambert, W.E. and Tucker, G.R. 1972: *Bilingual education of children; The St Lambert Experiment.* Rowley, Mass.

Lance, D.M. 1975: Spanish–English code-switching. In Hernández-Chavez, E. *et al.* (eds), *El lenguaje de los Chicanos* (Arlington) 138–53.

Larson, M.L. *et al.* 1981: Overview of the program of bilingual education in the Peruvian jungle. In Larson and Davis 1981, 37–252.

Larson, M.L. and Davis, P.M. (eds) 1981: *Bilingual education: An experience in the Peruvian Amazonia.* Dallas.

Le Compagnon, B. 1984: Interference and overgeneralization in second language learning: The acquisition of English dative verbs by native speakers of French. *Language Learning* 34, 3, 39–67.

Lefebvre, C. 1979: Quechua's loss, Spanish's gain, *Language in Society* 8, 395–407.

— 1984: Grammaires en contact: définitions et perspectives de recherche. *Revue québécoise de linguistique* 14.1, 11–48.

Lenneberg, E. 1967: *Biological foundations of language.* New York.

Leopold, W.F. 1939–49: *Speech development of a bilingual child: a linguist's record.* 4 vols, Evanston, Ill.

Le Page, R. and Tabouret-Keller, A. 1982: Models and stereotypes of ethnicity and language. *Journal of Multi-lingual and Multicultural Development* 3, 161–92.

Lewis, G. 1972: *Multilingualism in the Soviet Union; Aspects of language policy and implementation.* The Hague.

Lewis, G.L. 1975: *Turkish grammar.* Oxford.

Li, W.L. 1982: The language shift of Chinese Americans. *International Journal for the Sociology of Language* 38, 109–24.

Lieberson, S. 1970: *Language and ethnic relations in Canada.* New York.

Lieberson, S.J. and McCabe, E.J. 1982: Domains of language usage and mother-tongue shift in Nairobi. *International Journal of the Sociology of Language* 34, 83–94.

Lightfoot, D. 1979: *Principles of diachronic syntax*. Cambridge.

Lindholm, K.J. and Padilla, A.M. 1978: Child bilingualism: Report on language mixing, switching and translations. *Linguistics* 211, 23–44.

Lindsay, P.H. and Norman, D.A. 1977: *Human information processing* (second edn), New York.

Linguistics Minorities Project 1985: *The other languages of England*. London.

Lipski, J.M. 1978: Code-switching and the problem of bilingual competence. In Paradis, M. (ed.), *Aspects of bilingualism* (Columbia), 250–64.

Long, M. 1981: Variation in linguistic input for second language acquisition. Unpublished manuscript, School of Education, University of Pennsylvania.

—— 1982: Does second language instruction make a difference? A survey of research. Working Papers of the Department of English as a second language, University of Hawaii 1.2., 93–120.

Loveday, L. 1982a: *The sociolinguistics of learning and using a non-native language*. Oxford.

—— 1982b: Communicative interference: A framework for contrastively analysing L2 communicative competence exemplified with the linguistic behaviour of Japanese performing in English. *International Review of Applied Linguistics* 20, 1–16.

Lowley, E.G. *et al.* 1983: Ethnic activists view the ethnic revival and its language consequences: An interview study of three American ethnolinguistic minorities. *Journal of Multilingual and Multicultural Development* 4, 237–54.

McCormack, W.C. and Wurm, S.A. (eds) 1979: *Language and society; anthropological issues*. The Hague.

McClure, E. 1977: Aspects of code-switching among Mexican-American children. In Saville-Troike, M. (ed.), *28th Annual Round Table Monography Series on Language and Linguistics* (Washington, DC), 93–115.

Mackey, W. 1976: *Bilinguisme et contact des langues*. Paris.

—— 1977: The evaluation of bilingual education. In Spolsky and Cooper 1977, 226–81.

Mackey, W. and Ornstein, J. (eds) 1979: *Sociolinguistic studies in language contact*. The Hague.

McLaughlin, B. 1978: *Second language acquisition in childhood* (second edn, 2 vols, 1984, 1985). Hillsdale, NJ.

Macnamara, J. 1966: *Bilingualism and primary education*.

—— 1967: The bilingual's linguistic performance: A psychological overview. *Journal of Social Issues* 23, 59–77.

—— 1969: How can one measure the extent of a person's bilingual proficiency? In Kelly 1969, 79–97.

—— 1970: Bilingualism and thought. In Alatis, J.E. (ed.), *Report of the twenty-first annual round table meeting on linguistics and language studies* (Washington, DC), 25–40.

—— 1971: Success and failures in the movement for the restoration of Irish. In Rubin and Jernudd 1971, 65–94.

—— 1974: What can we expect from a bilingual programme? *Working Papers on Bilingualism* 4, 42–56.

MacNamara, J. *et al.* 1968: Language switching in bilinguals as a function of stimulus and response uncertainty. *Journal of Experimental Psychology* 78, 208–15.

MacNamara, J. and Kushnir, S.L. 1971: Linguistics independence of bilinguals: The input switch. *Journal of Verbal Learning and Verbal Behavior* 10, 480–87.

Meisel, J. 1975: Ausländerdeutsch und Deutsch ausländischer Arbeiter; Zur möglichen Entstehung eines Pidgin in der BRD. *Zeitschrift für Literaturwissenschaft und Linguisitik* 5, 18, 9–53.

—— 1977: Linguistic simplification: A study of immigrant workers' speech and foreigner talk. In Corder, S.P. and Roulet, E. (eds), *The notions of simplification, interlanguages and pidgins and their relation to second language pedagogy*. (Neuchâtel and Geneva), 88–113.

— 1980: Linguistic simplification. In Felix, S.W. (ed.), *Second language development; Trends and issues* (Tübingen), 13–40.

— 1982: The role of transfer as a strategy of natural second language acquisition/proceeding. Ms. Hamburg University.

Meisel, J. *et al.* 1981: On determining development stages in natural second language acquisition. *Studies in second language acquisition* 3, 109–25.

Meiseles, G. 1980: Educated spoken Arabic and the Arabic language continuum. *Archivum Linguisticum* 11 (new series), 118–48.

Mercer, N. *et al.* 1979: Linguistic and cultural affiliation amongst young Asian people in Leicester. In Giles and Saint-Jacques 1979, 15–26.

Moorghen, P.M. and Domingue, N.Z. 1982: Multilingualism in Mauritius. *International Journal of the Sociology of Language* 34, 51–66.

Morag, S. 1959: Planned and unplanned development in modern Hebrew. *Lingua* 8, 247–63.

Mühlhäusler, P. 1974: *Pidginization and simplification of language*. Canberra.

— 1981: Structural expansion and the process of creolization. In Valdman and Highfield 1981, 19–56.

— 1986: *Pidgins and creoles*. London.

Müller, K. 1934: *Die Psyche des Oberschlesiers im Lichte des Zweisprachen-Problems*. Bonn.

Muysken, P. 1981: Halfway between Quechua and Spanish: the case for relexification. In Highfield, A. and Valdman, A. (eds), *Historicity and variation in creole studies* (Ann Arbor, Mich.), 52–78.

Nadkarni, M.V. 1975: Bilingualism and syntactic change in Konkani. *Language* 51, 672–83.

Nair, K.R. and Virmani, V. 1973: Speech and language disturbances in hemiplegics. *Indian Journal of Medical Research* 61, 1395–403.

Naro, A.J. 1978: A study on the origins of pidginization. *Language* 54, 314–47.

Nishimura, M. 1985: Intrasentential code-switching in Japanese-English. Unpublished doctoral thesis, University of Pennsylvania.

O'Barr, W.M. and O'Barr, J. F. (eds) 1976: *Language and politics*. The Hague.

O'Grady, G.N. 1960: New concepts in Nyanumada: Some data on linguistic acculturation. *Anthropological Linguistics* 2, 1–6.

Oller, J.W. *et al.* 1977: Attitudes and attained proficiency in ESL: A sociolinguistic study of native speakers of Chinese in the United States. *Language Learning* 27, 1–27.

Osgood, C., Suci, C. and Tannenbaum, P. 1957: *The measurement of meaning*. Urbana.

Paradis, M. 1977: Bilingualism and aphasia. In Whitaker, H. and Whitaker, H.A. (eds), *Studies in neurolinguistics* Vol. 3 (New York), 65–121.

— 1980: Language and thought in bilinguals. *The Sixth LACUS Forum 1979*. (Columbia), 420–31.

— 1981: Neurolinguistic organization of a bilingual's two languages. *The Seventh LACUS Forum 1980* (Columbia), 480–94.

Pattanayak, D.D. 1981: *Multilingualism and mother-tongue education*. Delhi.

Paulsen, F. 1981: The recent situation of the Ferring language, the North-Frisian language of the islands Föhr and Amrum. In Haugen *et al.* 1981, 182–88.

Peal, E. and Lambert, W.E. 1962: The relation of bilingualism to intelligence. *Psychological Monographs* 76: 546, 1–23.

Pedrasa, P. Jr *et al.* 1980: Rethinking diglossia. In Padilla, R.V. (ed.), *Theory in bilingual education* (Ypsilanti, Mich.), 75–97.

Penfield, W. and Roberts, L. 1959: *Speech and brain mechanisms*. Princeton.

Pfaff, C. 1979: Constraints on language mixing: intrasentential code-switching and borrowing in Spanish/English. *Language* 55, 291–318.

— 1984: On input and residual L1 transfer effects in Turkish and Greek children's German. In Andersen, R.W. (ed.), *Second languages; A cross-linguistic perspective* (Rowley, Mass.), 271–98.

Philips, S.U. 1972: Participant structures and communicative competence: Warm Springs children in community and classroom. In Cazden, C.B. *et al.* (eds), *Functions of language in the classroom* (New York and London), 370–94.

Pitres, A. 1895: Etude sur l'aphasie. *Revue de Médecine* 15, 873–99.

Pool, P.A.S. 1982: *The death of Cornish*. Penzance.

Poplack, S. 1980: 'Sometimes I'll start a sentence in Spanish Y TERMINO EN ESPANOL': toward a typology of code-switching. *Linguistics* 18, 581–618.

Poplack, S. and Sankoff, D. 1984: Borrowing: the synchrony of integration. *Linguistics* 22, 99–136.

Potter, M.C. *et al.* 1984: Lexical and conceptual representation in beginning and proficient bilinguals. *Journal of Verbal Learning and Verbal Behavior* 23, 23–38.

Pride, J.B. and Holmes, J. (eds) 1972: *Sociolinguistics; Selected readings*. Harmondsworth.

Pulte, W. 1979: Cherokee: A flourishing or obsolescing language? In McCormack and Wurm 1979, 423–32.

Reinecke, J.E. *et al.* 1975: *A bibliography of pidin and creole languages*. Honolulu.

Revil, J.T. *et al.* 1968: A follow-up study of the Rizal experiment relative to achievement in English, Philippino, and content subjects at the end of the second year High School. Philippine Normal College, Manila.

Rindler Schjerve, R. 1981: Bilingualism and language shift in Sardinia. In Haugen *et al.* 1981: 208–17.

Ross, J.A. 1979: Language and the mobilization of ethnic identity. In Giles and Saint-Jacques 1979: 1–13.

Rubin, J. 1968. *National bilingualism in Paraguay*. The Hague.

Rubin, J. *et al.* (eds) 1977: *Language planning processes*. The Hague.

Rubin, J. and Jernudd, B. 1971a: Introduction: language planning as an element in modernization. In Rubin and Jernudd, 1971, XIII–XXIV.

—— (eds) 1971: *Can language be planned?* Honolulu.

Rūke-Dravina, V. 1965: The process of acquisition of apical /r/ and uvular /R/ in the speech of children. *Linguistics* 17, 56–68.

Ryan, E.B. and Carranza, M. 1977: Ingroup and outgroup reactions to Mexican American language varieties. In Giles, 1977, 59–82.

Ryan, E.B. and Giles, H. (eds) 1982: *Attitudes towards language variation*. London.

Saer, D.J. 1923: The effects of bilingualism on intelligence. *British Journal of Psychology* 14, 25–38.

Sanches, M. and Blount, B.G. (eds) 1975: *Sociocultural dimensions of language use*. New York.

Sankoff, D. (ed.) 1978: *Linguistic variation; Models and methods*. New York.

Sankoff, G. 1972: Language use in multilingual societies: Some alternative approaches. In Pride and Holmes 1972, 33–51.

—— 1980: *The social life of language*. Philadelphia.

Saunders, G. 1982: *Bilingual children; Guidance for the family*. Clevedon.

Scarcella, R. and Brunak, J. 1981: On speaking politely in a second language. *International Journal for the Sociology of Language* 27, 59–75.

Schachter, J. 1974: An error in error analysis. *Language Learning* 24, 205–14.

Schuchardt, H. 1890: *Kreolische Studien* IX, Vienna.

—— 1909: Die Lingua Franca. *Zeitschrift für Romanische Philologie* 33, 441–61.

Schumann, J. 1978: *The pidginization process; A model for second language acquisition*. Rowley, Mass.

Schwartz, A. 1971: General aspects of relative clause formation. *Working papers on Language Universals* 6, Stanford University, 139–71.

Scotton, C.M. 1976: Strategies of neutrality: language choice in uncertain situations. *Language* 52, 919–41.

—— 1979: Code-switching as a 'safe choice' in choosing a lingua franca. In McCormack and Wurm 1979, 71–87.

—— 1980: Explaining linguistic choices as identity negotiations. In Giles, H. *et al.* (eds), *Language, Social Psychological Perspectives* (Oxford), 359–66.

Sebba, M. 1984: Serial verbs: something new out of Africa. *York Papers in Linguistics* 11, 271-8.

Sebba, M. and Wootton, T. 1984: Conversational code-switching in London Jamaican. University of York.

Segalowitz, N. 1977: Psychological perspectives on bilingual education. In Spolsky and Cooper 1977, 119-58.

Segalowitz, N. and Gatbonton, E. 1977: Studies of the nonfluent bilingual. In Hornby 1977, 77-89.

Selinker, L. 1972: Interlanguage. *International Review of Applied Linguistics* 10, 209-31.

Serjeantson, M.S. 1968: *A history of foreign words in English*. London. (Original edition, 1935.)

Seuren, P.A.M. 1983: The auxiliary system in Sranan. In Heny, F. and Richards, B. (eds), *Linguistic categories: auxiliaries and related puzzles* Vol. II, (Dordrecht), 219-51.

Seuren, P.A.M. and Wekker, H. 1986: Semantic transparency as a factor in creole genesis. In Muysken, P. and Smith, N. (eds), *Substrata versus universals in creole genesis* (Amsterdam), 57-70.

Shuy, R.W. and Fasold, R.W. (eds) 1973: *Language attitudes: Current trends and prospects*. Washington, DC.

Silverstein, M. 1972: Chinook jargon: language contact and the problem of multi-level generative systems. *Language* 48, 378-406.

Simoẽs, A. Jr (ed.) 1976: *The bilingual child; Research and analysis of existing educational themes*. New York.

Singh, R. 1982: On some 'redundant compounds' in Modern Hindi. *Lingua* 56, 345-51.

Skutnabb-Kangas, T. 1978: Semilingualism and the education of migrant children as a means of reproducing the caste of assembly line workers. In Dittmar, N. *et al.* (eds), *Papers from the first Scandinavian-German symposium on the language of immigrant workers and their children* (Roskilde), 221-51.

—— 1983: *Bilingualism or not: The education of minorities*. Clevedon.

Skutnabb-Kangas, T. and Toukomaa, P. 1976: Teaching migrant children's mother tongue and learning the language of the host country in the context of the socio-cultural situation of the migrant family. University of Tampere, Finland.

Smith, M.E. 1939: Some light on the problem of bilingualism as found from a study of the progress in mastery of English among pre-school children of non-American ancestry in Hawaii. *Genetic Psychology Monographs* 21, 119-284.

Smolicz, J.J. 1983: Modification and maintenance: language among school-children of Italian background in South Australia. *Journal of Multilingual and Multicultural Development* 4, 313-37.

Snow, C.E. *et al.* 1981: The interactional origins of foreigner talk: Municipal employees and foreign workers. *International Journal for the Sociology of Language* 28, 81-91.

Soares, C. and Grosjean, F. 1981: Left hemisphere language lateralization in bilinguals and monolinguals. *Perception and Psychophysics* 29, 599-604.

Sobin, N.J. 1984: On code-switching within NP. *Applied Psycholinguistics* 5, 293-303.

Søndergaard, B. 1981: Decline and fall of an individual bilingualism. *Journal of Multilingual and Multicultural Development* 2, 297-302.

Spencer, J. 1974. Colonial language policies and their legacies in sub-Saharan Africa. In Fishman 1974, 163-75.

Spolsky, B. and Cooper, R.L. (eds) 1977: *Frontiers of bilingual education*. Rowley, Mass.

—— (eds) 1978: *Case studies in bilingual education*. Rowley, Mass.

Stölting, W. 1980: *Die Zweisprachigkeit jugoslawischer Schüler in der Bundesrepublik Deutschland*. Wiesbaden.

Stroop, J.R. 1935: Studies of interference in serial verbal reactions. *Journal of Experimental Psychology* 18, 643-61.

Swain, M. and Lapkin, S. 1982: *Evaluating bilingual education; A Canadian case study*. Clevedon.

Taber, C.R. 1979: French loanwords in Sango: The motivation of lexical borrowing. In

Hancock, I.F. (ed.), *Readings in creole studies*. (Ghent), 189–97.

Taeschner, T. 1983: *The sun is feminine; A study on language acquisition in bilingual children*. Berlin.

Tanner, N. 1967: Speech and society among the Indonesian elite: A case study of a multilingual community. *Anthropological Linguistics* 9, 3, 15–39.

Tauli, V. 1968: *Introduction to a theory of language planning*. Uppsala.

Teitelbaum, H. *et al.* 1975: Ethnic attitudes and the acquisition of Spanish as a second language. *Language Learning* 25, 255–66.

Timm, L.A. 1975: Spanish–English code-mixing: El porque y how-not-to. *Romance Philology* 28, 473–82.

—— 1978: Code-switching in WAR and PEACE. *The fourth LACUS forum*, 239–47.

Todd, L. 1974: *Pidgins and creoles*. London and Boston.

Tosi, A. 1984: *Immigration and bilingual education*. Oxford.

Toukomaa, P. and Skutnabb-Kangas, T. 1977: The intensive teaching of the mother tongue to migrant children at pre-school age. University of Tampere, Finland.

Turner, L.D. 1949: *Africanisms in the Gullah Dialect*. Chicago (reprinted, New York, 1969).

Unesco 1953: *The use of vernacular languages in education*. Paris.

Valdés Fallis, G. 1976: Social interaction and code-switching patterns; A case study of Spanish/English. In Keller, G.D: *et al.* (eds), *Bilingualism in the bicentennial and beyond*. (New York), 53–85.

Valdman, A. 1977a: L'effet de modèles culturels sur l'élaboration du langage simplifié. In Corder, S.P. and Roulet, E. (eds), *The notions of simplification, interlanguages and pidgins and their relation to second language pedagogy* (Neuchâtel and Geneva), 114–31.

—— (ed.) 1977b: *Pidgin and creole linguistics*. Bloomington and London.

—— 1979: *Le créole: structure, statut, origine*. Paris.

—— 1981: Creolization and second language acquisition. In Valdman and Highfield 1981, 297–312.

Valdman, A. and Highfield, A (eds) 1981: *Theoretical issues in pidgin and creole studies*. New York.

Veltman, C. 1983: *Language shift in the United States*. Berlin.

Veronique, D. 1984: The acquisition and use of aspects of French morphosyntax by native speakers of Arabic dialects (North Africa). In Andersen, R.W. (ed.), *Second languages: a cross-linguistics perspective* (Rowley, Mass.), 191–213.

Vildomec, V. 1963: *Multilingualism*. Leyden.

Vorster, J. and Proctor, L. 1976: Black attitudes to 'white' languages in South Africa: A pilot study. *The Journal of Psychology* 92, 103–8.

Vygotsky, L.S. 1962: *Thought and language*. Cambridge, Mass.

Weinreich, U. 1953: *Languages in contact: Findings and problems*. The Hague.

Weinreich, U., Herzog, M.I. and Labov, W. 1968: Empirical foundations for a theory of language change. In Lehmann, W.P. and Malkiel, Y. (eds), *Directions for historical linguistics* (Austin and London), 95–188.

Welmers, W.E. 1974: Christian missions and language policies in Africa. In Fishman 1974, 191–203.

Whinnom, K. 1971: Linguistics hybridization and the 'special case' of pidgins and creoles. In Hymes 1971, 91–115.

Whiteley, W.H. 1969: *Swahili: The rise of a national language*. London.

—— 1971: Some factors influencing language policies in Eastern Africa. In Rubin and Jernudd 1971, 141–58.

—— 1974: Language policies of independent African states. In Fishman 1974, 177–89.

Whitney, W.D. 1881: On mixture in language. *Transactions of the American Philosophical Association* 12, 1–26.

Wode, H. 1981: *Learning a second language; 1. An integrated view of language acquisition*. Tübingen.

Wölck, W. 1973: Attitudes towards Spanish and Quechua in bilingual Peru. In Shuy and Fasold 1973, 129–47.

Woolford, E. 1983: Bilingual code-switching and syntactic theory. *Linguistic Inquiry* 14, 520–36.

Workgroup on foreign workers' language (Werkgroep Taal Buitenlandse Werknemers) 1978: Nederlands tegen buitenlanders. Publ. no. 26 Institute of General Linguistics, University of Amsterdam.

Zobl, H. 1980: The formal and developmental selectivity of L1 influence on L2 acquisition. *Language Learning* 30, 43–57.

—— 1982: A direction for contrastive analysis: The comparative study of developmental sequences. *TESOL Quarterly* 16, 169–83.

Zuñiga, T.V. 1976: *El anglicismo en el habla constaricense.* San José, Costa Rica.

Index to languages and countries

Aboriginal languages 5, 55, 82
Africa 2, 57, 60, 69, 101, 129, 134, 139, 176
  East 52, 56, 134, 135
  West 5, 134, 177, 182, 183
African (North) immigrants (France) 91
African languages 1, 69, 181, 182, 183
Afrikaans 18, 110, 179
Afro-American 180
Albanian 155
America 5, 20, 48
  Central 6, 48, 185
  Central, immigrants (USA) 185
  North 6
  South 48, 51, 54, 130, 131
Amerindian languages 4, 14, 35, 37, 43, 53, 61,
    68, 127, 130, 131, 135, 139, 141, 146, 160,
    167, 168, 173, 181
Amharic 51
Amuesha 61
Anglo Saxon 166, 168
Arabic 34, 74, 87, 101, 132, 139, 147, 148, 149,
    159
  (Egypt) 26
  (Israel) 18
  (Sudan) 57
  Classical (Morocco) 19, 24, 27, 63
  Moroccan 19, 20, 24, 27, 42, 63, 86, 125 (see
    also Moroccan)
  Quranic 25
Aruba (Dutch Antilles) 179, 185
Asia 101, 179
  Central 53, 57
Atlantic Creoles 181, 183
Australia 5, 35, 37, 38, 42, 55, 125
Austria 1, 39, 40, 41
Austro-Asiatic 46
Austronesian languages 134
Aztec 1, 36, 42, 160

Bahasa Indonesia 48, 56, 134
Balkan 1, 6, 155

Baltic 155
Bantu 56
Basque 6, 62, 64, 101, 157
Belgium 4, 5, 11, 34, 57
  Brussels 120
  Flanders 28
Bengali 56
Berber 25, 27, 86
Bhojpuri (Mauritius) 22
Bokmål 52, 53
Bolivia 34, 161, 173
Bonaire (Dutch Antilles) 179, 185
Brazil, Amazon basin 5
Breton 32, 44, 101
Buang 28
Bulgaria 57
Bulgarian 155
Byzantine 180

Canada 4, 15, 16–18, 19–20, 29, 32, 34, 36, 66,
    67, 71, 92, 102, 105, 109, 110, 129, 133, 135,
    160, 161, 178, 185,
  Quebec 3, 29, 32, 36, 66, 67, 109, 132, 133,
    160, 161, 163
Cape Verdean Portuguese Creole 179
Caribbean 5, 6, 24, 176, 177, 178, 179, 182, 184
Cashubic, North 155
Castilian see Spanish
Catalan 47
Cayenne 178
Celtic 157
Central African Republic 169, 170
Cherokee 35
Chicano 12, 18, 19, 37, 132 (see also Spanish)
Chinese 80, 85, 86, 87, 89, 155
  (Hawaii) 104
  (USA) 33, 36, 92
Chinook 135
Chinook Jargon 135, 137
Colombia 54
Comanche 167, 168, 170, 172, 173

Cornish 32
Costa Rica 92, 169, 170
Cree 135
Cuba 135
Curaçao (Dutch Antilles) 179, 185
Czech 84

Danish 35, 52, 98, 155, 166
  (Greenland) 2
Denmark 52
Dravidian 5, 46, 158
Dutch 3, 11, 34, 42, 68, 86, 87, 91, 99, 101, 126,
    127, 133, 134, 143, 144, 145, 148, 150, 151,
    165, 172, 176
  (Australia) 35, 36
  (Belgium) 5, 11, 34, 101, 120
  (Dutch Antilles) 185
  (Japan) 168
  (Surinam) 59, 126, 127
  (USA) 37
Dutch Antilles (Aruba, Bonaire, Curaçao) 179,
  185
Dutch Creoles 179

Ecuador 34, 51, 52, 85, 130, 131, 141, 142, 154,
    155, 156
Egypt 26
English *passim*
  (Africa) 69
  (Australia) 35, 36, 42, 82
  (Costa Rica) 169
  (Canada) 17, 19, 29, 32, 36, 66, 67, 69, 92, 102,
    109, 110, 129, 133, 160, 161
  (France) 48
  (Hawaii) 104
  (India) 46, 56, 61, 65, 147, 148
  (Italian Americans) 15
  (Japan) 168
  (Jews USA) 15
  (Kenya) 41, 51, 56, 119, 134
  (London) 3
  (Mauritius) 22
  (Nigeria) 69
  (Philippines) 67, 68
  (Quebec) 3
  (Sudan) 57
  (South America) 54
  (South Africa) 18, 110
  (Tanzania) 28
  (West Africa) 134
  Jargon (West Africa) 183, *see* Pidgin English
  Middle 167
  Old 166, 167, 168
English Creoles 5, 178, 179, 183
Estonian 155
Ethiopia 51
Europe 6, 26, 33, 41, 60, 113
  North 148
European languages 4, 158, 176, 181, 182, 184

Fanakalo 177
Far East 177
Ferring 34
Finland 114
Finnish 98
  (Sweden) 59, 65, 70
Flemish 5, 11, 34, 101, 120
France 6, 26, 30, 34, 48, 91, 101, 164, 178
  Brittany 32, 44
  North African Immigrants 91
French 1, 2, 5, 30, 34, 44, 48, 74, 76, 77, 78, 80,
    81, 82, 89, 91, 117, 120, 121, 125, 131, 134,
    136, 151, 157, 166, 176, 178
  (Belgium) 5, 28
  (Canada) 3, 17, 19, 20, 29, 32, 36, 45, 66, 67,
    69, 92, 102, 109, 110, 129, 132, 133, 135, 163
  (Central Africa) 169, 170
  (Haiti) 26
  (Mauritius) 22
  (Morocco) 19
  (Switzerland) 5
  (USA) 14, 121, 135, 167
  Creoles 5, 178
French Guyana Creole 178
Frisian 6, 34, 51
  North 34

Gaelic 6, 43, 57
Garo 96, 97
German 3, 42, 49, 74, 78, 88, 89, 90, 96, 97, 98,
    101, 109, 138, 145, 151, 165, 182, 185
  (Austria) 39, 40, 41
  (Australia) 35, 36
  (Belgium) 5
  (Silesia) 113
  (USA) 37
  North 155
Germanic languages 5
Germany 34, 82, 89, 102, 113, 138, 143, 145,
    146, 185
Great Britain 5, 13, 23, 24, 51, 57, 70, 102, 114,
    115, 132, 147, 166, 167, 174
  Cornwall 32
  London 3, 14, 119, 185
Greek 155, 180
  (Australia) 35, 36
  (Great Britain) 51, 115
  (Homeric) 120
  immigrants (Germany) 90
  immigrants (Europe) 33, 90
Greenland 2
Guarani 25, 26, 51
Guinea, Gulf of 179
Guinea-Bissau 176
Gujerati 11, 32
  (Kenya) 41
  (Great Britain) 13, 32

Haiti 26, 178

Haitian Creole 26, 34, 178
Hausa 69
Hawaii 104
Hebrew 18, 54, 110, 117
Hindi 3, 46, 56, 61, 65, 131, 132, 159
  (Mauritius) 22
  (Surinam) 59, 126, 127
Hungarian 55, 97
  (Austria) 39, 40, 41
Hungary 39

Igbo 69
India 1, 3, 4, 5, 11, 32, 46, 56, 60, 65, 71, 96, 97,
  132, 147, 149, 155, 158, 159
  Maharashtra 14
  Tamil Nadu 14
Indian Ocean 177
Indians (South Africa) 177
Indo-Aryan 46
Indo-European (India) 5, 155, 159
Indonesia 48, 56, 134
Inuit 2
Irish 57
Israel 18
Italian 33, 41, 59, 74, 106, 120, 148
  (Australia) 35, 36, 42
  (Great Britain) 41, 42, 70, 102, 114
  (Switzerland) 85
  (USA) 15, 114, 132
Italy: Sardinia 33, 41, 59

Jamaica 178, 180, 185
Jamaican Creole 178
  (London) 14, 119
Jamaican immigrants (Costa Rica) 169
Japan 168, 169, 170
Japanese 87, 89, 128, 143, 146, 149, 150, 168,
  169
  (USA) 114, 115
Javanese 56, 135
  (Surinam) 56, 135

Kannada 158, 159
Kenya 51, 52, 56, 134
  Nairobi 41, 134
Kikuyu 119
Kiungaja 52
Konkani 156, 158, 159
Krio 178
Kwega 51

Landsmål 47, 52
Langue d'Oil 26
Langue d'Oc 26, *see* also Occitan
Latin 124, 148, 157, 158, 166
Latvian 97
Lettish 155 (*see also* Latvian)
Lingala 177
Lingua Franca 177, 182

Lithuanian 155
Lotuho 82
Louisiana French Creole 178
Luxembourg 113

Macao Portuguese Creole 179
Macedonian 155
Malay 56, 134
Malaysia 56
Maltese (Australia) 35
Marathi 14, 158
Mauritian Creole 22, 178
Mauritius 22, 178
Media Lengua 130, 131, 156
Mexican immigrants (USA) 23, 64, 67, 122
Mexicano 36, 42
Mexico 1, 12, 19, 36, 70, 159, 160
Michif 135
Middle East 148
Mongol 6
Moroccan (Netherlands) 11, 42, 68, 86, 87, 91,
  113
Moroccan immigrants (France) 23
  (Belgium) 23
  (Netherlands) 11, 23, 24, 42, 68, 86, 113, 144,
  146
Morocco 19, 20, 25, 26, 68
Mozambique 48, 70

Nahuatl 36, 37, 42, 70, 159, 160, 162
Navaho 127, 128
Negerhollands 179, 183
Netherlands 3, 6, 11, 23, 24, 27, 34, 42, 51, 68,
  70, 86, 87, 113, 132, 140, 141, 143, 144, 145,
  146, 150, 185
New Guinea 28, 58, 178
Niger Congo languages 169
Nigeria 60, 69, 70, 134
Nilo-Saharan 51
Norway 52, 53
Norwegian 47, 52, 53, 55, 155, 156
  Bokmål 52, 53
  Landsmål 47, 52
  Nynorsk 52, 53
  Riksmål 52, 53
Nyaumada 55
Nynorsk 52, 53

Occitan 26, 120

Pacific 5, 176, 179
Pakistan 147, 159
Palestine 47
Papiamentu 179, 185
Papua New Guinea 28, 58, 178
Paraguay 25, 26, 51
Pennsylvania Dutch (German) 37
Persian 87, 159
Perso-Arabic 132

Peru 20, 34, 44, 61, 68, 69, 70
Philippine Spanish Creole 179
Philippines 52, 54, 60, 68, 69, 70
Philippine languages 52, 54
Pidgin Deutsch 185
Pidgin English (West Africa) 134
 (Hawaii) 104
Pilipino 54, 67, 68
Poland: Silesia 113
Polish (USA) 132
Portuguese 5, 57, 74, 153, 157, 176, 179
 Jargon 183
 Creoles 5, 179, 183
 (Japan) 168, 169
 (Mozambique) 48
Provençal 26, 120
Puerto Rico 130
Puerto Rican Spanish (USA) 119, 120, 122, 130

Quebec, *see* Canada
Quechua 137, 171, 172, 173, 174
 (Bolivia) 161, 162, 173
 (Ecuador) 51, 52, 53, 85, 130, 131, 141, 142,
  154, 156, 174
 (Peru) 20, 44, 45

Reunion 178
Riksmål 52, 53
Roman Empire 6, 157
Romance languages 5
Romanian 155, 157
Romansch 5
Russian 53, 60, 75, 97, 117

Sango 169, 170
Sao Tomense Creole 179
Saramaccan 153
Sardinian 33, 41, 59
Sarnami 59, 126, 127
Semitic languages 51
Senegal 176
Serbian, South East 155
 (Germany) 42, 108
Serbo-Croatian 33, 108
Seychelles Creole 178
Shona 70
Sierra Leone 178
Slavic languages 155
South Africa 18, 110, 177, 179
South Asian immigrants (Mauritius) 22
Soviet Union, Udmurt ASSR 13
Spain 6, 47, 48, 54, 62, 143
Spanish 5, 74, 84, 85, 86, 87, 96, 117, 121, 134,
  140, 142, 157, 165, 171, 176, 179
 (America) 20, 34, 44, 45, 159, 160
 (Bolivia) 161, 173
 (Costa Rica) 169
 (Ecuador) 53, 85, 130, 131, 141, 142, 154, 156,
  171, 174

(Japan) 168
(Paraguay) 25, 26
(Puerto Rican) (New York) 23, 173
(Peru) 20, 44, 45, 61, 68, 69
(Tex-Mex) 19
(USA) 2, 12, 14, 18, 20, 23, 33, 34, 60, 62, 64,
  66, 67, 102, 104, 111, 113, 119, 120, 121,
  122, 123, 124, 127, 128, 130, 167, 173, 185
Spanish Creoles 5, 179
Sranan 126, 127, 132, 133, 153, 178, 183, 185
Sudan 57
Surinam 59, 126, 127, 153, 178, 185
Surinamese immigrants (Netherlands) 132, 133
Swahili 28, 52, 55, 134
Sweden 59, 66, 70
Swedish 97
 (Finland) 114
 (USA) 37
Swiss German 85
Switzerland 5, 62, 85

Tagalog 67
Taki-Taki *see* Sranan
Tamil 14, 56
Tanganyika 52
Tanzania 28, 52, 55, 56, 58
Third World 6, 46, 60, 62, 67, 71, 101, 185
 languages 4, 119
Thracian 157
Tibetan 155
Tibeto-Burman 46
Tok Pisin 28, 178, 184
Tsonga 59
Turkey 11, 57, 68, 101, 141
Turkish 76, 86, 87, 155, 158, 159, 162
 (Bulgaria) 57
 (Germany) 82, 89, 90, 102, 138
 (Great Britain) 51
 (Netherlands) 11, 68, 86, 87, 91, 113, 141, 150
 immigrants (Europe) 33, 102, 103

Udmurt 13, 14
Uganda 134
Ukrainian 34
Urdu 3, 159
USA 4, 11, 14, 18, 33, 35, 36, 60, 62, 64, 66, 67,
  90, 92, 102, 105, 114, 119, 130, 135, 167,
  168, 174, 178, 180
 California 64, 66, 67, 70
 Florida 60
 Hawaii 104
 New York 2, 15, 119, 130, 173, 185
 Pennsylvania 37
 Texas 104
 Virgin Islands 179
USSR 53, 55, 56, 60

Vietnamese 34
Virgin Islands 179

Wales 16, 36, 43
Welsh 6, 17, 36, 43, 98, 108
West Indian immigrants (London) 23
West Indians (Great Britain) 13

Yabem 28
Yiddish (USA) 14, 85

Yoruba 69, 134
Yugoslavian immigrants (Europe) 33
(Germany) 42, 108

Zaire 177
Zulu 177, 178

Subject index

accent, ethnic 132–3, 137
accommodation 22f, 28, 167, 168, 170
acculturation 167–8
acquisition 157
  simultaneous 94f, 103–4, 109–10
actuation problem 162–3
adaptation 138
addition vs. substitution in the lexicon 165
additive bilingualism 102
affective meaning 77
Afro-genesis hypothesis 181–3
agglomeration problem 163
anterior tense 178
anti-neutrality 159
apathic reaction (of bilinguals) 114
approximative system 182
areal feature 155–6
assimilation 62, 63, 65, 93, 113–14
  cultural 62–3, 93
  linguistic 62–3
assimilationist model of bilingual education 65
associative response 76–7
Atlantic mono-source hypothesis 183
avoidance of structures 87

baby talk 139–40, 181–2
balance hypothesis 104
base/host language in code-switching 121–3
Basic interpersonal Communicative Skills (BICS) 105–7
behaviourist learning theory 84
behaviourist view of language attitudes 16f
bilingual brain 73f
bilingual education, models of 65
Bilingual Education Act 59
bilingualism, additive 102
  compound 75–7, 79
  coordinate 75–7, 79
  individual 2f
  psychological 3
  psychopathology of 113–15
  societal 1f

sociological 3
subordinate 75, 77
subtractive 102, 108, 111–12
bio-programme hypothesis 181, 183
borrowing 153, 154, 156, 157, 158–63

calque, see loan shift
categorial hierarchy 170–1
circumlocutory expressions 167–8
code-mixing 116–28, 159, 172–3
code-switching 80, 108, 116–28, 130
codification 51–3
cognates 98, 103
Cognitive Academic Language Proficiency (CALP) 105–7
cognitive effects/ability 108
cognitive flexibility (of bilinguals) 108, 111
common social context 184
Common Underlying Proficiency (CUP) 106–7
communication, context-embedded 105–6
communicative competence 146, 148 (see also functional competence)
competence 146
component 153
compound bilingualism 75–7, 79
computation time 80–1
conceptual organization 75–9
constraints problem 162–3
content words 172
context-reduced communication 105–6
continuum 184–5
Contrastive Analysis Hypothesis 84–8
convergence 154–6, 159
  (in speech accommodation) 28
coordinate bilingualism 75–7, 79
copula 139
core vocabulary 165
creative construction 85–6
creole 175–86
critical period 94–5
cross-cultural communication 138–51

cross-language interference 78 (*see also* interference)
cross-sectional research 86
cultivation 53–5
cultural assimilation 93
  identity 12
  presuppositions 145–6
  shock 61

decision tree 22f
decreolization 184
definition of bilingualism, sociological 3
  psychological 3
denotation 77
density 135f
dependency 123, 126
developmental errors 88
developmental interdependence hypothesis 61, 105, 112–13
differential 74
diglossia 22, 24–6, 82, 102
directive function 29–30, 119, 166
discourse 151
  markers 172
distance 94, 95, 143, 150
divergence (in speech accommodation) 28
domain 22–4
dominant language 102, 103
doubling 135, 137
dual system hypothesis 75

early immersion programmes 66
elaboration 53–5
embedding problem 162–3
emblematic switching 118, 137, 172
equivalence constraint 123, 124
equivalents, interlingual 98
errors 85, 88
ethnic accent 132–3, 137
  group 12
  identity 12, 85, 86, 130, 143–4
  loyalty 132–3
ethnicity, definition of 12
ethnolect 132–3
ethnolinguistic group 12
  vitality 33
evaluation of language planning 55
evaluation problem in linguistic change 162–3
expanded pidgin 176
expressive function 30, 119, 166, 170
extended system hypothesis 75

fluent switcher 120–1
foreigner talk 133–4, 137, 138–43
formal competence 146, 148
fossilization 92, 181–2
Free Morpheme Constraint 127
fricativization 154
function words 172

function, expressive 30, 119, 166, 170
  integrative 29–30
  metalinguistic 30, 120
  phatic 30, 119
  poetic 30, 120
  referential 29, 118, 119, 166, 172
  directive 29–30, 119, 166
functional competence 146, 148
  separation 75–9
  specialization 22f, 29f
functionalist 153, 154, 156, 157, 158–63

generalization strategy 90–2
genetic feature 155–6
government 124–5
grammatical borrowing 162f
graphization 52–3
group 12

helping verb 126–7
hemispheric dominance 73–5
heterogeneity, synchronic 41
high variety 24f
holistic 153
home–school language mismatch 59
homogenization 155
homophonous diamorphs 126
hybrids 165

identity 85, 86, 130, 143–4
immersion model 59, 66
imperfect L2 learning 181–2
implementation (in language planning) 55
importation 164
imposed norm hypothesis 19
in-group communication 129
in-group reaction of bilinguals 114
inactive language 79
individual bilingualism 2f
inherent value hypothesis 19
input switch 79–81
instrumental motivation 92–4
integrative motivation 92–4
intelligence, verbal 108–9
  nonverbal 109
inter-sentential code-mixing 118, 137
interaction rules 143–51
interethnic communication 138–51
interference 78, 82–100, 149
intergroup communication 129, 133f
interlanguage 83–92, 139–40, 157
interlingual equivalents 98
  errors 85
intermediate system 83, 88, 89
internal motivation 158–62
Interpersonal Speech Accommodation
    Theory 28
intra-sentential code mixing 118, 137, 172
intralingual errors 85

jargon   135, 175, 183

koine   180

L1 = L2 hypothesis   85–6
L1 influence, indirect   86
Language Academy   48
language attitudes   16f
  attrition   173–4
  border   5
  death   32f, 43–5, 173f
  development   48, 52–5
  loss   32f, 42–5
  loyalty   20
  maintenance/preservation   32–8
  planning   46–58
  planning, individual   47
  planning, national   47
  policy   46
  selection   48
  shift   32, 38–45, 102
  varieties   15
late immersion programmes   66
lateralization   94–5
lexical borrowing   120–1, 131, 164–74
  expansion   53–5
  interference   165
linearity   123, 126
lingua franca   22, 134–5, 137, 176
linguistic levelling   155–6
linkage   135
literary standard   48
loan blends   165
loan translation   165
loanshifts   165
loanwords   164–5
logical operators   15
longitudinal   86
low variety   24f
loyalty, ethnic   132–3

maintenance model of bilingual education   65
marked choice   27
marked structures   135
matched-guise technique   16f
mental lexicon   78, 79
metalist view (of language attitudes)   16
  (of learning)   87
meta-comment   119–20
metalinguistic ability   109–11
metalinguistic function   30, 120
minority language treatment   48, 51
mixed reduplication   131–2
models of bilingual education   65
modernization   53–5
modularization   153
monostylism   44–5, 144–5
morphological integration   169, 172–3
morphological simplification   43–4

motivation   92–4
multi-level generative system   135

negative transfer   84
neural processing   75
neutralization   126–8, 129–37, 139
non-core vocabulary   165, 170
non-dominant language   102, 103
non-prestige language   17
nonce borrowing   165

objectivist approach (to ethnicity)   13
one-store hypothesis   78–9
output switch   79–81

paradigmatic   153–72
parallel recovery   74
partial immersion programmes   66
paternity   12
patois   185
patrimony   12
phatic function   30, 119
phenomenology   12
phonological adaptation   169, 172–3
picture–word interference test   78
pidgin   151, 170, 175–8, 183, 185–6
pidgin English   104
plural   139, 179, 180
pluralistic model of bilingual education   65
poetic function   30, 120
Portuguese monogenesis hypothesis   181, 183
post-creole continuum   176, 184–5
post-nominal articles   155
post-pidgin continuum   176
power dimension   145, 150
prestige language   17, 158, 162
primary accommodation   167–8, 170
proficiency   150
  score   85–6
Progressive Matrices Test   109
pronominal
pronoun usage   140, 142, 145
psychological distance   94, 95, 143, 173
psychopathology of bilingualism   113–15
purism   164

questionnaire   17

rank order of morphemes   86
reaction of bilinguals, apathic   114
  rebel   114
rebel reaction (of bilinguals)   114
recovery   74
reduction   162, 175
reduplication   131–2, 179, 182
referential function   29, 118, 119, 166, 172
reflexive   156

register 140-3
relative clause 158-62
relativized constraints 126-8
relexification 42-3, 130, 137, 156-7, 159, 183
repidginization 176
resyntactization 159
retroactive inhibition 76
ritual function 14
rudimentary pidgin 176

Sapir-Whorf Hypothesis 115, 168
secondary accommodation 167-8
 articulation 136
selective recovery 74
self-rating tests 103
semantic differential scale 17, 77
 memory 78, 79
 transfer 90
 transparency 181
semilingualism 63, 107, 108
sensitive period 94-5
Separated Underlying Proficiency (SUP) 106-7
serial verb 178, 179, 180
simplification 43-4, 83, 90-1, 108, 139-40, 151, 162, 180, 181, 182
simultaneous acquisition of two languages 94f, 103-4, 109-10
single switch hypothesis 79-80
social distance 94, 95, 143, 173f
 event 29
 meaning 11, 28
 network 39-40
 planning 50
 situation 29, 184
social-psychological variables 90, 92, 109
societal bilingualism 1f
solidarity dimension 145
solidarity scales 20
speech accommodation, *see* accommodation
 acts 147-8, 150
Sprachbund 155-6
stable pidgin 176
standardization 51-5

status scales 20
stereotypes 139-40
Stroop procedure 78, 79-80
structural motivation 158-62
structure avoidance 87
stylistic differences 144-5, 148, 157
sub-set hypothesis 75
subcategorization 124-5
subjectivist approach (to ethnicity) 13
submersion education 67
subordinate bilingualism 75, 77
substitution 164, 165
substrate 157
subtractive bilingualism 102, 108, 111-12
successive pattern 74
synergistic recovery 74
syntactic borrowing 156f
 parsing 123-4
syntagmatic 153

TAG-switches 118
threshold hypothesis 112-13
topic-related switching 118-19
topicalization 15
total immersion programmes 66
trade language 183
transfer 83-90, 97-8, 149, 157
transition problem 162-3
transitional model of bilingual education 65
translation ability 81
 level 61
triggering 125-6

universalistic hypothesis 85, 86, 180-1

variation 180
variety, high 24f
 low 24f
vernacular language approach 60-2, 67-71
vitality, ethnolinguistic 33

X-bar theory 136

Author index

Aitchison, J. 163
Alatis, J.E. 71
Albert, M.L. 81
Albó, X. 165
Alisjahbana, S.T. 56
Alleyne, M.C. 181, 186
Anderson, R. 100, 181
Anderson, A.B. 36
Anisfeld, M. 18
Appel, R. 42, 68, 87, 91, 113
Apte, M.L. 14, 56
Arthur, B. 140

Baetens Beardsmore, H. 9
Barkowsky, H. 146
Ben-Zeev, S. 110
Bender, M.L. 51
Bentahila, A. 19, 125
Bickerton, D. 175, 180, 181, 186
Birnbaum, H. 155
Blom, J.-P. 29
Bloomfield, L. 2, 3
Blount, B.G. 151
Bouchard, D. 160, 161
Brown, R. 145, 184
Brunak, J. 147
Burling, R. 96, 97
Burt, M. 85, 86, 90, 100

Cairns, C.E. 76
Cairns, H.S. 76
Canfield, K. 127
Carlock, E. 132
Carranza, M. 18, 19, 20
Carrow, Sister M.A. 104
Casagrande, J.B. 167, 168, 173
Chan, M.C. 80
Charry, E. 133
Child, I.L. 114
Chomsky, N. 124, 146, 153
Christian, C.C. Jr 61

Civian, T.W. 155
Clark, E.V. and H.H. 78
Clyne, M. 33, 35, 37, 38, 45, 125, 126, 151
Cobarrubias, J. 58
Cohen, A.D. 64, 66, 67
Cohen, M. 7
Cooper, R.L. 45, 71
Crama, R. 117, 126
Crawford, J. 135
Cummins, J. 61, 71, 104–7, 111, 112, 115
Cziko, G.A. 65, 69

Dalbor, J.B. 84
Darcy, N. 108
Davies, E.E. 125
Davis, F.B. 68
Davis, P.M. 68, 69
Day, R.R. 18
De Houwer, A. 99
De Saussure, F. 121, 137, 153
DeBose, C.E. 151
DeCamp, D. 175, 185
Defoe, D. 139
Del Rosario, G. 54
Di Sciullo, A-M. 124, 125, 127
Diaz, R.M. 108, 109, 111
Diebold, A.R. Jr 113
Diem, W. 26
Dittmar, N. 143, 185
Dolson, D.P. 113
Domingue, N. 22
Dorian, N. 43, 44
Doron, E. 117, 123
Dressler, W. 32, 44
Dulay, H. 85, 86, 90, 100
Duskova, L. 84

Eastman, C.M. 58
Edelsky, C. 108
Edwards, J.R. 14, 19, 62
Ehri, L.C. 78, 79

Ellis, H.C. 84
Ellis, R. 100
Ervin-Tripp, S.M. 76, 114, 115
Everts, H. 113
Extra, G. 151

Faerch, C. 90
Fasold, R.W. 9, 16, 17, 20
Feinstein, M.H. 15
Fellman, J. 47
Ferguson, C.A. 22, 25–7, 53, 55, 130, 138, 140, 142, 151
Fishman, J.A. 9, 12, 13, 15, 22, 23, 24, 27, 31, 45, 58, 130
Flores, N. de la Zerda 19
Fonck, A. 148
Foster, C.R. 71

Gaarder, B.A. 33
Gal, S. 39, 40, 41, 45
Gardner, R.C. 81, 92, 93
Gatbonton, E. 133, 144
Giles, H. 11, 19, 20, 21, 22, 28, 33, 36, 119
Gilman, A. 145
Glazer, N. 12, 33
Grosjean, F. 9, 73, 74, 128
Guboglo, M. 13
Guitarte, G.L. 48, 54
Gulutsan, M. 111
Gumperz, J.J. 20, 27, 29, 31, 118, 119, 121, 122, 146, 147, 148, 151

Hakuta, K. 87, 109, 111
Hall, R.A. Jr 186
Halliday, M. 22, 29, 118
Hancock, I.F. 181
Hartford, B. 71
Hatch, E. 85, 142
Haugen, E. 7, 49, 50, 52, 164, 170, 171, 174
Havelka, J. 81
Heller, M. 29
Hernández-Chavez, E. 27, 118, 119, 121, 122
Herzog, M.I. 162
Hesseling, D.C. 7, 180
Hewitt, R. 14, 16
Highfield, A. 186
Hill, J. 36, 37, 42
Hill, K. 36, 37, 42
Hopper, R. 19
Hornby, P.A. 115
Hymes, D. 28, 31, 146, 153, 186

Ianco-Worrell, A. 109, 110

Jakobson, R. 22, 29, 118, 155
Jarovskij, A. 97
Jernudd, B. 50
Jones, B.L. 43
Jones, W.R. 108
Joshi, A. 123, 124

Karttunen, F. 159
Kasper, G. 90
Kelly, L.G. 116
Kessler, C. 111, 112
Kiers, T. 42
Kim, T.W. 168
Kishna, S. 126
Klavans, J.L. 125
Klein, W. 185
Kloss, H. 37
Kolers, P. 76, 77, 78, 79, 80
Krashen, S.D. 94, 100
Kremnitz, G. 26
Kushnir, S.L. 80

Labov, W. 122, 133, 162
Lado, R. 84, 85
Lakoff, G. 145
Lalleman. J. 150
Lambert, W.E. 16, 17, 18, 20, 66, 76, 81, 92, 93, 102, 105, 109, 112
Lance 117
Lapkin, S. 71
Larson, M.L. 61, 68, 69
Le Compagnon, B. 88, 89
Lefebvre, C. 44, 45, 161, 163
Lenneberg, E. 94, 95
Leopold, W.F. 96, 109, 110
LePage, R. 13
Lewis, G. 53
Lewis, G.L. 159
Li, W.L. 33, 36
Lieberson, S.J. 15, 36, 41
Lightfoot, D. 163
Lindholm, K.J. 97, 99
Lindsay, P.H. 78
Linguistic Minorities Project 51
Lipski, J.M. 122, 123
Long, M. 140, 143, 151
Loveday, L. 143, 144, 146, 149, 150, 151
Lowley, E.G. 14

Mackey, W. 9, 70
Macnamara, J. 2, 57, 65, 77, 79, 80, 104, 109
McCabe, E.J. 41
McClure, E. 120
McCormack, W.C. 9
McLaughlin, B. 83
Meisel, J. 87, 90, 143, 151
Meiseles, G. 26
Mercer, N. 13
Mittner, M. 151
Moorghen, P.-M. 22
Morag, S. 47
Moynihan, D.P. 12
Mühlhäusler, P. 29, 175, 186
Müller, K. 113
Muysken, P. 85, 124, 125, 127, 130, 171

Nadkarni, M.V. 158

Nair, K.R.   74
Naro, A.J.   181
Nishimura, M.   128
Norman, D.A.   78

O'Barr, J.F.   58
O'Barr, W.M.   58
O'Grady, G.N.   55
Obler, L.K.   81
Oller, J.W.   92
Ornstein, J.   9
Osgood, C.E.   17, 76

Padilla, A.M.   97, 99
Paradis, M.   74, 75, 79, 81
Pattanayak, D.D.   71
Paulsen, F.   34
Peal, E.   109, 111
Pedrasa, P. Jr   121, 130
Penfield,   79
Pfaff, C.   90, 122, 123, 124, 128
Philips, S.U.   146
Pitres, A   74
Pool, P.A.S.   32
Poplack, S.   118, 119, 123, 124, 127, 128, 173
Potter, M.C.   79
Proctor, L.   18
Pulte, W.   35

Quinn, M.E.   111, 112
Quintero, R.T.   48, 54

Reinecke, J.E.   186
Revil, J.T.   68
Rindler Schjerve, R.   33, 41
Roberts, W.   79
Ross, J.A.   12, 14, 15
Rubin, J.   26, 50, 58
Rūke-Dravina, V.   96, 97
Ryan, E.B.   18, 19, 20, 78, 79

Saer, D.J.   108
Saint-Jacques, B.   20
Sanches, M.   151
Sankoff, D.   122
Sankoff, G.   22, 27, 181, 184, 186
Saunders, G.   97, 98, 99, 100
Scarcella, R.   147, 148, 149
Schachter, J.   87
Schaffer, D.   124
Schuchardt, H.   7, 153, 180, 182
Schumann, J.   90, 94, 185
Schwartz, A.   161, 185
Scotton, C.M.   118, 119, 129, 134, 137
Sebba, M.   119, 120, 178
Segalowitz, N.   75, 77, 78, 111, 132, 133, 134
Selinker, L.   83
Serjeantson, M.S.   166
Seuren, P.A.M.   181

Shuy, R.W.   20
Silverstein, M.   135
Singh, R.   124, 125, 127, 131, 132, 171
Skutnabb-Kangas, T.   9, 61, 63, 71, 77, 104, 105, 108, 112, 115, 116
Smith, M.E.   104
Smolicz, J.J.   42
Snow, C.   141, 142
Soares, C.   74
Sobin, N.J.   124
Sondergaard   89
Spencer, J.   57
Spolsky B.   71
Stewart, W.A.   108
Stölting, W.   42, 108
Stroop, J.R.   78
Suci, C.   17
Swain, M.   71

Taber, C.R.   165, 170, 171
Tabouret-Keller, A.   13
Taeschner, T.   96, 100
Tannenbaum, P.   17
Tanner, N.   135
Tauli, V.   49
Teitelbaum, H.   92
Teunissen, J.   113
Timm, L.A.   117, 122
Todd, L.   186
Tosi, A.   41, 42, 114
Toukomaa, P.   61, 104, 105, 112
Troike, R.C.   65, 69
Trubetzkoj, N.S.   155
Tucker, G.R.   66
Turner, L.D.   7

UNESCO   60

Valdés Falis, G.   117
Valdman, A.   71, 151, 181, 186
Van Gelderen, H.   117, 126
Veltmann, C.   45
Veronique, D.   91
Vildomec, V.   101
Virmani, V. 74
Vorster, J.   18
Vygotsky, L.S.   110

Weinreich   3, 6, 7, 75, 77, 82, 84, 85, 86, 113, 162, 165
Wekker, H.   181
Welmers, W.E.   58
Whinnom, K.   181
Whiteley, W.H.   52, 54, 56, 57
Whitney, W.D.   7, 170
Whorf, B.L.   168
Wodak-Leodolter, R.   32, 44
Wode, H.   87, 88
Wölck, W.   20, 132

Woolford, E. 123
Wootton, T. 119, 120
Workgroup on Foreign Workers' Language 140
Wurm, S.A. 9

Yeni-Komshin, G. 18

Zobl, H. 88
Zuñiga, T.V. 169